COMPOSING A NEW SONG

Stories of Empowerment from Africa

Hope Chigudu, *Editor*

Contributors
Makanjuola Olaseinde Arigbede
Tomson Dube
Patrick Kiirya
Leila Sheikh
Emily Sikazwe

MWENGO

THE COMMONWEALTH FOUNDATION

WEAVER W PRESS

First published in 2004 by
The Commonwealth Foundation
Marlborough House
Pall Mall
London
SW1Y 5HY

Weaver Press
P. O. Box A1922
Avondale, Harare, Zimbabwe

Fountain Publishers
P. O. Box 488
Kampala
Uganda

Distributed outside Africa by
African Books Collective
www.africanbookscollective.com

Typeset by Fontline Electronic Publishing Pvt Ltd., Harare
Cover Design: Inkspots, Harare

ISBN: 1 77922 015 4

Table of Contents

List of Acronyms

AACC	All Africa Conference of Churches
AIDS	Acquired Immune Deficiency Syndrome
BAKWATA	Muslim Council of Tanzania
BRAC	Bangladesh Rural Advancement Committee
CBDIBA	Centre Béninois pour le Developpement de Initiatives à la Base (Benin)
CBO	Community Based Organisation
CDF	Community Development Foundation (Nigeria)
CDRN	Community Development Resource Network (Uganda)
CEDAW	Convention on the Elimination of all forms of Discrimination Against Women
CFO	COPODIN Family of Organisations
CFWRZ	Community Foundation of the Western Region of Zimbabwe
CHAWATIATA	Traditional Healers Association of Tanzania
CIDA	Canadian International Development Agency
COPODIN	Coalition for Popular Development Initiatives in Nigeria
CRC	Convention on the Rights of the Child
CSO	Civil Society Organisation
CUSO	Formerly: Canadian University Service Overseas
DENIVA	Development Network of Indigenous Voluntary Associations
DFID	Department for International Development (UK)
DSA	Development Support Agencies
DTV	Dar es Salaam Television
EAII	Egbe Alafowosowopo fun Isegun Ise ne Ilee Naijairia (Nigeria)
EZE	Protestant Association for Cooperation in Development (Evangelische Zentralstelle für Entwicklungshilfe)
FOS	Federation for Open Scouting (Federatie voor Open Scouting)
IDASA	Institute for Democracy in South Africa
FABE	Family Basic Education (Uganda)
FAVDO	Forum for African Voluntary Development Organisations
FemAct	Feminist Activist Coalition (Tanzania)

FUPRO	Féderation de Unions de Producteur de Bénin
GADC	Give-a-Dam Campaign (Zimbabwe)
GAMA	Groupe d'APPUI au Mouvement Associative du Niger
GDNM	Grassroots Development and NGO Management
GTZ	Deutsche Gesellschaft für Technische Zusammenarbeit
HIV	Human Immunodeficiency Virus
HIVOS	Humanistic Institute for Cooperation with Developing Countries (Netherlands)
IITA	International Institute of Tropical Agriculture
IMF	International Monetary Fund
IRED	Innovations et Réseaux pour le Développement
LABE	Literacy and Basic Adult Education (Uganda)
LDC	Least Developed Country
LitNet	Uganda National Literacy Network
MMD	Movement for Multiparty Democracy (Zambia)
MORIBEN	Féderation des Unions des Groupements Paysans du Niger
MTEA	Multipurpose Training and Employment Association (Uganda)
NAF	New Age Foundation (Nigeria)
NAVISOC	Network for Alternative Vision of Society (Nigeria)
NEB	National Executive Board (of LABE)
NGO	Non-Governmental Organisation
NLC	Nigerian Labour Congress
NOVIB	Netherlands Organisation for International Development Cooperation
NPA	Norwegian People's Aid
OAU	Organisation of African Unity
OD	Organisational Development
ORAP	Organisation of Rural Associations for Progress (Zimbabwe)
PAD	Philisisizwe Association for Development (Zimbabwe)
PEM	Participatory Education Methodologies
PERFORM	Poverty Eradication Forum (Nigeria)
PLA	Participatory Learning and Action
PO	People's Organisation
PRA	Participatory Rural Appraisal
RDCC	Rural Development Coordination Council (Zimbabwe)
REFLECT	Regenerated Freirean Literacy through Empowering Community Technique
SAP	Structural Adjustment Programme
SCF	Save the Children Fund
SNV	Organisation Nederlandaise de Developpment

SOSPA	Sexual Offences Special Provisions Act (Tanzania)
TAMWA	Tanzania Media Women's Association
TANGO	Tanzania Association of Non-Governmental Organisations
TAWLA	Tanzania Women Lawyers' Association
TGNP	Tanzania Gender Networking Programme
TVT	Television Tanzania
UNDP	United Nations Development Programme
UNECA	United Nations Economic Commission for Africa
UNICEF	United Nations Children's Fund
UNESCO	United Nations Educational, Scientific and Cultural Organisation
UPE	Universal Primary Education (Uganda)
WEDUREC	Workers' Educational and Recreational Centre (Nigeria)
WFC	Women For Change (Zambia)
WLI	World Learning Incorporated (USA)
WSSD	World Summit for Sustainable Development
WUS	World University Service

CONTRIBUTORS

Hope Chigudu who was born in Uganda but lives and works in Zimbabwe is a gender specialist and co-founder of the Zimbabwe Women's Resource Centre. As well as being a grassroots activist, Hope has advised national governments and worked for the United Nations, and specialises in strategies for organisational development and change. She has published widely on gender and civil society development. Hope is the African member of the Commonwealth Foundation's Citizens and Governance Programme team.

Dr Olaseinde Arigbede (Nigeria) is a full-time development activist, who originally trained as a doctor of medicine and a neuro-scientist. After some years as an inspector of mines and a lecturer in anatomy, he moved into rural development work. For the past 25 years, he has worked exclusively on issues of poverty eradication, gender justice, self-reliance of peoples, and the empowerment and self-management of civil society. His commitment to village communities began with the clinical care of poor peasants, and he and his wife were founder members of COPODIN. Subsequently, he has been involved in developing appropriate small-scale technologies for grain agronomy on peasant farms. He has facilitated three civil society associations in search of alternative paradigms of development, as well as a major peasant federation in Nigeria. In addition, he has helped to link grassroots initiatives in civil society in Africa; and has been keen to source and promote traditional knowledge and skills, especially in the health terrain.

Tomson Dube (Zimbabwe) has a degree in religious studies from the University of Zimbabwe, and has studied international and intercultural management in the USA. He began his career by teaching English in a secondary school and in 1993 he joined ORAP as the Information and Documentation Coordinator. In this capacity he was involved with the advocacy and lobbying activities of the organisation. Later he became the Academic Director of Zenzele College, an institution within ORAP that offers training in NGO management. In addition to undertaking some lecturing duties and acting as an academic advisor, he is also responsible for the recruitment of students and for financial management. In his spare time Tomson is involved in church and community activities, while his work has provided opportunities for overseas travel and networking.

Patrick Kiirya (Uganda) trained initially as a teacher and later took a degree in social work and administration at Makerere University in Kampala. He started his career as a secondary school teacher, and spent some years teaching and training teachers in Kenya. Gradually he developed an interest in educating adults, and retrained in order to become engaged with adult literacy and education. He was a founder member of LABE and started work with the new organisation in 1989 as a Literacy Instructor/Coordinator. Having dedicated his career to LABE for more than a decade, he eventually took up the position of Director. Patrick has been an enthusiastic campaigner for improved adult education in Uganda and has collaborated with the government to achieve LABE's goals. He has served on educational committees and networks, at national and regional level.

Emily Sikazwe (Zambia) is an agronomist by profession. For several years, from 1985 to 1992, she worked for the Zambian Government, serving with the parastatal responsible for improving cotton production. This involved her in a variety of activities, including the supervision of technical programmes and the support of smallholder cotton farmers through community programmes. In 1992 she moved across to the NGO sector and in 1993 she became the Executive Director of Women for Change, which is dedicated to encouraging the empowerment of women in rural communities and their participation in their own development. Emily is a stalwart of the NGO community in Zambia, and has campaigned to influence policy change on issues of gender and sustainable development. She has travelled both in southern Africa and the wider world, and in 2000 she received the Woman of the Year Award from the American Biographical Institute.

Leila Sheikh (Tanzania) is a journalist by training, with degrees in politics and African studies. She was a founder member of TAMWA and has worked with the organisation since 1989, raising public awareness about violence against women through the media. For several years she coordinated research within TAMWA and edited its publications, including the magazine *Sauti ya Siti*. She ran the Pathfinder Programme on Family Planning/Reproductive Health Rights during 1995-96 and she was the Co-ordinator of TAMWA's Crisis Centre from 1990 to 1996 during the campaign against violence. In 1996 she became the Executive Director of TAMWA. Leila is a gifted journalist, and she has devoted her professional and leadership skills to improving the lives of women in Tanzania. She has been a prominent campaigner for women's rights and has written many pamphlets and papers on issues relating to women.

FOREWORD

This book is the outcome of the Commonwealth Foundation's third NGO Documentation Fellowship programme, which was held in the African region from September to December 2000. It is part of a Commonwealth-wide series on the theme of *Lessons in Empowerment*. Having been preceded by volumes from the Caribbean and Asia, it will be followed by a further volume from the South Pacific.

The Foundation is an intergovernmental organisation resourced by and reporting to Commonwealth governments. It works with civil society in the Commonwealth to facilitate connections between people, their associations and communities, so as to encourage mutual learning in the fields of professional and community development.

To this end, it initiated this documentation programme in 1998 with a view to publishing material about the work of NGOs especially in developing countries, which is written not by outsiders, but by people working within these organisations.

This annual Documentation Fellowship has provided a selected group of four or five prominent NGO leaders an opportunity for analysis and documentation of their experience; the exchange of ideas; and the publication of their stories in a book. The Fellowship has been organised regionally, and the first programme took place in the Caribbean, with participation from Belize, Guyana, Jamaica, and Trinidad and Tobago. The reports of the four Caribbean Fellows on their advocacy and development work were published in April 2000 under the title, *Spitting in the Wind*. A further volume from Asia, entitled *Improving People's Lives*, is being published in 2003, containing reports from India, Malaysia, Pakistan and Sri Lanka.

This African volume documents NGO work in Commonwealth countries right across the continent. It reflects the diversity of this work in the countries of Nigeria, Tanzania, Uganda, Zambia and Zimbabwe; and draws out important lessons for empowerment in the areas of rural development, adult education, networking among people and the rights of women. The Foundation is indebted to the five Fellows for recording their stories, and to the Editor, Hope Chigudu of Zimbabwe, for helping to shape their material.

One important feature of this scheme is that the Foundation seeks publishers within the region of each Fellowship programme. Thus the Caribbean book was brought out by Ian Randle Publishers of Jamaica and the Asian book by Sage Publications India. The Foundation has been pleased to collaborate with Weaver Press, based in Harare, to produce this African volume.

Colin Ball
Director, The Commonwealth Foundation

INTRODUCTION

Hope Chigudu

A Picture of Africa

The African continent brims with diverse populations of richly varied colour and identity. These people are deeply spiritual, recognising one another as 'kindred spirits' who accept the intrinsic and eternal harmony between the living, the dead and their spirits. The continent's tenacious life force throbs with a rhythmic passion. Africans exude a love for family, for traditions that confirm a heritage, for the gods and spirits, for people and for the land – in fact, a passion for everything that epitomises life.

Despite living through centuries of migration, slavery, colonisation, political struggles, nationalist movements and severe underdevelopment, Africa has overcome these obstacles to emerge into the present community of independent nations. The people of Africa believe in humanity, kindness towards others, a communal sense of responsibility, and hospitality towards guests. Africans are imbued with an enduring spirit, strong social values and proud traditions of respect for the human being. The resilience of the African human spirit is illustrated in the long and heroic political struggles of the women and men who made sacrifices for the emancipation of self and country. Among these, personalities like Graca Machel, Mbuya Nehanda, Nelson Mandela, Mwalimu Julius Nyerere, Jomo Kenyatta, Winnie Mandela, Kwame Nkrumah and Steve Biko have become household names and icons of the strength of Africa. They personify the quality for which Africans are known all over the world – the strength to survive against all odds.

This African streak also saw the making of famous African scholars and writers like Chinua Achebe, Ayi Kwei Armah, Bediako Asare, Kofi Awoonor, Amilcar Cabral, Tsitsi Dangarembwa, Cyprian Ekwensi, Luis Bernardo Honwana, Chenjerai Hove, Mazisi Kunene, Ali Mazrui, Micere Mugo, Flora Nwapa, Oginga Odinga, Yambo Ouologuem, Okot P'Bitek, Mwangi Ruheni, Wole Soyinka, Ngugi wa Thiong'o and many others.

Africa is a vast land of colour and contrasts. It is bordered to the east by the Indian Ocean, to the west by the Atlantic and to the north by the Mediterranean Sea. The Organisation of African Unity (OAU), at its formation in 1963, recognised an Africa of 53 independent states spanning the Arab nations of the North, the mainly French-speaking West African states, the Swahili-speaking countries of East and Central Africa and the predominantly Bantu Southern African states. Inheriting artificial boundaries – which often cut across ethnic lines, fomenting internal conflict – the OAU set out to perform the daunting task of keeping Africa's more than 50 countries and surrounding islands together. The outsider looking in may be forgiven for thinking that Africa is an unwieldy outcome of nature's tectonic accidents and migration. Yet in Africa's diversity of peoples and cultures there is some unity in concept and practice.

The blended cultures of Africa

The Africa we speak of in the year 2002 has many non-indigenous faces. In the east and south of the continent, the settler phenomenon of earlier centuries led to the expansion of Africa's cultures and peoples. It is, therefore, quite common to find a Caucasian African of Irish descent or an African of Asian extraction in countries such as Kenya, Lesotho, Malawi, Mozambique, Namibia, South Africa, Swaziland, Zambia or Zimbabwe. With further adulterations from the two religions of Christianity and Islam, the Africa of today is a volatile but beautiful pot-pourri of west, east and indigenous African traditions and cultures.

Africa's architecture has also developed along the lines of this blend of cultures. While many parts of Africa have maintained their heritage of traditional building technology and lifestyles, it is very common to find a replication of European or Asian housing designs, township layout and infrastructure in conurbations such as Cape Town, Abuja, Johannesburg, Durban, Nairobi, Harare, Windhoek or Accra. In most African cities, instantly recognisable central business areas with concrete high-rise buildings can be found. Yet for cities like Lagos, Kampala, Cairo, Addis Ababa, Ibadan, Mombasa, Lusaka and Freetown the unique housing designs and pattern of development leave one with no doubt that this is Africa.

In the countryside, natural settings of lush green tropical vegetation, multicoloured deserts or flaming savannah grasslands create breathtaking backdrops for traditional homesteads of mud huts and intricate grass thatch. African rural dwellers live in villages closely knitted together by their kinship and culture, where everyone is their 'neighbour's keeper' and family members depend on each other for social security.

The mention of African cuisine brings thoughts of hot spicy food, exotic mixtures of colour that stimulate the taste buds or of the rare-meat eating Masaimara and the Zulu wild game pot roasts. Above these qualities, most African foods have medicinal and curative value, especially the West African herb-laden stews and soups. Many Africans use food to prevent and treat illnesses. Therefore preparation and consumption methods are learned through well-established oral traditions and practice. The primary ingredients of sub-Saharan African meals are starch filler foods eaten with soups or stews made from meat or fish and vegetables. In

Eastern and Southern Africa, the influence of Caucasian and Asian settler populations can be tasted in the steaming dishes of curried meat, poultry and fish which have become very popular at fast food outlets.

Next to its human and natural resources, some of Africa's greatest exports have been in the area of music and fashion. The music of Africa rocks many leisure spots around the world. Known for its fast beat and bass drums, African music has lost neither its appeal nor its originality. Sweeping through West African high life sounds to the Central African Kwasa Kwasa, modern N'dombolo beats and the southern Kwaito and Mapansula jives, African rhythm reverberates with a living culture that evokes a wholesome passion for the good life and defines the undying soul of its people. The continent of Africa has produced great musical giants and ensembles. For example, Hugh Masekela, Ladysmith Black Mambazo, 'mama Africa' songbird Miriam Makeba and Brenda Fassie (all from South Africa); the late Fela Anikulapo 'Ransome' Kuti with his notorious 'Kalakuta Republic' music and King Sunny Ade and his juju music (both from Nigeria); and the late Pepe Kale, Kanda Bongoman, Mbilia Belle and Kofi Olomide (all from Central Africa). Not to be outdone by others, the 1990s saw the rise of Zimbabwe's musical talents in the persons of Thomas Mapfumo, Oliver Mtukudzi, the effervescent Simon Chimbetu and many younger stars of Chimurenga music, who pack halls of entertainment at home and abroad, with 'sold out' shows.

African fashion has made its mark on the world's markets and is easily recognised by its spectacular colours. African fashion and fabrics are now exported to all parts of the western world. Combined with handicrafts, the African fashion and fabric industry accounts for over 40 per cent of income generating activities for many women's groups, clubs in rural areas and the urban proletariat. Although these activities have economically empowered more rural women, civil society organisations (CSOs) have realised that this industry has failed to realise its potential owing to poor marketing and insignificant exports, hence, more recently, there has been a shift to more sustainable forms of income generation.

Africa's natural resources: wealth or woe?

Africa is blessed with abundant human and natural resources. Famous for their mineral wealth are countries like Ghana and South Africa (gold ore), Angola and Nigeria (crude oil), Botswana and Namibia (diamonds), and Zambia (copper ore). The countries of sub-Saharan Africa boast at least 40 different mineral ores which are mined and marketed worldwide.

For most of the twentieth century, the economies of African countries were dependent on agriculture. Consequently, many African countries invested in developing their agricultural sector, particularly cash crop production. Africa's land mass and favourable weather conditions – warm to hot, with an absence of extremely cold temperatures – suit most of its countries to growing crops for domestic use and export. Agricultural outputs include animal products, cocoa, coffee, cotton, tropical fruits, maize, oranges, pineapples, rubber, sorghum, sugar, tobacco and vegetable oils.

The awesome natural endowments and wealth of Africa have too often attracted the undesirable attention of economic mercenaries, megalomaniacs and kleptocratic leaders. Many of the continent's natural resources were, and still are, being shipped off cheap to the more industrialised countries for processing and subsequent resale in Africa as highly priced processed goods. This creates a discrepancy in balance of payments and fuels the debt crisis of African countries, as governments have to borrow in order to procure much needed machinery or processed goods. In spite of all their natural wealth, African countries have a long journey ahead in the quest for economic development and industrialisation.

The increasing indebtedness of African countries has brought new challenges in the widening gap of world trade and North–South relations as underdeveloped African countries press for debt relief and better terms of trade from the industrialised nations of Europe and North America. Backed by the alliances of industrialised nations, international financial institutions stand in the gap attempting to usher in 'well behaved' African countries to the first world. Yet, for most of Africa, the crossing point is but a mirage, an endless painful journey tempered by the occasional presence of donors and welfare organisations.

Africa's population pressure

The biggest concern in writing this introductory chapter on Africa is how to represent Africa's 700 million people living in over 50 countries. To call Africa's population a conundrum is an understatement. In some African cultures it is disrespectful to count the numbers of children in a family. Yet in order to plan well, it is necessary that countries state population figures with a high degree of accuracy. African countries struggle to meet this planning requirement by conducting resource depleting national censuses, ignoring the fact that traditional sources could provide more useful population figures locally, at minimal cost. Of all the countries in Africa, only the formerly segregated societies of southern Africa managed to establish and maintain credible national registration systems, thereby producing near accurate population figures with which they monitored and controlled the movement of the black people. From such records, countries like Zimbabwe, Kenya, Namibia and South Africa developed good population registers. However, most African countries battle to update and maintain their population statistics as the cost of registration of births and deaths, population censuses and development of voters' rolls escalate.

With the above scenario in mind, it is recognised that Africa's population debate is not just an issue of numbers. It is about populations versus resources.

As the old cliché of Africa's 'population pressure' is gradually eroded by high death rates owing to disease, war and famine, the debate shifts to the effects of population migration. With so many constraints, the ability of African states to plan ahead to absorb their educated, but unemployed, youth and other migrants into the existing urban centres, has been questioned. More recently there has been a mass exodus of African economic refugees away from depressed, rural areas, as well as to international destinations. The last two decades of the twentieth century saw many economic migrants from Africa move to the more developed economies of Europe and North America. This trend of migration is responsible for the 'brain drain' of the continent. Because most African countries lack the necessary resources to maintain accurate population data, they are unable to devise mechanisms to cope with this loss of people and skills.

AIDS in Africa

Recent UN reports emphasise the extent to which HIV/AIDS is eroding economic, health and educational development in Africa by wiping out its human resource base. Except during the slave trade, Africa's population has never suffered as much shock as is being experienced now with the threat of HIV/AIDS. The extent of the fear which the HIV/AIDS pandemic has struck in the hearts of most Africans can be seen in the countless euphemisms by which the disease has come to be known in different countries – 'the slow leak', 'slimming disease', 'slow puncture', 'the modern disease', 'the silent killer' – as if mentioning the name would aggravate its incidence. HIV/AIDS is hitting Africa where it hurts most – the family. From the early 1980s of outright denial or nervous half-hearted acknowledgement of the disease, to the late acceptance and hypocritical enforcement of 'non-disclosure' policies, African countries allowed HIV strains to permeate their societies. Waking up from their self-delusional stupor in the 1990s, many African countries found their societies decimated by the loss of their young and most productive people to the disease, while numbers of AIDS orphans skyrocketed with the attendant social welfare implications. Since then, governments of countries such as Botswana, Nigeria, South Africa, Uganda, Zambia and Zimbabwe have taken steps towards curbing HIV/AIDS by designing bold policies and mounting aggressive campaigns against the spread of the disease. Their efforts, assisted by foreign aid, churches and CSOs have gone a long way towards educating the public, supporting the already infected, curbing infection rates, and forcing governments in many countries of sub-Saharan Africa to 'act lest they die'.

A dehumanising kind of poverty

When westerners describe 'poverty', they do not speak quite the same language as Africans. Poverty in Africa is an all-embracing term which summarises the whole human being, sealing the fate and state of the individual referred to. Imagine being so poor as to be almost non-existent physically, socially and spatially. This is the state of the poor in Africa. This poverty is so dehumanising that one might be naked (therefore hides away from sight), starving (cannot pursue normal social activities), and unreachable (therefore can neither access nor be accessed) owing to remoteness from the seat of government.

Much has been written, debated and 'workshopped' regarding Africa's poverty crisis. One of the donor community's favourite 'conditionalities' for development programmes on the continent has been poverty eradication. To provide for cases of failure within project lifespans, donor project planners resort to buzz terms like 'poverty alleviation' or 'poverty focus'. Several government conferences and workshops are held annually to discuss the African debt crisis and poverty in the posh halls of power while the real poor languish with only a faint hope of being reached by some humble local non-governmental organisation (NGO) or other welfare agent. Even the numerous investment initiatives and the economic reforms imposed by the whizz-kids of the Bretton Woods Institutions have done little, if anything, to ease the struggles of the African masses against poverty.

Predictably, the poorest groups in Africa are women and children. By the end of 1999, over 100 million African children lived below the poverty line and two out of every five children were malnourished. Africa's declining economic growth rates and per capita income confirm this poverty trend which is compounded by gender biases, illiteracy, corruption and population dispersion. Yet, hopeless as the situation seems, African civil society organisations (CSOs) and the international community continue courageously to battle this plight of the poor African, as seen from the papers in this publication.

A matter of good governance

Since the end of the cold war, and as a result of political changes taking place in Eastern Europe, the western world has turned its attention to Europe, forcing the countries of sub-Saharan Africa to get their act together and manage their public affairs better. For countries such as Tanzania, Uganda, Nigeria, Zambia and Zimbabwe, whose stories are told in this publication, bad governance and the inability of the public sector to provide adequate services have provided excellent opportunities for community action and citizens' intervention through CSOs and NGOs. Interventions such as the African Capacity Building Initiative have also taken up the challenge to develop countries in the region through management and administrative reforms, with significant success.

What seems to be lacking in most African states is the political will to put public good before private partisan interests. For example, African governments' rhetoric and promises of 'food security' have done nothing to improve the reality on the ground, undermined primarily by bad management and the corruption of governments. While recurrent droughts, crop failures, and livestock depletion render people vulnerable to poor nutrition and famine, the onus for civil protection in times of need falls on governments which often fail to ensure adequate disaster preparedness. As a result, countries have been forced to swallow the bitter pills doled out to their people in the name of structural adjustment and economic reforms by international finance.

The women of Africa

Gender bias in the African lifestyle is rooted in the African concept of social order and form, buttressed by traditional spirituality. The marginalisation of women in Africa is taken for granted and argued forcefully on the premise of 'our culture' and patriarchy. Even in matrilineal societies of Africa, the relative power of a woman is measured by her reproductive capacity, and her access to resources is often guarded by a male authority figure. Many African societies gloss over the history of female disempowerment by listing the resources and 'imagined power' their mothers had within the traditional setting. They quickly excuse the oppression of women in modern-day Africa, stating that this has come about because of change processes, urbanisation and a perceived loss of traditional values in the new order. There is no attempt to interrogate the issues of women's actual access to resources or their power over 'own resources' which was never assured in the past. Hence African women continue to struggle within very oppressive social systems and governments.

While education and empowerment of women has achieved much for some individual women, the position of women in the wider society is still lamentable. They are still marginalised in most African countries in the economic, professional, social and political spheres. Political relegation is the bane of the African woman as she is shorn of the ability to participate in making the decisions that most affect her. In most African countries, global initiatives toward improving the condition of women by enforcing their rights, affirmative action, equal opportunity policies, eradication of gender prejudiced legislation and improving reproductive health are often undermined by economic problems as women and children always bear the brunt of declining national or domestic financial resources. The girl child is the first to be withdrawn from school as family incomes dwindle; women's reproductive health suffers whenever health systems fail; and women have to sustain their sick and dying family members as governments abdicate their health delivery responsibilities in the guise of 'home-based' health care.

Efforts to correct this situation and their level of success vary from country to country. Countries that have made successful attempts are Uganda, South Africa and Nigeria. Uganda was the first to implement affirmative action and, as a result of a deliberate quota system, one third of the National Assembly is made up of women. Later, in South Africa and Nigeria, successful attempts were made in different regimes to increase the representation of women in national forums, including parliament and the executive. Botswana, Namibia, Zimbabwe, Malawi and others have benefited from women's activism and participation in political struggles, wars or social protests, to a point where laws have been enacted and the status of women upgraded. Women in these countries now have 'equality before the law'. Their major legal status now allows them to push for actual access to resources and opportunities for equality through political processes. But they still have a long way to go to achieve equality in many respects because women are often sidelined in the fight for fair political or legal representation. Africa has yet to have a woman president.

An image for Africa

Africa's media image has undergone rapid changes in the last two decades. For most of the twentieth century, the western press created pictures of mysterious peoples with even more mysterious languages and cultures. During this period, it was not uncommon for a Zimbabwean from Harare to be asked in Galveston, Texas, whether she knows 'a fellow who comes from Africa ... yes ... perhaps from Abidjan' with an African sounding name thrown in. However, from the 1980s political events in the sub-Saharan regions and the trend towards globalisation led to a considerable makeover of the continental face of Africa. No more the tales of primitive people engaged in dark practices and superstitions that transported many film-makers to the limits of their imagination. This Africa is the continent which supplied slave labour to the western civilisations, the fertile ground for western colonial expansionist experiments and the motherland of most black peoples of the world. By the turn of the millennium, the African continent and Africans had finally come out of the dark media stereotype. Today, Africa is better known but even more misunderstood than before. Torn by civil strife, poverty and harsh climatic conditions, yet so alluring in its beauty, Africa looms large with a potential for rapid development or disastrous decline, depending on one's point of view.

True lessons in empowerment

Few stories of attempts at empowerment from the African continent leave room for hope. Often we read about CSOs or NGOs in Africa struggling to bridge the gap of poverty that marginalises the rural poor. Reports of an African continent plagued by starvation, poverty, corruption, violent civil strife, wars, conflicts and genocide are the order of the day. CSOs or NGOs often regurgitate these apocalyptic images of Africa in undignified attempts to attract donor funding for empowerment. Such grim stories might indeed be true but the stories told in this publication give much hope for the empowerment of rural Africans. They trace the experiences of five NGOs to provide at least twenty lessons of successes and challenges of the empowerment process within the African context. They combine historical analyses and plural research methodologies to produce a publication that provides insight for the reader.

Efforts in adult functional literacy and poverty eradication

Patrick Kiirya tells of Uganda's challenges of empowerment through education in a continent where literacy levels are far below world standards. Uganda's Universal Primary Education (UPE) policy is critically analysed to expose the weak linkage with adult basic education, which had hitherto been regarded as a separate and inferior system of educational activity.

When the government of Uganda announced and commenced its UPE, it was in keeping with many African countries which concentrated on children and ignored the productive adult population. However, following the Dakar conference on Education for All, the Literacy and Adult Basic Education Organisation (LABE) set out to illustrate that, complementing the UPE, adult basic education 'is a must for sustainable development' in Uganda. The paper sets out to document LABE's case for a shift from the optional basic education of every citizen to a deliberate system of education for all which is legally binding as a basic human right under national and international laws. In other words, African governments should require all citizens to receive mandatory basic education and should make it unlawful for any citizen to refuse such education. Although it is yet to take root in African governments' agendas, this exciting concept is pursued by Kiirya through considerations of diverging interpretations of human rights.

Experiences documented in this paper include the Ugandan government's commitment to UPE, its policies of decentralisation and poverty eradication, and its efforts at promoting private-public sector partnerships with CSOs and NGOs. LABE believes that, in this era of pluralism, diversified educational models are the answer to Uganda's disparities in the prioritisation of basic education. The paper also looks at the role of funding agencies such as the World Bank in defining directions for adult basic education, as well as the dialectics surrounding the influence of the family and local community in primary school learning achievements, and the formal institutions that are the custodians of learning materials and instruction. The narrowness of definitions of 'adult basic literacy' to mean 'literacy for adults' is questioned as Kiirya states, 'Even with adults, it is not only the illiterate who have basic learning needs. Government planners often forget this.' He bemoans the absence of a 'literate environment' owing to the overarching focus on the 'written word'.

LABE has become Uganda's biggest national network in basic education, making more NGOs visible in the delivery of this educational initiative. The organisation has also contributed to improving literacy rates from 54 per cent to 65 per cent, while selling its services to international NGOs such as the United Nations High Commissioner for Refugees, organisation Nederlandaisede Developpment (SNV) and Save the Children Fund (SCF) as well as partners in Kenya, Sudan, Burundi, Malawi and South Africa. Kiirya situates his organisation within the struggle to redistribute power between adult and youth, non-literates and semi-literates; the democratisation of basic education process; and building a self-help perception for otherwise marginalised groups.

Women working for empowerment, development and change

Two of the papers describe the state of women's professional, socioeconomic and political empowerment.

From Tanzania comes the story of gender-based violence and discrimination which fires up the Tanzania Media Women's Association (TAMWA). This is an urban professional association of women working in the media in Tanzania with the main aim of advocating women's and children's rights. The mission of the association is to sensitise society in general on gender and development issues while specifically lobbying for policy changes and favourable legal amendments to protect the rights of women and children. Their position in the media profession provides ample opportunity to carry out this task. TAMWA runs seminars, workshops, media events and programmes, and disseminates information to accessible communities. The group also run crisis and drop-in centres, providing legal aid and counselling services to women and child victims of gender-based violence. Their success is confirmed by figures given of visitors to the centres as well as their linkages with stakeholders and partner organisations to address gender and human rights issues.

Although membership of TAMWA has increased from twelve to 150 with ties that spread across East, Central and Southern Africa, it has had its share of challenges and threats to its structure. Through the trying times of any membership organisation, TAMWA withstood the test and is proud to record a significant contribution towards empowerment of Tanzanian women by the enactment of the Sexual Offences Special Provisions Act (SOSPA) in 1998. Having scored this major success, TAMWA is not sitting on its laurels but is extending the horizons of advocacy by looking into access of women and children to the legal system and instruments. For TAMWA this is the true crux of empowerment.

In contrast to TAMWA, Zambia's Women For Change (WFC), a rural-based NGO, deals with issues of empowerment for women in the most depressed areas where access poses a problem. WFC has a founding philosophy of reaching hard-to-reach groups of women, hence the strategy of identifying 'remote rural areas of the country where the organisation might work and where few, if any, other development organisations are present'. WFC's grassroots approach seeks first to animate and mobilise all sections of the communities identified to recognise their human resource potential and ensure the full participation of both men and women. Once the area is identified, assessments are carried out to establish and prioritise the needs or problems of the people. The organisation uses a simple participatory rural appraisal (PRA) matrix to determine existing resources and problems faced. The participating communities pass through the complete continuum of the empowerment process, from identifying and 'owning' their problems to making conscious decisions to change their conditions and implementing their 'own projects' using their 'own resources'. This is the community capacity building approach of choice in many southern African countries today as governments fail to discharge their responsibility to their people and donor funding for development projects slowly dries up. NGOs such as WFC have realised the untapped potential of even depressed areas and how to effectively engage rural people in the very serious venture of self-determination.

The cultural approach to empowerment

The Organisation of Rural Associations for Progress (ORAP) is a Zimbabwean NGO based in the southern town of Bulawayo, with three international merit awards to its credit. ORAP's goals are to fight poverty in both rural and urban communities and to empower the rural poor within their cultural context to improve their livelihoods. The paper traces the history of the organisation through its formation, the tensions of pre-independence political activity, the banning/unbanning of the association and its subsequent expansion. With a firm belief in development for and by the people, ORAP's experiences in community empowerment for sustainable rural livelihoods, food security, natural resource conservation and environmental protection provide clear evidence that self-reliance can be achieved even amongst the poorest groups. ORAP harnesses the people's culture and knowledge of their environment to empower them. This results from a conviction that 'rural people are economically poor because they have been dispossessed of their traditional knowledge, language and way of life'. The writer explains that the organisation's vision emanated from the resilience shown by the rural people through the liberation struggles, persistent droughts and political challenges faced by the southerners in the early post-independence years of Zimbabwe.

Key terms from the Ndebele language of southern Zimbabwe are used to conceptualise ORAP's development approach. They emphasise self-reliance, self-employment, and the social mobilisation of 'own' mental and cultural resources to implement a collective savings scheme. As stated in the paper, 'The concepts originate from people's own practices rooted in their language and culture.' ORAP's approach encapsulates the modern strategies of institutional support for human capacity building. It also incorporates gender considerations, recognising that rural women play a very proactive role in the social mobilisation process amongst the communities that they operate in.

The organisation's mission is characterised by the use of phrases like 'turning their swords into ploughshares', rooting out poverty and building development on the strength of the people's culture, knowledge, skills and experience. It also seeks to uphold meaningful democratic values of participation, transparency, accountability and intra-community linkages. These mission statements are followed up with strategic objectives stretching over three-year planning cycles.

Being so close to the community, ORAP has achieved much success in establishing viable and sustainable projects in response to its felt needs and aspirations. ORAP taps into the passionate and firm African belief in the family to establish organisational structures that have proved effective for the challenges of managing service provision to rural communities. The organisation also raises funds and other resources for its membership and endeavours to build beneficial relationships with funding agencies.

CSO partnerships: PERFORM and the miracle of poverty eradication

The case of Nigeria's COPODIN (Coalition for Popular Development Initiatives in Nigeria), an organisation linked to the Poverty Eradication Forum (PERFORM), starts with an assertion that 'the abiding impoverishment of large segments of society remains the principal cause of disempowerment of peoples'. This conviction is the essence of COPODIN in its search for what the writer calls 'dignifying development'.

The paper deals with the 'dependency-for-empowerment problematique which concerns civil society organisations' today. While acknowledging that CSOs and NGOs require funding and donor support to carry out development activities and empowerment, the writer disputes the efficacy of an empowerment process premised on donor dependency, particularly as it relates to North–South donor politics. The story looks at questions of donor funding versus the self-liberating drive of recipient communities, and queries whether empowerment activities can indeed be carried out in the absence of donors. Given the poor resource bases of

African communities and the diminishing financial resources of their governments, the paper explores alternative ways towards the transnational solidarity promised by donor relationships.

COPODIN's two decades of work brings forth several lessons in empowerment which the story explores. It is suggested that the South's historically induced self-denigration through receipts of donor funds is anathema to empowerment. Fully aware that the organisation was navigating uncharted waters, the paper analyses the outcome of this organisational choice for fund raising and the lessons learned in implementation. An idea-based foundation for CSO intervention in self-empowerment is explored within the historical, cultural, social, economic and political context of the people's organisations (POs).

The research methodology mixes historical documentation of the experience through interviews with relevant people, and the compilation of existing documentation and questionnaire-based surveys of views and opinions of a wide spectrum of NGO leaders. A special workshop on Self Reliance and Donor Support was used to obtain the views of CSOs on coalition and partnerships for self-empowerment. An analysis of information from national and international conferences on the issue of donor funding of development activities is also made.

This story of COPODIN illustrates the determination of poor people and local CSOs in Nigeria to overcome a situation of powerlessness and poverty through self-transforming group effort, minimal external financial support and partnerships for development. It contains poignant lessons in the complex phenomenon of empowerment which many community-based CSOs and NGOs in Africa are bound to recognise and utilise effectively.

COPODIN FAMILY: DARE TO BE DIFFERENT

Makanjuola Olaseinde Arigbede

A most important walk

We stopped the car and started walking in the direction of the village. Our mission: to offer our services as doctors and, in turn, to learn from the villagers. Once in the village, we would introduce ourselves as 'their sons and daughters' come to find out how we might be useful to the people. We had calculated that most of these poverty stricken communities would want health services as a priority. We had visited thirteen communities that year, 1973. Without fail, they asked for help with medical services.

Only one of the communities did not – the one we reached that afternoon at the end of our walk. The chief of this village told us to 'go to hell'. He made it clear that even were we to enact magic, he would not want our help.

We decided immediately that this would be the community for our baptism in direct service to the people and our classroom for learning their ways. Six months later we found out why we had encountered this hostility from a people who were so evidently in need of help. It turned out that their caution – what we had regarded as hostility – made a lot of sense in a country where the well-off seek to exploit the denied.

The national context

Nigeria gained independence on 1 October 1960, after being thoroughly milked by the colonising power and the West in general for five centuries. In 1914, what had been three separate major nationalities and many smaller groups were amalgamated by Britain into a single country with one destiny. By so doing, the colonising power planted a time-bomb of discord for the future and provided successive ruling élites with a convenient excuse for not delivering on the promise of independence.

At independence, despite the colonial plunder, Nigeria would still have had enough resources to carry it forward and to help it become a 'good society' had it been blessed with an élite that could deliver good governance. The immediate post-independence period was one of rising hope for the country. The economy was reasonably buoyant even though it relied on primary commodity exports. A wide variety of export crops as well as enough food crops to make the nation food self-sufficient were produced. Nigeria also had considerable mineral resources which had the potential to enhance the accumulation of wealth for developmental purposes. The technology that the country did not have was expected to be developed rapidly to satisfy the needs of agriculture which, in turn, would provide the raw materials for expanding industrial production. Neither did the new nation fare badly in the area of high-level skills as it rapidly developed a large pool of highly trained personnel as the human engine for its development aspirations.

The ruling élite thus started out with credit in material and human resources, productive capacity, the sort of favourable bipolar geopolitical ambience that gives small and weak nations some leeway in international relations, and a trusting, hard-working and responsive citizenry. It could most certainly have successfully midwifed the birth of a good society but it didn't. By the end of six years:

- Nigeria had slid into an economic rut characterised by stagnating agricultural productivity, dwindling commodity export capacity, failure of the much-anticipated technological take-off, and a poorly performing industrial sector.
- The economy had become catastrophically reliant on crude oil to the utter neglect of agriculture and, despite the discovery of larger and larger deposits of crude oil, ordinary Nigerians had become poorer and more desperate, food security had become precarious and food importation had begun.
- National debt, which was hitherto unknown, had slowly risen in the wake of ever increasing borrowing for white elephant projects.
- The private sector, that should have been forging ahead with innovative productive projects and creating new job opportunities had instead become more and more comprador, content with importing and marketing goods produced elsewhere.
- The politics of intolerance and unbridled power was gradually tearing apart the fragile fabric of the nation and political parties had become vituperative ethnic platforms.
- The time-bomb of ethnic divisiveness and suspicion ticked ever closer to explosion point, urged on by the greedy élite in their struggle for power and wealth.

By the end of 1965 it was clear that something had to give, and what gave was the sovereignty of the people and their right to democratic governance. The chaos in the nation gave the signal to the only organised and ideologically disciplined faction of the élite – the military – that it could, without much opposition, and even with justification, enter into the realm of politics.

The first coup d'état occurred in January 1966. Then, a long night of brutalisation descended as one coup succeeded another. Before the present transition from military to civilian rule in May 1999, civilians had ruled Nigeria from 1

October 1960 to 14 January 1966, and from 1 October 1979 to 30 December 1983, a period of nine and a half years, while the military had held sway for the remaining 29 years since independence.

The Nigeria that the people welcomed in 1960 with great joy and expectation fell from being 'the land of hope and promise' to become a nightmare.

The practical implications of this comprehensive wastage of a nation by those called upon to lead it are evident in every aspect of Nigeria's life and the experiences of its people. Today Nigeria is among the world's twenty least developed countries, with 33.8 per cent of the total population not expected to survive to the age of 40 and 49 per cent having no access to health services or safe water.

Citizens' responses and the formation of the new age foundation

The people of Nigeria have not capitulated meekly to the injustices and oppression inflicted upon them by successive ruling élites. Inya Eteng puts it like this:

> Popular mass organs have also developed as institutions for confronting economic and political injustice throughout the colonial period and in more recent times. The Iseyin-Okeiho and Egba risings of 1916 and 1918, respectively, the Aba Women's Riot of 1929–30, the Agbekoya peasant revolt of 1968–69, the Bakolori revolt of 1980, the Etchie incident of 1990, and the Ogoni and similar revolts by communities in the southern oil-bearing enclave since the 1990s strongly indicate the potency of mass movements emanating from popular organisational participation *(Adedeji et al., 1997)*.

The Agbekoya peasant struggle of 1968–69 was masterminded by citizens from the south-west of the country, specifically the Yoruba, and waged against a government that was not only Yoruba but which based its credentials on the protection of Yoruba interests. The peasants made a valiant effort to involve a wider spectrum of suffering smallholder farmers across the country and across ethnic lines but their success was limited. By the end of the uprising, the peasants had amply demonstrated that they could make a serious effort to rid the country of misgovernance. This sacrifice by the poorest segment of Nigerian society had also exposed a painful paradox: although the country was ostensibly very rich because of its huge deposits of crude oil, poverty was more and more becoming the lot of the majority of citizens.

This situation received the most vociferous attention on the campuses of the few tertiary institutions then in existence in the country, in particular at the University of Ife, Ile-Ife (later renamed Obafemi Awolowo University). At the same time, internationally, progressive academics had to unequivocally pitch their tents either with the capitalist camp, which was blamed for colonialism and neocolonialism, or with the supposedly more progressive and humanist socialist camp.

The challenge for this small group of academics and activists was to find a practical expression for their high sounding 'concern for the poor'. As a first step, they formed themselves into an organisation called the New Age Foundation (NAF). At this time (1973) in Nigeria, non-governmental organisations (NGOs) were almost unheard of. The government agency charged with the task of registering such bodies recognised only charities and, since the NAF claimed that its intention was to engender the conditions which would make the giving and taking of charity unnecessary, the agency simply did not know what category of social organisation to slot it into.

Early in 1973, after sharp internal disagreements on the way forward, NAF underwent a reorganisation. One faction of NAF firmly believed in exposing its members to the acid test of actual immersion amongst the impoverished rural population as a basis for learning the necessary lessons in empowerment and self-empowerment. Some members of this faction finally made the move to establish practical connections with living communities.

Guiding principles

By the time we had made our way to the village to offer our services, and to be taught in turn, we had agreed upon certain guiding principles:

- The centrepiece of our *modus operandi* would be assimilation and mutual learning, with the academics being both learners and teachers, not 'infallible bringers of uncommon wisdom'.
- At no point in our relationship with the people must our own ideological preferences be allowed to take precedence over what the people were comfortable with doing.
- We must come ready to give service to the people on the basis of unforced self-sacrifice and without expecting any returns from the people beyond being given the opportunity to become increasingly united with them.
- The social empowerment effort would develop on the basis of an ever widening alliance that would bring together citizens from different class backgrounds, always and only on the basis of a shared commitment to the aims and objectives of the effort.
- As the effort gathered momentum and more cooperative production groups were established by the peasants, participants who joined from the middle class must be absorbed as full members, on an equal footing with the peasants.

COPODIN's (EAII's) evolution from NAF

The first two years in the villages saw intensive work on the part of the activists to change the economic, political and social conditions that underpinned mass impoverishment. The principal tool for achieving this goal was an alliance of all those who rejected these dehumanising conditions. The peasant protagonists named this alliance Egbe Alafowosowopo fun Isegun Ise ni Ilee Naijiria (EAII).

They wanted to transmit the message that change has to be conceived within the framework of an organisation (*egbe*) and that organisations have rules of performance, expectations, rights and sanctions. *Alafowosowopo* means 'endless hand linking' and emphasises the prime importance placed on solidarity, cooperation and sharing as the critical characteristic of this *egbe*. The concept *isegun* was the rallying cry of the people that the way to uprooting poverty from their lives, the lives of their children and the lives of unborn generations, was through proactive, determined struggle to 'overcome'. *Isegun* means 'overpowering or eradicating'.

By choosing the word *alafowosowopo*, the peasant founders foresaw the 'family solidarity' that has characterised the organisation over the last three to four decades. Using the concepts of *egbe* and *alafowosowopo*, the peasant leaders tried to transmit, particularly to their daughters and sons bearing 'the mark of foreign cultures', their understanding of the relations and status within an *egbe* that has solidarity at its heart. In the organisation, all had to be equal but without prejudicing the special respect and consideration given to those in whom the aspirations and authority of the *egbe* are concentrated as leaders. Leadership would under no circumstances mean 'book knowledge'.

(For the sake of consistency, we will be referring to EAII from now on as COPODIN, 'Coalition for Popular Development Initiatives in Nigeria', although it was only in 1990 that the organisation was formally renamed.)

COPODIN's ethos and the work of volunteers

All governments of the South have had to come to terms with the unrelenting pressure from countries and agencies of the North, on whom they depend for assistance, to cede space to 'approved' civil society organisations (CSOs) in development planning and execution. The CSO and NGO sector has gained immense stature and support in the last decade, to the point where it is fast becoming a substitute for governments that are generally regarded as inefficient and corrupt. However, the essential qualities that distinguish these organisations from their private and public sector counterparts have gradually but unrelentingly been effaced. The recognition and support granted them have been won at the expense of visionary energy, self-sacrificing zeal, and cultural rootedness and relevance.

The individual as visionary, committed leader inseparably fused with the people has disappeared and has re-emerged in a business suit as the efficient, paid and instructed member of staff. Where the original visionaries and assimilated leaders are allowed to persist at all, there is unrelenting pressure to convert them into temporary fixtures whose tenure is determined by what is fast becoming a universally uniform set of rules.

COPODIN is not, in the generally accepted meaning of the term, an NGO. It has pursued its struggles without seeking donor funding. The spirit that informed the earliest stages of the effort meant that volunteers were central to the organisation's human resource perspective as it has never been in a position to offer monetary incentives in place of ethical or moral ones. This perspective is linked directly to the way in which a persistent state of underdevelopment is seen by civil society activists. If we are underdeveloped and immersed in poverty because we lack the skills to manage ourselves and our businesses then, perhaps, so-called 'capacity building' and 'training' spearheaded by NGOs would be the antidote. If, however, our state is due more to unrelenting factors of the political economy of domination, both among and inside countries, then traditional NGO initiatives cannot be relied upon to release us.

COPODIN, CSOs, NGOs and POs: What's the difference?

In telling the story of COPODIN, as a CSO that dared to be different by pursuing its struggles without seeking donor funding, we need to explain how we see the organisation. Characteristically, NGOs are 'intermediary organisations' of civil society which position themselves between accessible resources and other CSOs that need these resources. When so conceived, they may even generate resources which they then pass on to their partners, but they are principally 'conduit organisations', created by and dependent upon funding. Given this conception of NGOs, it would be rather strange to claim that they can be run without funding. It is very important to clarify this issue and emphasise that the story of COPODIN is not simply that of an NGO that was operated without funding. COPODIN is what is properly called a 'people's organisation' (PO), one that could, depending upon its needs and philosophy, use the services of NGOs. It is not burdened by the vocational responsibility of accessing resources so as to then transmit these to needy organisations but is, itself, an organisation that has needs and must find the resources to meet those needs. It can choose to approach this task, the way COPODIN has done, relying totally on its own resources, or lack of resources.

The principal challenge of COPODIN's story is that, while CSOs must expend material and other resources on their empowerment efforts, they cannot be indifferent to the nature of the funding that they seek or accept. Funding that obscures the true nature of the causes of poverty and lulls the people into a contented dependency cannot be empowering funding and serious CSOs, including NGOs, must shun it. Funding that completely ignores endogenous capabilities and resources in favour of easy-to-access foreign or other donor funding not only perpetuates the present culture of dependency that afflicts our societies at all levels but also postpones the possibilities for true development. NGOs, like other CSOs, can and must do their work without dependence on foreign donor funding.

It is important to mention here our deep respect for those of our colleagues who take donor funding but manage to maintain the ideational, programmatic and cultural autonomy of their organisations and the people they work with. The critique raised by our story does not seek to belittle the substantial achievements of these activists. However, they are exceptions to the rule that dependency on donor funding means, either subtly or more overtly, the surrender of autonomy over the development process, the paradigms upon which it is based and the limits that are set for it.

The volunteers' initial work

The initial years saw spirited work in the following areas of development practice:

- Provision of free curative and preventive medical services and the mobilisation of communities for the provision of safe drinking water and other social services denied them by incompetent and insensitive governance. This effort obliged the team of volunteers and their rural peasant 'team mates' to learn and apply skills for dealing with government bureaucracy.
- Vigorous efforts to stimulate and develop a critical appreciation of the prevailing economic, social and political status quo, as a means to understanding the forces that generate and entrench mass impoverishment in the country. The state as well as the government needed to be thoroughly demystified in order to raise the level of self-confidence of the peasants.
- An intensive adult literacy campaign, carried out in tandem with the task of generating a critical understanding of the political economy of the country. This task necessitated the development of a manual of alphabetisation in Yoruba.
- Development of fairly large-scale cooperative production enterprises, not yet on a large enough scale to meet the yawning needs of the people but of a favourable size by comparison with the smallholder mode dominant among the peasants.
- Reproduction of successful methodologies as the volunteers became more confident and the alliance with the rural peasant communities grew more secure. This entailed launching a Youth Volunteer Development programme which, for the first phase, focused on students in local tertiary institutions.

A celebration and an invitation

At the end of April 1975, my partner and I were rejoicing at the birth of our second and last child, a divinely lovely daughter and according to the traditional ways of our forebears the naming ceremony came up when she was eight days old. The peasant leaders we had been working with came to grace the occasion. At the end of the formal ceremony, the peasant chairperson made a brief speech to express some thoughts entrusted to him by the other members.

> We appreciate very deeply the sacrifices that you have both been making on our behalf for some years now and we would like you to know that we remember you and your household in prayers all the time. May God, in His infinite mercy, always repay you bountifully. It is clear that if a man spends his time watering the garden of others so that they may live happily, it is God himself that waters the garden of the selfless man. However, we have one small observation to make that we hope you would take very seriously. It seems to us unavoidable that you would have great difficulties understanding our 'tongue' so long as you are staying so far way from us, in a universe where you may turn on electricity in the day time. We would like to assure you on this very special day that should you decide to move closer to us and directly experience our universe, we would be only too happy and prepared to provide support for you and your children to the utmost extent possible under our circumstances.

His words could have only one meaning. Despite our efforts to work closely with the peasants, we were still very much strangers while we held our university jobs. As we ourselves had already begun seriously to question the morality of our staying in these jobs, we responded positively to the challenge, resigning from the comforts of campus existence and moving to live in one of the village communities to continue our work. The other activist who wanted very much to make the move at the same time could not, however, gain the cooperation of his partner and had to give up the idea.

This move was absolutely decisive for the next phase of the effort and the extent of our own relevance. It also opened to us new doors of learning.

Agents of change and personal poverty

Perhaps one of the most contentious issues among civil society activists is the question of how much privation activists can or must permit themselves to experience in the course of accompanying the impoverished people who are their constituents. My partner and I, as the convenors of COPODIN, had simply leapt into the fray, not stopping to check what the price would be. On the economic front, our own purses, which had almost solely supported the efforts, became so lean that our families began to utter groans of neglect and incipient hunger. Part of the price was also the unhappiness of parents who had hoped, after producing such high level professionals, to be proud of them and to be free of poverty themselves; the disappointment of many siblings who felt abandoned because of this 'selfish' decision; and the consternation of friends who could not understand such masochism. However, because we were also exposed at the same time to discoveries of the most profound and enriching sort, it was not possible for us to view the privations as 'suffering' as we worked with the impoverished citizens of our country, sharing dreams and plans, suffering disappointments, and enjoying rare moments of success with them.

I remember a meeting on Sagakope Island, just outside Accra, where I raised the question of the ethics of personal affluence for the activist in the midst of deepening poverty for the grassroots and a major storm broke. I was later to pay for this impetuous intervention by being denied treatment for an attack of malaria as my host had been so incensed by my comments that he could barely bring himself to care for me.

The free clinic and the strategic review

COPODIN has always insisted that our people not only deserve free medical services, and should actually enjoy these as a right, but that such services could readily be provided. Its Community Free Medical Services began on 11 March 1973 and ran with great success in the south-west of the country. Many innovative approaches had to be adopted, and a few pressure group actions mounted, to secure the medical supplies needed for the effort. The success and publicity of the programme caused a groundswell of requests from other communities near and far – a development that greatly alarmed the peasant leaders of the first village community who would have preferred to be given a period of uncontested monopoly.

In short, the contradictions inherent in the manner in which we had leapt into the fray and breathlessly run along to 'the promised land' came home to roost with great force. Difficult questions demanded immediate answers and our class assumptions ran into stiff critique, especially from our most valued allies, the peasants.

These experiences, when taken together, compelled us to undertake a strategic review of the effort on all fronts. Thus, for the next few months, the participants engaged in profound and protracted criticism and self-criticism. All ongoing programmes and alliances, as well as their ideational underpinning, came up for detailed analysis. For many of us who had come into the effort from a middle class intellectual background, this was a traumatic but healing experience. We had, up until then, paid only lip service to 'being accountable to the grassroots'. After the strategic review, the participants decided on a number of new steps to strengthen the effort in the future:

- The organisation would respond to the impulse for expansion but with great care to not overload its own capacities. This was therefore a period of controlled expansion of the coverage of the programme.
- We would proceed on the basis of internally generated resources and what we could, through pressure group work, squeeze out of various government agencies and other institutions.
- We would embark on a large and diversified agroproduction enterprise. In order to both raise the productivity of labour and reduce the drudgery of farming for the members, an intensive programme of training for peasant and non-peasant members of the organisation was begun in collaboration with the Farm Technology Unit of the International Institute of Tropical Agriculture (IITA) in Ibadan and the Faculty of Technology of the University of Ife, Ile-Ife. For the purposes of this programme, the literate members were trained by agricultural engineers at the IITA. They, in turn, not only trained the peasant members but also provided the dynamo for the equipment fabrication programme of the organisation. Many very useful and effective agricultural tools were designed and made by this combined team of peasants and middle class intellectuals.

The collaborations sought and used for this programme were by no means fortuitous or accidental, but part of a clear choice to proceed on the basis of ever-widening functional alliances, both political and technical. Many years of isolation and exclusion had conditioned the peasants to seek change in terms of alliances 'always forming a fist to thump one's chest credibly', as our people are fond of saying.

Nobody does anything for nothing ... what do you want?

When the free clinic was established, it enjoyed maximum support from the peasant communities. Often we would run the clinic using lanterns for illumination, well into the gathering darkness of nightfall and people came from near and far to take advantage of the facility. After some months, however, attendance at the clinics dwindled noticeably until virtually nobody came forward to be treated. This obvious general boycott called for a public meeting and we all sat in the shade of our 'conference tree' to find out what the matter was. After a few oblique comments, very characteristic of the ever diplomatic Yoruba people, the truth came out: nobody does anything for nothing and every action such as ours must have an underlying objective. The people wanted to know what our objective was so as to determine whether or not they could afford the service. The villagers had good grounds for their question as, prior to our arrival, another doctor, using similar words to ours, had robbed them of their 'living banks', their domestic animals. In reply to their question, we requested farmland for a cooperative production enterprise whose proceeds would give the community ownership over the service even though the income would probably be nominal.

Not to speak up is to condemn oneself to expiring with one's travails

The low-key advocacy carried on in the programme at the beginning came forcefully under critique in the strategic review and a firm decision was reached, under pressure from the peasant leaders themselves, who argued, as the Yoruba have done for ages, that 'not to speak up is to condemn oneself to expiring with one's travails'. In justifying the emphasis that would henceforth be placed on advocacy and self-advocacy, the strategic review argued that the fundamental conflict in society derives from the injustices and denial of rights meted out to the vast majority of citizens by the élite. The misgovernance emanating from this monopoly of political, economic and social power by a few has been responsible for reducing the country and the majority of its citizens to abject poverty. The impoverishment and general disempowerment of the citizenry, coupled with the ignorance across a broad range of issues that afflicts people thus excluded, represent colossal problems that must be overcome if poverty is to be banished from society. While CSO projects and other development interventions definitely bring succour to a small percentage of citizens, the fundamental changes that must be made for society to be truly humane can only be achieved by training the people to conduct vigorous and sustained self-advocacy in the quest for good governance and sustainable livelihoods.

The programme therefore strove to:

- conscientise the peasantry, and the rural community in general, towards a clear understanding of the true causes of their impoverishment;
- demystify the much respected Yoruba belief in *akunleyan* (destiny) as the final arbiter of human earthly possibilities;
- practise the principle of accountability both in our general politics and in the relations between the élite and the peasantry;
- create avenues for peasants to influence policy making, especially in relation to agricultural matters;
- enhance the self-regard and self-confidence of peasants in relation to other social groups;
- overcome the sense of futility and fatalism which afflicts the people, especially non-literate peasants and other rural dwellers; and

- entrench in the collective psyche of the peasants their inalienable right to demand and obtain explanation and accountability from their rulers, and encourage them to use this right.

The key to this programme was the recognition that those elected to public office, at least during the cracks in the military dictatorship era in Nigeria, could be pressured into responding to calls from the grassroots as long as they desired to return to power at subsequent elections. The peasants used this leverage most effectively and the experience of having those they had regarded as being beyond the reach of ordinary mortals come to meet with them and be grilled by them greatly enhanced their confidence. Another level of officialdom that came under the pressure of the peasants at this time were the bureaucrats who run the various governmental agencies that deal directly with peasants. These often petty tyrants found themselves cornered once their minister or commissioner had come to honour the call of the peasants and they were left no choice but to respond as well.

The self-advocacy programme involved intensive use of the mass media, particularly radio and television. This was run as a Speak Out programme which sought to project the voice of the voiceless through direct involvement of peasant representatives and spokespersons on statewide media, analysing and highlighting matters of interest to the rural populace and beyond. The experience garnered from the early programme of self-advocacy work by the peasants has been very useful in the present effort to mobilise a wider spectrum of citizenry for a massive advocacy drive to overcome poverty and bad governance.

Many other programmes were launched in this period to strengthen the organisation's poverty eradication drive. These were:

- a modified health service programme, which focused more on accessing the services that ordinary citizens should have as their right;
- cooperative ownership of patent medicine stores, which helped reduce the problems faced in accessing medical supplies;
- efforts to recover traditional knowledge in medicines and general health care, in collaboration with like-minded traditional medical practitioners and NGOs, both local and international;
- development of cadreship among the peasant leaders to generate a corps of dedicated and critically aware peasant leaders as disseminators of the principles and practice of COPODIN for the building of a truly just and humane society; and
- the Youth Volunteers Development programme aimed at producing people, trained in rural communities and poor urban agglomerations under the close watch and guidance of the grassroots leaders, who would take over from the present generation of activists and carry the effort to new heights.

No money for COPODIN

In 1978 the strategic review recommendation that financial assistance be sought, was implemented. Through the assistance of partners living in England, the National Coordinator of COPODIN travelled to Europe to seek financial assistance for the peasant federation's work. The trip took him from one donor agency to another and, although these potential partners differed in their focus, ideologies and preferences, they all had one thing in common: their unbending refusal to entertain any request for assistance from a Nigerian organisation. The reasons given were that Nigeria was a rich country by all the assessments available at the time and that there were many other really needy countries in Africa to which assistance should properly go. It was also said that Nigerians themselves should learn and apply the practice of generous giving to the less privileged instead of the dominant tendency for them to be selfish.

The National Coordinator returned home without raising any assistance and the organisation had to contend with this disdain and lack of interest. While it was true that Nigeria was already beginning to be seen as one of the major crude oil producers in the world, a factor that should have made the country rich, it was patently false to conclude from this that Nigerians were rich and could fend for themselves. This reductionist perspective totally failed to take account of the fact that it is not the quantum of resources but the prevailing social relations that determine what citizens actually receive from the common wealth. In 1978, Nigeria was already under military dictatorship and her citizens had little or no opportunity to participate in determining the way the country would be run. With the euphoria of crude oil wealth already relegating the productive agricultural sector to the background, and the ruling élite beginning to consume every resource in sight, the ordinary citizens had precious little left to nibble on. Under these conditions of mass exclusion, life had become exceedingly difficult for the majority of the people.

The neglect of the international community, along with the organisational tendency towards self-reliance, explains the beginnings of our determination to pursue our work without recourse to donor funding. Besides this, we were obliged to take seriously the adage of our people that 'the pest which consumes the life force of the vegetable is located within and among its leaves'. It was clear that we should:

- collaborate, on the home front, with other CSOs and NGOs (irrespective of whether they agreed with our perspective that overall change and not minuscule alleviation of poverty should be our vocation) in building and nurturing a strong national network to act as a vehicle for civil society interventions in policy formulation;
- extend the necessary 'networking for change' to other peasant federations, inside and outside the country;

- open out to the wider world so that the little that CSOs can hope to achieve locally would be strengthened by work in collaboration with other organisations globally;
- attract like-minded individual activists and organisations to begin to build a series of organisations that derive their raison d'étre from the same ideational foundations, thus beginning the creation of the COPODIN Family of Organisations (CFO);
- intensify our cooperative agricultural production effort so as to reach economies of scale at which level our organisations would be self-supporting;
- convince other networks and organisations to work in favour of fundamental change instead of minute sectoral improvements; and
- make policy advocacy the central hub of our work.

The home-focused struggle

Once the decision had been taken to forge ahead without making any special effort to attract donor funding, with all the implications that had for institution building, COPODIN activists, both peasants and non-peasants, knuckled down to prepare a home-focused struggle. Our analysis led us to conclude that, so long as the economy of the country was enslaved to middle agents of all kinds and at all levels, the real producers could not expect to earn enough from their sweat to justify their daily effort. Peasants already knew that, from cacao to corn, from coconut to tomatoes, when the producing farmer made an income of ten naira, the middle agent would make one hundred naira. And there were times when even the government, through devices like commodity boards, was the middle agent.

We also understood that, as long as policies regulating and promoting agricultural production were made by a ruling élite to favour large-scale farmers, hunger, food insecurity and poverty would be the harvest that peasants and smallholder farmers would reap. Unless policy making for agricultural production benefited significantly from the accumulated knowledge and humble tastes of the peasants, who presently produce 85 per cent of all the food that gets to our internal markets and onto our tables, the livelihoods of ordinary people would continue to be in jeopardy. Agricultural production, especially by dedicated smallholder farmers, had to be given the necessary boost and be restored to its place of pride as the mainstay of the economy. It had become very clear that unless we built the agricultural sector, irrespective of what was earned from the extractive industries, our industrial manufacturing efforts would be a mirage and unemployment and general misery would be the outcome.

The associative movement needed to come to terms with its responsibility in the task of achieving good governance for the nation. Until bad and corrupt governance was arrested through citizens' action, all the little gains made on the basis of small

NGO projects would be doomed to reabsorption into gloom. And, so long as donors continued to swish their fingers about in our national soup pot in the name of 'development partnership' and a few dollars, our development efforts would lack focus and be capable of nurturing only subsistence and dependency.

The above reasoning underpinned our entry into the second phase of the work of COPODIN. We did not lose sight of the need to find ways of reducing the pressure of poverty on the lives of the people through basic needs projects but we said very clearly that these unrelenting needs would continue to hold people hostage until the fundamental issue of power sharing in society was attended to. Therefore, while seeking ways of overcoming the pangs of hunger in the short run, we worked in the long term to enlarge the scope and reach of advocacy and the building of organisations of scale through networking.

Networking

One of the immediate effects of the decision to embark upon a wider partnership in the associative movement in Nigeria was the vigorous effort made by COPODIN to link up and network with other NGOs in the country. Besides bilateral networking with specific organisations, the peasant federation invested huge human and material resources in building a national umbrella organisation for CSOs. The energy brought to the task by COPODIN was based on its conviction that a vibrant and dynamic national umbrella could and should become an instrument for the promotion of NGOs and their work, an effective 'voice of the voiceless', and a major contributor to the civil society self-advocacy drive. The federation believes that there is a compelling case for a national organisation that brings all CSOs and their various networks together. Such an umbrella recommends itself not only to governments, with whom the sector must interact with some predictability and uniformity, but also to private, bilateral and multilateral development support agencies (DSAs).

For the NGOs, this umbrella is often a 'home' in which they can enjoy the widest possible exchange and learning and on which they can depend for protection from the 'frost', or even total freeze that sometimes attends relations with governments. It is a home within which they can shelter from the harsh rainstorms and blistering heat that descend upon them from erstwhile development partners and in which they might gather the critical mass necessary for the effective projection of a credible voice of the people. Finally, it is the home within which they might nurture a durable and self-sustaining institutional memory, character, and set of norms and standards.

Given the way in which poverty has ravaged people's lives, and the tendency of ruling élites to be self-serving, especially in Nigeria, a voice strident enough to project the needs and aspirations of the grassroots is truly indispensable. Also, given the extreme demobilisation and cultural denial of vast segments of civil society, it is the voice of the voiceless that must lead advocacy and popular education tasks. However, despite two major attempts in the last decade and a half, the struggle for a national consortium has still not been won.

Apart from networking at home, COPODIN has worked hard for the realisation of major cross-border networking among peasant federations in the West Africa subregion. The problems confronting peasants in the different countries of Africa are similar and a great deal of progress would be made in each country through greater cross-border collaboration among peasant federations. A brief description of this important and growing network shows how COPODIN views self-empowerment.

The peasant solidarity network without borders: COPODIN–MORIBEN

The two peasant federations, COPODIN and MORIBEN (Féderation des Unions des Groupements Paysans du Niger), had worked exclusively within their own national borders, utilising whatever resources they could obtain from the public domain to foster their productive efforts. Indeed, they knew nothing about the problems of the peasants in contiguous countries. But in 1991, through the networking efforts of IRED (Innovations et Réseaux pour le Développement), an international networking organisation that had relations with both federations, the peasant leaders of the two movements came to recognise not only their essential unity but also those common problems which consigned them to misery.

On learning that rural youth in Niger are underemployed or unemployed for over half of the year due to the inclement climate, the leaders of COPODIN formulated a collaboration programme which would be empowering for both federations. It was agreed, on the basis of several meetings of peasant leaders, that COPODIN's aspiration for agricultural production according to economies of scale, which was being held back by labour shortage, could benefit from collaboration with MORIBEN, and that MORIBEN, whose youth needed employment, could also benefit from collaboration with COPODIN.

In 1993 the leaders of both federations met in Niamey to hold discussions with MORIBEN members in five rural communities. The details they worked out included alternative marketing, with maize produced on COPODIN farms being exchanged for livestock from MORIBEN. This made the most of the comparative advantage of each organisation to strengthen the other.

The two peasant federations came to this collaborative effort in response to their need to be able to effectively generate the bulk of the resources needed for their ongoing self-transformation struggles from their own productive effort. The objectives of their effort went beyond the generation of income as they sought to:

❑ produce the means for the self-transformation of members and their association through cooperative agricultural production;

- do the above on economies of scale which would lift the producers above mere subsistence and produce funds needed for effective organisational development and work;
- establish enterprises of a scale which would provide employment for unemployed rural youth, particularly from ecologically disadvantaged geographical locations;
- promote the self-training of peasants through exchange and new production practices;
- establish production relations based on solidarity and cooperation rather than exploitation and conflict;
- engage in a mutually enriching exchange on all cultural levels across national borders;
- establish mutually beneficial alternative marketing practices and principles;
- establish links of solidarity between peasant federations in contiguous countries, irrespective of geographical or linguistic differences;
- foster the controlled, peasant-to-peasant and country-to-country, transfer of plant genetic material to enhance agroproduction;
- provide important experience for IRED in facilitating the work of organisations of peasants through functional productive networking; and
- provide experience for both IRED and the two federations in capacity building for POs, by the organisations themselves and their partners.

The programme started in Ode-Omu, Osun State of Nigeria, in 1993, with twenty young men coming from MORIBEN into the COPODIN family as 'brother workers' who were housed, fed, cared for medically, given subsistence allowances and paid an agreed terminal wage. In return, they worked alongside the members of COPODIN on enlarged mixed farms with special emphasis on maize production. The activities that were necessary during the planning and implementation of the initiative included:

- the preparation by COPODIN of the social infrastructure to receive the participating youth into the programme at its base in Ode-Omu;
- the employment of the young men from MORIBEN on COPODIN farms, on fraternal terms, over the span of two planting seasons;
- in the second year, a smaller negotiating team of COPODIN leaders being hosted by MORIBEN with assistance from COPODIN to renegotiate the terms of the programme after a joint evaluation of the first year's experiences;
- the participation of 14 young men in a similar programme in the second year;
- a vigorous production effort focusing on the production of maize and cassava on much larger scales than had ever been attempted by COPODIN;
- mid-course and emergency evaluation meetings held in Ode-Omu between the leaders of the two collaborating organisations and their partner IRED, to jointly

find solutions to emerging problems and keep the programme firmly on the rails;

- vigorous and continuing lobbying efforts to obtain official blessing for the cross-border trading component of the collaboration in view of existing prohibition by the Nigerian government of grains transfer across borders which severely affected the exchange programme; and
- the intensification of the construction of grain storage facilities to support the people-to-people trading between the two peasant federations.

Lessons learnt from the first two years of collaboration

The first two years offered important insights into the complexities and difficulties that such an ambitious undertaking entailed. In the first year, the batch of young people sent to COPODIN came from the rural areas and had been farmers themselves. They worked very efficiently and were well attuned to the environment and the form of work required of them. However, the group that came into the programme in the second year, 1994, mostly comprised youth who had migrated to the capital city, Niamey, and developed a totally different set of attitudes and tendencies. These made it difficult for them to adapt to the rural setting and the peculiar discipline of agricultural production.

The programme demonstrated that it is feasible to anticipate significant income generating capacity on a collective basis once the correct scale of production has been reached. It also showed that it was possible to contribute significantly to solving the unemployment problems faced by youth in Niger.

The programme also underlined the necessity of cross-border trading between grassroots entities to find ways and means of overcoming governmental obstacles to legitimate people-to-people trading. The lesson here seems to be that, whatever else civil society entities do, they must take self-advocacy on a significant scale very seriously.

Forming a peasant federation

After assimilating the lessons learnt from the first phase of the peasant collaboration effort, a new step was taken in 1995. The collaboration was developed into a formal network through the following processes:

- The number of federations was increased to three with the entry of FUPRO (Féderation des Unions de Producteur du Bénin).
- To enhance the effort of the peasant federations that were recognised as the principal protagonists, NGOs were brought in as partner organisations with CBDIBA (Centre Béninois pour le Developpement de Initiatives à la Base) from

Benin, GAMA (Groupe d'Appui au Mouvement Associative du Niger), the Swiss Cooperation (Niger), and SNV (Organisation Nederlandaise de Developpment) joining IRED in providing support services to the peasants.

❑ The programme, which had begun as a semi-formal collaboration, metamorphosed into a formal and structured network whose institutional framework would, in the beginning, be flexible without formal organs of control.

Responsibilities within the network were apportioned as follows:

❑ SNV and other donors would see to the financing of the programme.
❑ IRED, CBDIBA, GAMA and SNV would ensure technical support and institutional strengthening of the peasant federations.
❑ IRED would take responsibility for the gathering and circulation of information.
❑ The peasant federations would, with IRED, be responsible for the network's newsletter.
❑ The peasant federations would also be responsible for planning and implementing the commercial exchange programme and the development of women's skills.

To utilise the human resources of the network efficiently, a technical committee of peasant federations, as voting decision makers, and support organisations, as observers, was formed that would meet every two months to examine policies in detail, follow-up the execution of tasks, promote research, liaise with other organisations etc.

In 1996 the network adopted a programme of the following activities:

❑ a follow-up market research study to underpin the commercial exchanges among the federations;
❑ a study of peasant organisations in Nigeria;
❑ a study of peasant movements in Benin;
❑ launching of the network's newsletter;
❑ producing the final version of the network's charter; and
❑ commencement of commercial exchanges among the peasant federations.

In November 1996, at its general meeting held in Ode-Omu and hosted by COPODIN, the network adopted the name 'Peasant Solidarity without Borders Network/Réseau Solidarite Paysanne Sans Frontiere'. FUPRO, in Benin, was designated to house the temporary secretariat. The network continues to expand by including more peasant federations from other countries of the subregion.

Recognition

COPODIN did not merely neglect to publicise itself, it assiduously rejected publicity, either through the media or by way of brochures and other publications meant to endear it to funders and others. This posture was totally in keeping with the rejection by its leadership of all those attitudes and practices that might foster 'developmental tourism'. However, organisations that worked closely with COPODIN and accompanied it in its struggles had ample opportunity to view its nature, spread and characteristics at every stage of its development.

In 1988, the government of Oyo State made a grudging concession to the efforts of the COPODIN activists. Though more than a little unsure of the real motives of the activists in the organisation, the government decided to honour COPODIN with a state merit award. The citation read: 'In recognition of outstanding contribution to social and community development…selfless contribution towards improving the quality of human lives in rural areas', and acknowledged that 'the health of the people could hardly be sustained in the presence of poverty and malnutrition'. Unfortunately, the gesture did not do much to repair the mistrustful attitude that peasants had toward governments in general, especially those imposed by the military.

As it turned out, the much-touted merit award was no more than a wooden plaque garnished with some high-sounding words that were far from profoundly meant by the state. This recognition was given to the peasant federation not because its development work was truly applauded by the government, but as part of a general anodyne concession to civil society. The National Coordinator of COPODIN was, therefore, tasked with making a protest to the government, while thanking it for the award. An extract from the Coordinator's letter to the State Governor gives an insight into how the peasants saw the event and why the mistrust persisted.

> For a programme of self-development like ours, it is not enough for a merit award to proffer moral approbations only. It is also very important that such recognition should materially assist these, often bootstrap efforts, to greater heights. Apart from our free medicare services, for which we expect no material support (in recognition of the problems of government in this area), all other areas of our work stand in dire need of meaningful assistance.

Then, in 1992 COPODIN's main international NGO partner, IRED-International, conducted a competition among its more than 1,000 partners worldwide for the Chandra Soysa Prize. This prize was named for the first president of IRED-International, who gave his life and work totally and unstintingly to the cause of emancipation of the grassroots people of the world. IRED urged COPODIN to participate in the competition.

The decision of the international committee to give the prize that year to COPODIN greatly enhanced the organisation's self-confidence and a memorable ceremony was held at the national headquarters of COPODIN during which COPODIN received the cheque for the prize.

Opening out to the world and a new name

Prior to 1990, except for the brief journey undertaken to Europe to seek funding, we had operated entirely within Nigeria. In the first five years of the life of COPODIN, there was really little to network with at home as the development of the NGO sector was still very much in its infancy and, except for church-based efforts, real self-aware NGOs were few and far between. But, as the true picture of the country's mass misery began to dawn upon the world, donor and other development agency attention shifted in its direction. Foreign NGOs and some bilateral donors started taking an interest in the plight of a people who were condemned to suffer such deprivations in the face of what the world had thought to be a very rich natural legacy. COPODIN came in for some attention and potential interest at this time but, due to its stance on donor funding, it was soon left well alone. However, as the interest of the development community shifted more directly to this potentially great country, the first few real development NGOs began to be nurtured and promoted for international attention. These newcomers to the development scene were encouraged to begin processes of networking with their counterparts in the North as truly indigenous initiatives, not branches of foreign NGOs. By 1989 this process had advanced to the point where Nigerian development NGOs were taking part in plans for global summits.

Another factor that played a major role in stimulating this outward direction was the initiative of NGOs in other parts of Africa, particularly the Sahel, where the abject condition of the populace in the wake of the near total collapse of nation states had produced NGO action well ahead of that in Nigeria. The Forum for African Voluntary Development Organisations (FAVDO), headquartered in Dakar, Senegal, played a key role in stimulating Nigerian NGOs to 'take on the world'. When, in 1990, a major international conference on popular participation was organised by FAVDO and the United Nations Economic Commission for Africa (UNECA), COPODIN was invited not only to participate, but to give one of the major papers. It was as we accepted this challenge that we decided to adopt the name COPODIN (Coalition for Popular Development Initiatives in Nigeria) to facilitate communication with a global reality and the different cultures that would be encountered in Dakar. This was to be the beginning of a major and sustained exposure of COPODIN to the global arena of NGO initiatives in development.

Since that first exposure, COPODIN has had the privilege of participating in an increasing number of international collaborative initiatives which have given us the opportunity to challenge, and be challenged by, a wider spectrum of serious activists for authentic development in Africa and beyond. The experience that came with this opening out to the wider world of CSO activity has greatly strengthened the resolve of our organisation to pursue the course of intensifying advocacy and influenced the rather rigid attitude of COPODIN to donor funding.

The organisation has striven to become more open and to join others in seeking development alternatives worthy of our dignity by networking and broadening our contacts.

One of the aspects of this opening out which has been highly stimulating for COPODIN concerned regional religious institutions. The collaborative work done with the Continental Church, within the ambit of the All Africa Conference of Churches (AACC), has given COPODIN important experience that stands it in good stead. At home, the organisation has worked to weld into a unified force, citizens whose main source of social energy is the spiritual anchorage of their lives. Buffeted and confused as they are by social, economic and political forces that are often difficult for them to properly comprehend, many ordinary citizens seek refuge in and respond readily to spiritual stimulation. Any change process that ignores this fact of their lives would find it difficult to secure their attention long enough for change to be possible. COPODIN conducted a programme of pressure group building and advocacy skills development among peasant leaders in Nigeria using religion as a take-off point. This task, undertaken in collaboration with the Institute of Church and Society in Ibadan, benefited immensely from the continental initiatives carried on with the AACC. The role of the World Council of Churches, with progressive influences like those of the late Paulo Freire, cannot be ignored in the thrust of the regional body at this most crucial period for the development of our interaction with the AACC. Although religious institutions and leaders tend to fix their gazes on eschatological concerns and the promise of miraculous release, it is important for secular activists engaging the people in self-empowering social action to take account of this phenomenon and develop the skills needed for successful collaboration with religious institutions of all faiths.

Developing a 'family' of change organisations

Truth would have COPODIN activists of academic, middle class extraction admit that it was the unwritten wisdom of the peasants, accumulated over many years of deprivation and learning to survive the impact of unrelenting disempowerment, that impelled COPODIN to engage in 'family building' to achieve the desired change. Well before activists of academic background were able to reach non-sectarian perspectives, the peasant activists were keeping up steady pressure to ensure that the effort was not sealed off in a sectarian box and thus made ineffectual. The peasants had always believed in the efficacy of large scale mass movements to achieve society-wide changes and their organisation moved in that direction. Below we examine more closely two outreach initiatives undertaken by COPODIN.

The producers' and consumers' joint organisation

In its drive to collaborate with other social groups that might contribute to the change effort from the same perspective, COPODIN had identified the mass of workers as its primary ally. Workers are the principal consumers of what the peasants produce and both groups suffer from the machinations of middle agents. The first phase of this process saw the two allies organising a collaborative effort for procurement and purchasing. Stable associations were jointly established wherein representatives of workers and peasants analysed the food commodity needs of the consumers and the food production capacities of the peasants. Funds needed for the support of production were provided, in part, by payment in advance by workers for projected needs, thus reducing the dependence of peasants on the cut-throat usurers who ruled the rural landscape. The relationship made it possible to control the cost of food items for the members while assuring producers of fair prices for their commodities. In this collaboration, the counterparts of COPODIN for the workers were their consumer cooperative associations.

This grassroots-generated solution to the perennial twin problems of lack of access to production credit for smallholder agricultural producers and food insecurity for all owing to artificial hikes in commodity prices worked very well in practice. Indeed, it is one of the cardinal lessons that the self-empowerment effort has to offer. If the necessary support and commitment by CSOs and other sectors of society were forthcoming, the present overblown and donor dependent solution of micro credit provision as an instrument of development would be largely unnecessary. It should also be stressed that this is a political solution that effects a shift of power over so-called 'market forces', from middle agents, élites and governments, to the grassroots of society. The most generous and elaborate micro credit schemes backed by donor funding cannot hope to achieve what this option offers the disempowered peasants and their allies in political terms. This scheme depends for its success on the workers being paid and on a vibrant agricultural sector. If the workers are not paid, the credit on which the programme depends is threatened.

In the face of unrelenting government attacks on the programme in which peasants and workers saw a lot of advantages for themselves under the impetus of their own commitment and mutual solidarity, the process gradually but surely shifted in a more political direction. The workers felt impelled to move beyond the confines of the consumer associations to a more overt and self-aware organisation for their salvation. As a result, the first of the organisations which constitute the CFO was born as the Workers' Educational and Recreational Centre (WEDUREC). This organisation, established in 1984 in Lagos and the south-west of the country, sought to use self-mobilisation of the grassroots through education and self-advocacy to raise the level of the struggle significantly. The orthodox trade union movement could not be utilised for this effort which was essentially domicile based and aimed to encourage a much wider, less strictly class specific, membership. Despite its humble and harmless origins, it was still possible for the apologists of military dictatorship to attack the nascent organisation and accuse it of attempting to establish a parallel Nigerian Labour Congress (NLC). WEDUREC was very clear in its published statements and emphasised that, 'This organisation will not compete with the NLC; it is not an attempt to form a rival labour centre; yet, it is not an arm of the NLC.' It went further to stress that: 'It is an organisation in which rank-and-file workers run their own affairs.'

Peasants reach out to the intelligentsia

The peasant leaders knew that somehow they must establish a close relationship with the intelligentsia, the *alakowes* (the lettered), in order to build the alliance that would achieve the change they desired and needed. After all, trustworthy or not, these schooled daughters and sons are none other than their own offspring. At every learning meeting, the peasant leaders put pressure on the, by now few, middle class activists to engender a forum that would bring a wider spectrum of 'people like themselves' to the effort.

While direct work among peasants and the rural communities was not exactly an everyday undertaking among the middle class in Nigeria, it was not too difficult to identify women and men of integrity who also felt deep concern for the plight of the grassroots in society. The intention that was presented to those invited to begin the new organisation was more extensive than accompanying peasants and their struggles; it was a call to be involved in the wholesale overhaul of our society. Those invited came not simply as individuals but as activists in their own right, bringing into the new effort their various organisations as well. The new organisation was called the Network for Alternative Vision of Society (NAVISOC).

The entry point chosen by the participating activists was understandably cerebral, given the perception the middle class holds of itself as the 'intellectual promoter' of social change. It was felt that the first step should be to facilitate a broadly based definitional task in civil society, in which members of the major stakeholder sectors came together to reflect on what type of society they would like to live in. The picture painted by members of each 'class' would then be blended to produce a comprehensive document describing what Nigerians would like their country to be like. NAVISOC believed that those who were drawn into the process of 'defining the nation' would be more easily encouraged to become part of the next phase of this social enterprise.

It is important to point out at this stage that, like most social change efforts championed by middle class elements that oppose the misgovernance of the country, the NAVISOC initiative sought to find a middle way between capitulation to the ruling élite and overthrowing it. While most of them would readily understand the cataclysmic events of 1968–69 when peasants rose to throw off their misery by resorting to violence, they could not participate in promoting such methods of social change and preferred to look for non-violent means. All the interventional steps taken by this organisation, both directly in support of the actions of the peasantry and in other social categories, bore this hallmark.

In the event of actual social contest, however, the actions of the ruling élite, under its most brutal governance structure to date, gave NAVISOC and all other such initiatives a rude awakening. The government of the day gave up all pretence at civilised governance and, led by the most brutal expression of its military wing to date, the ruling élite unleashed terror on the country and proclaimed an unchallengeable monopoly over the right to define what the country would be like. Aided and abetted by the International Monetary fund (IMF) and the World Bank, the government decreed a programme for the country which it called 'Vision 2010'. This move took the wind out of the NAVISOC's sails and a process of rethinking became mandatory for the organisation. Suffice to say, such efforts never really die, they merely recede into the background. As our people say, 'the retreat of the bull ram has only one purpose – to build up greater momentum for another engagement.'

Working without money: COPODIN's work in advocating funding with dignity

Despite the explosion of the NGO sector in Nigeria, the proportion of impoverished people touched by donor largesse is two to five per cent of the entire population. There is, therefore, no reason for those who remain outside of this warm blanket of support to feel especially isolated or unfortunate.

The problems leading to and perpetuating the poverty of our peoples derive from inequitable social arrangements and power distribution, criminal corruption, bad governance, sustained military dominance and grossly unjust global economic and political interference in the internal affairs of poorer countries by the economic giants of the North. Dependence on donor funding can only obscure the outlines of these forces and prevent a people from overcoming their problems through their own efforts and those that could be derived from networking between deprived nations. What our peasants lose in small handouts, they more than make up for in the development of capacity and correct leadership for self-advocacy and the creation of sustainable and just social arrangements.

At present, the main route by which community-based organisations (CBOs) gain access to credit for their productive enterprise is through the intermediary role of NGOs. Many arguments are offered as justification for this choice and they are probably valid, up to a point. The experience of COPODIN has, however, generated a strong challenge to this dominant paradigm in the micro finance sector. The organisation sees with great clarity the fact that, without meaning to, NGOs that play the intermediary role in micro finance may end up actually perpetuating subsistence among their grassroots partners. When an NGO accesses a credit fund for transmission to CBOs (whose number could be large, given the struggle of the intermediary to be seen to command a large constituency), such funds are often too little to properly capitalise the enterprises of its constituency. Most of the CBOs that are served by NGOs, after the intermediary organisation has extracted its own overheads and 'legitimate' share, end up not getting enough to raise their enterprise to reach economies of scale. Subsistence is kept alive and well among the people who are, however, thankful that they receive anything at all.

People's organisations that work without donor funding can concentrate on developing coping mechanisms that make it possible for them to meet the conditions set down by credit institutions, both of the developmental and orthodox private varieties. Such self-empowering organisations may need the services that professional NGOs can offer but they are also able to 'buy' such services if they have to.

COPODIN is able to record some success in this regard. After so many years of self-denial, it is now possible for the COPODIN Family of Organisations to access production support credit with dignity. An important aspect of the extensive networking in which COPODIN has been involved over more than two decades is the realisation in Nigeria of perhaps one of the most efficient and effective micro finance institutions anywhere. This organisation, the Community Development Foundation (CDF) – the only indigenous credit wholesaling organisation in the micro finance sector in Nigeria – now makes it possible for advanced ideas to be entertained and tested in the task of providing credit support to grassroots associations. COPODIN, alongside other important civil society activists and their organisations, played a significant role in this development, which was underwritten principally by the Ford Foundation of the USA and Evangelische Zentralstelle für Entwicklungshilfe (EZE) of Germany.

COPODIN mounted intensive advocacy within CDF for the direct funding of CBOs. Such funding, it has argued, guarantees economies of scale as it effectively capitalises the CBOs' enterprises. The above advocacy has been taken very seriously by the CDF, and grassroots organisations, including the POs nurtured in the COPODIN perspective, are taking advantage of this 'credit with dignity' programme.

Eradicating poverty from Nigeria: a task that must be done

In 1999 COPODIN, in collaboration with the United Nations Development Programme (UNDP) and the wider CSO community in Nigeria, embarked on the

Nigerian Poverty Eradication Forum (PERFORM). For us in COPODIN it was a natural extension of our lifelong work and direction, and it represented a berthing for a ship that had roamed the seas widely. COPODIN was not only the designated national partner but its National Coordinator took on the responsibilities of coordinating this initiative that brought together a wide spectrum of stakeholders to attack mass poverty. The peasant federation thus found a wider alliance than it had worked with in the past and we plunged into the new collaboration with great zeal.

In principle, the initiative accepts the inevitability of dialogue and some measure of cooperation among the three main stakeholders in society: civil society, the private sector, and government. However, it insists that if civil society is to fully and effectively participate in such tripartite dialogue it must first be strengthened and have its capacity built up in an all-round manner. This implies, for instance, that in order for smallholder farmers to effectively participate in dialogue with government and the private sector in agricultural policy making, the farmers must 'beef up' their organisations and learn the 'tricks' of policy advocacy. COPODIN is particularly well prepared by long experience to be able to tackle this responsibility and the organisation views the PERFORM initiative as the last member, for now, of the COPODIN Family of Organisations. COPODIN is not in any doubt as to what its own role and expectations are from this multi-stakeholder civil society entity that gives us, for the first time, the opportunity to plan and execute programmes of social change in direct collaboration with many other marginalised sectors of society, at the same time and within the same overall programme. This is certainly very important for the scaling up of the work that we have been engaged in for three decades. Indeed, it is ironic that it is the smallholder farmer sector, with which COPODIN has always worked, that is charged with the coordination of this important process.

The most important unifying factor for all the programmes of PERFORM is that advocacy and other activities must be based in and on the people themselves, stimulating them to take the responsibility for corrective action in society. The effort must never be based on a collection of a few outspoken citizens who would 'speak for the people' on matters of poverty eradication or monopolise the right to dialogue with governments 'on behalf of the people' in search of pro-poor policies. Rather, it is expected to engender a process that will strengthen civil society entities, build their capacities for self-advocacy and pursue training programmes designed to promote the negotiating powers of civil society groups, especially at the grassroots level. In tackling the responsibilities of coordination, COPODIN is aware that tension must be expected among the different social groups represented in a broad coalition such as PERFORM. However, the test of the viability of the alliance of these groups for social change is the extent to which these tensions can be used creatively to promote change.

Lessons and challenges

The experience of the COPODIN Family of Organisations is still very much an unfolding one and the lessons also continue to evolve with some becoming obsolete and untenable as new challenges and insights emerge to invalidate them, and others, thought to be wholly unlikely, taking on profound relevance.

The desired change

We have no hesitation in saying that the first lesson that this struggle to rehumanise the country teaches is that minute incremental projects, such as NGOs are eternally engaged in, never make fundamental changes. This is especially so in societies already scored with deep clefts of human misery from injustice, bad governance and class exploitation. The tiny ruling élite that controls power, that consumes most of the resources and that is mainly responsible for the misery and poverty of the majority of the people, will resist fundamental change with all the power at its disposal. Change activists must constantly be aware that, when the status quo holds them up as shining examples worthy of emulation, their work has ceased to make any fundamental claims on the system that manufactures our peoples' poverty.

While it is true that the benefits that accrue to a small proportion of the citizenry from NGOs are good, and in some cases necessary, the change that activists must work for goes well beyond this. It is no more than cruel cynicism to argue that the people we regard as poor may actually not regard themselves as poor. Our peoples are poor but they are impoverished by factors and social arrangements that can be successfully combated if only we focus on them and are determined to defeat them.

The modest improvements that the work of NGOs bring about in the livelihoods of our people might have been acceptable in the long term if the larger social system allowed them to reach their potential. However, any honest activist would attest to the fact that the unrelenting misgovernance of the nation, with its dire economic implications, always manages to swoop down just when we are about to sing 'hallelujah' for the successful upliftment of peoples beyond subsistence. Hence, the changes that COPODIN has decided to work for are those that actually reverse the motor of decay, and do so in a sustained way.

In order to get the change process right, it is necessary to unite with our impoverished peoples, both rural and urban, listen attentively to their wisdom and totally commit ourselves to the change effort. Only by so doing can we all, together, discover the correct paradigms to drive the change effort. We must resist the fashionable advocacy in some quarters to the effect that 'people should stop seeking to change the world and be satisfied with the little that they can do and do very well'. This covert form of the irremediably bankrupt 'trickle down' theory must be exposed and rejected whenever it rears its ugly head.

Those who choose to accompany the struggles of our people for a more humane and just Nigeria, and who elect the NGO approach, must reject the donor-driven and false wisdom that seeks to turn them into strangers and outside experts in the homesteads of their own mothers and fathers. I refer to the clearly ideological push for us to regard our interventions in our peoples' struggles as temporary when we are asked, in the name of making way for the people to manage themselves, to organise them on a short-term basis – three to five years at most.

Agents of meaningful change

Change, if it is to be meaningful, cannot be circumscribed by any form of sectarianism. It is not enough to simply mouth 'popular participation' while fronting as messiahs of the people. Messiahs are not good for the people as they merely end up disempowering them. The tendency must be resisted for any part of the CSO movement, on the basis of fund-induced visibility or vociferousness, to arrogate to itself 'champion of the people' status. We must all take seriously the wisdom demonstrated by the peasants of the CFO that only a broad alliance of all those who hate the degeneration in our society can make the desired change.

It is important that we embrace functional networking in various forms and on the widest variety of issues as the way to forge an organisation of the scale that the effort needs for success. Knowing how to constantly expand the population of change agents is the secret of successful fundamental change.

Without abandoning the 'basic needs' struggles that most NGOs are involved in at the micro level, it is of decisive importance for the future of our country and peoples that the larger task of 'systemic change' be kept in sight and promoted at all times. Only by so doing can we guarantee that the good small happiness that we bring into the lives of our people will blossom and proliferate to cover the entire country.

The myth of the 'efficient institution', that is sold to the civil society and in pursuit of which well-meaning and serious activists spend their entire lives, must be carefully critiqued by activists. Yes, it is important to be efficient, to build institutions that last, to practically demonstrate accountability and democracy, to present organisations that are fundable. Beyond this however, the extent to which funder approbation domesticates organisations, and renders them ineffectual in terms of fundamental change, must be appraised constantly and critically. As things stand today, Nigerian NGOs are not agents of fundamental change but of system-approved, possible change.

Funding for change

The question of how to secure funding for the development efforts of civil society remains the decisive one. It should receive the most critical attention of all those who engage the conundrum of social change. Otherwise, they will easily come to grief. The presently dominant paradigm of development funding which depends on donor charity – a profoundly dubious proposition especially coming from the North – can never lead the South out of its quagmire of underdevelopment.

Our modest achievements in COPODIN give us full confidence in saying that the often neglected 'small monies' or 'widowers/widows mites' that members of the grassroots would happily contribute provided they are satisfied that the organisations are their own, can achieve wonders. After all, before the days of the petro-naira, which gave governments a major instrument for the penetration of mass and other movements, the small monthly contributions of workers more than effectively supported their trade unions. How such small contributions can be galvanised into a mighty ocean of funding remains a major challenge that any serious activist must take on.

Our experience has also shown quite convincingly that solidarity or functional networking among grassroots organisations represents an untapped mine of development funding. Direct linkages between and among peasant federations, as in the Peasant Network without Borders, and between peasant producer cooperatives and workers' consumer associations to bypass the middle agent, lead to what could turn out to be major accumulations for development and other purposes.

A matter of ethics, culture and solidarity

Put very starkly, we must admit that the NGO 'world' is fast becoming a rich peoples' club and, for many NGO leaders, it has turned out to be a lucrative endeavour indeed. In this country, and in other countries of Africa, precisely this problem has been part of the reason that governments move to control the funds coming in for development – never mind their empty verbiage about responsibilities of government to coordinate and regulate for the sake of efficiency. For civil society activists, it should be a matter for serious concern that those of us who offered to serve the people and accompany them out of their impoverishment seem to have done much better for ourselves than for our constituency. Unless we resolve this ethical question, we run the risk of being lumped with the parasites that must eventually be subjected to a 'pesticide' attack by the people.

The last area in which we see a major challenge for CSOs is that of the weak, and often nonexistent, solidarity binding the various entities together. It is true that the funds brought in from outside alter the equation and engender what often turns out to be unwholesome competition among anxious NGO leaders. It is also true that the lack of a clearly articulated and universally supported code of ethics for donors leaves room for a lot of unfortunate practices in the field. However, it must be emphasised that, without unifying, historically grounded and culturally self-aware solidarity among the different entities in the development CSO movement, we will forever play second fiddle to a North that works instinctively and consciously in its own interests. This is, of course, without prejudice to the examples of mutually beneficial partnerships that exist globally. Even in our own countries, it is easy for us to listen to donors who preach some quasi-democracy, argue that a country as large as ours cannot, and must not, seek to have one national umbrella organisation. It seems extremely difficult for us to construct a national movement or solidarity across sectoral specialisations and interests, that is, until a predatory government moves to attack us in our atomised state and our vulnerability suddenly becomes evident to us.

Conclusion

The story of the COPODIN Family of Organisations, as vehicles of people's self-empowerment, is an unfolding one and it would be false and out of place to attempt to write a final conclusion to it. In order, however, to bring the present account to a meaningful point that assists the reader to draw useful lessons from the experience, some closing remarks are presented that indicate the present profile of the movement.

COPODIN has developed in response to a specific set of historical and environmental conditions that have ineluctably determined its choices as it struggled for self-empowerment. Its beginnings responded to the logic of the alliance between the impoverished masses of rural dwellers in a well-endowed country and progressive academics fired by a determination to practically contribute to the enthronement of justice, equity and profound respect for humanity. As it confronted the self-empowerment enterprise, its failure to raise the resource support it had assumed it needed compelled it to shift its focus inwards, both in terms of the source of material support for its work and in its conviction that self-advocacy, coupled with self-reliance, must be its principal tools. As it continued its effort, the organisation had to cope with a society that was becoming increasingly polarised between the thin crust of those who wielded power and the majority who suffered the abuses of that power. At every level, the usual 'safety valves' that such societies have to prevent explosion – minimal upward social mobility for citizens; a reasonably fulfilling existence for the people, particularly the middle class; levels of material poverty that do not compel a majority to suffer the lowest levels of subsistence; some modicum of respect for the rights of citizens, at least sociopolitical rights; the availability of 'reasonable hope' for the youth etc. – all collapsed. COPODIN, like any civil society entity, had no option but to 'adapt' to these changes if it were to stay alive and functional.

The conditions experienced by Nigerians between 1967 and 1999, during which period governance moved from the incompetent and corrupt civilian variety to the horrific and pillaging military one, were truly phenomenal. In these circumstances, an organisation like COPODIN, made up as it was of impoverished peasants who could be expected, sooner or later, to resist their wholesale destruction, had no option but to incline towards a political solution to the problems confronting the poor. Its political attitude, part of which was the refusal to become donor-dependent and donor-driven, meant that it could not be trusted by government to be of good behaviour. In the circumstances, the organisation got off very lightly, perhaps as a result of being imbued with the legendary patience and forbearing spirit of peasants the world over.

The writing of this experience has been a great challenge, not only to the writer, who is the National Coordinator of COPODIN and whose life has been intricately and completely woven into the destiny of the organisation, but also to the movement itself. An experience that departs so sharply from the norm is difficult to write about, especially in a period when those who undertook it are going through profound self-examination and evaluation to determine what attitudes will need to be adopted in the present and future political atmosphere. COPODIN is involved in critically analysing the prevailing national situation, especially now that our unfolding transition to democracy has survived the buffeting of the 'old power blocs' for one year. The organisation remembers, however, that it came in for 'painful' notice of state security, under both civilian and military governments, and nothing can be taken for granted.

Owing to the options that it felt compelled to embrace, this family of organisations cannot parade the usual appurtenances of NGOs. In fact, we are now pursuing a greater opening out to civil society, at home and abroad, in a way that allows us to make a modest contribution to the continuing struggle to overcome mass impoverishment and give citizens the opportunity to truly empower themselves. We continue to move civil society away from the past misleading recommendations that it must be non-political to be relevant and fundable, towards a more realistic stance. Civil society in Africa must come to recognise that the struggle to humanise our society is an intrinsically political act of the people. The kind of politics it embraces must be determined by the general social, political and economic ambience of each country.

As a group of organisations, the COPODIN family continues its work in relatively good health, considering the problems it has had to deal with. Each member of the family continues to be guided by its leaders, some of them, like COPODIN itself, having national boards made up principally of grassroots leaders while others are 'looked after' by a body of volunteers and grassroots cadres who maintain the spirit of the effort through thick and thin. The community-based peasant associations that constitute the basic building blocks of COPODIN have begun to be able to access credit support for their production and other enterprises in a manner that does not put their dignity and self-respect at stake. It is envisaged, as one of the outcomes of the ongoing self-evaluation of the movement, that the inevitable greater opening out to civil society will lead to the different units taking on the more orthodox outward manifestations of CSOs.

Bibliography

Adedeji, A. *et al* 1997, *Nigeria: Renewal from the Roots? The Struggle for Democratic Development*, Zed Books, London.

Arigbede, M. O., 1990, 'Popular participation—by whom and how?: Towards a collective understanding of the concept', paper presented to the UNECA and FAVDO international conference on popular participation in the recovery and development process in Africa.

IRED *Forum* No. 45, 1992.

Langley, P. 1996, 'Strengthening peasant organisations in Niger: A study of potential exchanges with peasant organisations in Nigeria', unpublished study on COPODIN.

LABE: BEATING THE COMMUNITY DRUMS

Patrick Kiirya

The national context

In 1908, when Sir Winston Churchill described Uganda as 'truly the pearl of Africa', he was referring to the country's ever-lush vegetation, fertile soils, abundance of food, gentle people, mild climate and abundant freshwater lakes and rivers. During colonial times, and for the first decade after independence (1962–1972), Uganda continued to be known as the 'pearl of Africa'.

However, the period from 1973 to 1990 was characterised by institutional abuse of power, murder, torture, war, looting and general decline. These were wasted years for Uganda that saw the collapse of government services in several fields, including education. This total disruption of society is the reason that Uganda, which in 1960 had the highest literacy rate in East Africa, had the lowest by the close of the century.

In 1996 the government of Uganda designated poverty eradication as the major focus of its overall development strategy. Here, as elsewhere, non-literate people are more likely than not also the poorest. With enhanced literacy and numeracy skills, the non-literate poor are better able to participate meaningfully in their own economic, sociocultural and political transformation, and that of their country.

A key challenge for both the government and its citizens is to make up for lost time in various sectors including education. Given its limited resources, the government's priority is to provide primary education to all children up to fourteen years old. This means that adult basic education has become the concern of non-governmental organisations (NGOs). One agency providing literacy training is a national, indigenous NGO called Literacy and Adult Basic Education (LABE).

Building LABE

LABE started in 1989 as a modest venture in which students at Makerere University gave literacy lessons to people living in the neighbourhood. It became a conventional 'project' between 1993 and 1995, supported by World University Service (WUS)UK and the Canada Fund. Perhaps it would have remained in this stage for some years were it not for its open approach to new ideas early on in its life. In 1994 LABE brought in Professors Lalage Bown and Jassy Kwesiga, two visionary academics who are also very practical in the field of adult education, to evaluate its work and help it chart a way ahead.

Professor Lalage Bown has over 30 years' experience in adult education in Africa. Her probing and challenging words still ring in my ears.

'LABE, you say you are "not just a project of international agencies", then, what are you?'

After toying with some answers, wishing to impress and murmuring words like 'grassroots development', 'people's organisation', 'bottom-up approach', I spoke from my heart.

'Lalage, my colleagues and I wish to build LABE as the leading indigenous national NGO whose first interest and focus is literacy.'

'Thank you very much. Now I can confidently write this report for I know you have a vision,' replied Lalage with a wide smile.

Professor Kwesiga cautioned LABE about not becoming operational if we wished to be national, but aiming to become an NGO that serves other NGOs and community-based organisations (CBOs). This is what LABE has become over the years. From a group of adult education students, to a literacy class, to a project, to the only indigenous national NGO in Uganda whose focus is literacy.

LABE's vision and mission

LABE's vision is to have an informed, literate society able to participate in and direct its own development. Our mission is to promote literacy and basic education choices for women and men in Uganda by working through and strengthening innovative community initiatives.

During my interaction with many local NGOs, I have noted that one of their fundamental weaknesses is an inability to articulate clearly their own vision and mission. But for LABE, the clarity of our vision and mission, which we explain in terms of addressing the specific problem of illiteracy, is a motivating and binding factor. This does not mean that we have not experienced problems related to vision and mission perceptions, especially as new staff members joined or as our stakeholders voiced different interpretations of the concept of 'literacy'. Because the three concepts, 'functional literacy', 'adult literacy' and 'literacy' can each be interpreted differently, it has been important to have inbuilt mechanisms to reassess and revise our vision and mission statements. As the founders, we have had to contextualise our original dreams as changes have gone on around us. There have been new ideas in development thinking, increased provision of basic education services to the Ugandan public, innovations in adult literacy thinking and changes in the demands made by our clients – the literacy learners, literacy workers, literacy organisations and the government.

Like many local NGOs, all our dreams and ideas would have come to nothing were it not for our success in interesting multiple donors in reasonably long-term funding relationships. Being young in the complex world of donor funding, and not wishing to be distracted by time-consuming donor resource mobilisation tasks, we decided to win the confidence of an intermediary NGO whose major interest is development education, WUS(UK). Through them we have approached various funders, including the Department for International Development (DFID), the European Union and Comic Relief. We also approached the Netherlands Organisation for International Development Cooperation (NOVIB) independently. NOVIB agreed to pool their resources with those of other donors into one LABE envelope and accept a unified reporting system. Later, we gained funding support from World Learning Incorporated (WLI), USA, and we are currently discussing the possibilities of funding with Irish Aid. World University Service, NOVIB and WLI have been surprised at our insistence that we do not want a relationship that ends at LABE receiving funds only. So, already, there have been visits from the three agencies and some joint activities. NOVIB, in particular, is excellent at advocacy and lobbying work and we are benefiting from their experience.

LABE operates by promoting literacy choices through partnerships. Its objectives include:

- enhancing the effectiveness of agencies engaged in literacy education through training and follow-up;
- promoting collaboration by providing meeting opportunities for literacy educators to facilitate necessary joint actions;
- advocating for an improved literacy rate;
- influencing policy at local, district, national and regional levels;
- providing consultancy services to NGOs and other institutions in areas related to literacy, education programme design, management, monitoring and evaluation; and
- supporting others in designing diverse, tailor-made, participatory training programmes.

Much talk, little action

Adult literacy is supposed to be an integral part of the vision of achieving 'education for all', initially by 2000 and now by 2015. But there has been little commitment by donors, NGOs or governments to achieving the targets set out in eleven international conferences and workshops held in various parts of the world from 1990 to 2000.

In 1990 governments and other agencies set out to reduce adult illiteracy rates by 50 per cent over the next ten years. The target was not achieved. Were there feelings of guilt and panic? No. We went to another conference, this time in Dakar, Senegal, where we extended the deadline for Education for All from 2000 to 2015.

I was in Dakar during the World Education Forum. Drama ensued as NGOs were about to be blocked from the forum. Pressure was exerted and, eventually, the bureaucrats gave in and 'allowed' NGOs to participate. I had managed to sneak to Dakar because, at the last minute, Oxfam (UK) and ActionAid, Uganda, decided to sponsor me. During a national assessment exercise at the International Conference Centre, Kampala, a week before the Dakar forum, I had openly demanded accountability from the government, donors and other agencies:

> 'Madam Chair, when the representative of the Minister of Education says the Uganda education assessment was the most outstanding in sub-Saharan Africa, may I know what was outstanding? The report? The education outputs? In spite of the wonderful report we have been told about today, where was it compiled, who did it and when? May I request that whoever represents us in Dakar be modest and sincere, and say, "Sorry, in Uganda, we have not done much about adult literacy."'

In Dakar I was shocked to find that adult literacy was referred to only in passing in the draft pre-Dakar framework paper. Although there was a tremendous amount of detail on child education, illiterate youth and adults were mentioned as a 'by the way'. I developed a headache. How could adult literacy be removed from the world education agenda? Other NGO adult literacy delegates were also concerned that adult literacy was being pushed aside. However, after much lobbying, we were successful in that one of the six goals coming out of the Dakar World Education Forum reads: 'Achieving a 50 per cent improvement in levels of adult literacy by 2015, especially for women, and equitable access to basic education and continuing education for all adults.' Adult literacy was back on the agenda, at least on paper.

The Uganda Ministry of Education and, to some extent, the Ministry of Gender, Labour and Social Development, where the Adult Literacy Department is housed, have tended to formulate policies and plans without consulting national civil society organisations (CSOs). They have, more than willingly, consulted (or taken instructions from) bilateral donors but avoided national CSOs, especially NGOs.

I would like to remind these government departments of a statement in relation to adult literacy from the final Dakar document which reads, 'The scaling up of practical, participatory learning methodologies developed by non-governmental organisations, which link with empowerment and local development, is especially important.'

The government of Uganda seems to have read the message clearly. On return from Dakar, I was appointed to a five-member task force by the Ministry of Education. I am the only local NGO person selected alongside the United Nations Children's fund (UNICEF) and Save the Children Fund (SCF) personnel to formulate a policy framework for educationally disadvantaged groups. The Ministry of Gender, Labour and Social Development has also said that, as soon as the government has resources, I will be requested to be part of the team to formulate a national adult basic education policy framework. All this shows that LABE has come a long way in its relationship with government officials and government departments. It is encouraging to be facilitated in doing something positive; for a long time we felt as though, in licensing us to operate, the government had given us baskets of salt and then sent rainmakers following us.

NGOs should work with, and where possible within, government to influence policies to be pro-poor. I also believe that national civil society must courageously challenge government if need be. Of course, this is easier said than done.

Decentralisation of governance: limitations and prospects for NGOs

Like many countries in sub-Saharan Africa, Uganda has undergone a process of decentralisation. The political aim is to widen and increase people's participation in decision making through the local government system. In the Local Government Act of 1997, there arose opportunities for different stakeholders to negotiate mutually agreeable outcomes. The consequences of decentralised governance on development planning and how these have fostered the development world of NGOs are discussed below.

All local districts are now expected to formulate development plans reflecting the needs of grassroots people. Those of us in the NGO fraternity had been claiming that our programmes are based on grassroots people's aspirations and that this was what distinguished us from the centralised planning approach of civil servants who were answerable to central government.

The changes compelled NGOs to search further. It was no longer anything new to have plans that mentioned 'grassroots participatory development' because local government councils at district and subcounty level were also making the same claims. An initial step taken by LABE was to ally ourselves to local government to better access the financial resources in the districts we wished to work in. In the past, donor assistance initially had to be based on agreements between foreign donors and the central government before it could reach districts, but this too has changed. However, inside districts, a form of 'recentralisation' took place as resources had to be negotiated with local officials who work under a lot of local political pressure. We started talking to the relevant district departments about whatever financial resources we had and the districts then used the LABE resources as leverage to negotiate for further assistance from the central government in Kampala. From 1999 our line ministry, the Ministry of Gender, Labour and Social Development, let go of its bureaucratic control. In fact, recognising that LABE is a formidable stakeholder in the districts in which it works, the central government now coordinates some of its communication through LABE.

However, new challenges have cropped up for LABE. While we avoided the centralisation in the capital, LABE still needed to create opportunities for local people and institutions – community groups and local NGOs – to express their views on local development planning. Many local community associations were initially set up as service delivery groups, so to transform them into groups that demand accountability from local public servants and local politicians has not been easy. Training, monitoring and information exposure were necessary if the partners in local civil associations were to utilise the opportunities created by decentralisation. LABE saw itself as a national NGO that should nurture local-level civil society to counterbalance state monopoly while, at the same time, exploring areas of cooperation with central and local government.

By early 1999 we discovered that we had been too ambitious. Central and local state structures were not expecting us to confront them. It was not expected that, under the Local Government Act and the NGO registration laws, NGOs would go beyond service delivery. LABE realised that it needed to link up with other NGOs, especially under the leadership of the Development Network of Indigenous Voluntary Organisations (DENIVA) to demand a revision of the decentralisation laws to recognise the advocacy role of NGOs. At the time of writing this paper, the NGOs had not been successful; in fact, there were signs of more control being demanded by both local and central government. Patron-client relationships still characterise the relationship between NGOs and government structures. When NGOs are asked to contribute resources, they are called 'partners' but partners should not be there just to receive instructions from the other side.

The agenda for the future is still extensive and demanding. Planning, even at district and lower levels, demands a high enough level of Western education for a participant to be invited to the now numerous 'participatory planning workshops'. Most of LABE's constituents, the non-literate or semi-literate, are excluded. This means that LABE has to vigorously advocate for truly non-élitist participatory techniques and models that do not need sophisticated literacy skills. LABE has been at the forefront of promoting Participatory Rural Appraisal and Participatory Learning and Action (PRA/PLA) planning techniques with plenty of visualisation, mapping, graphics and pictorial representations. When discussing budgeting, for example, a LABE facilitator will make a pie chart from banana fibres, grasses and other local materials.

LABE method of using budgets in literacy and numeracy sessions

Local people contribute to local council budgets through an annual graduated tax. The local council officials are in charge of budgeting and spending. This situation raises various issues of empowerment, transparency, participation and choice making.

Below is an example of some LABE literacy and numeracy sessions based on budgeting.

Step 1 (2 hours): Budgets and expenses Literate and non-literate group members are encouraged to discuss their personal budgets (with or without figures). Often it becomes clear that participants do not budget, but spend resources as and when they come in. Personal experiences of the dangers of this approach to running one's life are shared. The facilitators openly admit that they too make mistakes.

Step 2 (2–3 hours): Household budgets Household budgets are discussed as a way of starting from what the learners understand. This later forms the basis of understanding how budgets operate at national level. Estimated figures for various household expenses are volunteered by the learners and written on cards by literacy facilitators. Discussions are then held to establish links between personal incomes and household budgets. It is here that gender issues emerge around who makes decisions about what household income will be spent on. Control and ownership of assets and incomes between household members, including between parents and children, usually generates plenty of discussion.

Step 3 (2–3 hours): Local council budget This session looks at budgets using familiar graphics. We often use a tree, with the roots as the income. In this case, the roots are the items that bring in income for a local council. These are the graduated tax, an education grant and a health grant. Amounts are written on cards for each of the roots. Then the tree branches are used to show the expenditures of the councils: roads, protected springs, furniture for the local primary school, a local police guard, entertainment of central government visitors, pest and vermin control etc.

Step 4 (15–20 hours): Analysing and understanding the local budgetary processes The next few days, or even weeks, are spent on analysing and understanding the local budgetary processes. The non-literates learn figure recognition and basic addition and subtraction. Sessions on efficient resource use, and how this can be achieved, are mainly for those who are literate or semi literate.

Over the years, we have established the linkage between people's oral and mental numerical abilities and their practical literacy and numeracy skills, i.e. the method enables learners to articulate those things that they already know. People's confidence is built as they transfer learning from understanding a local council budget to understanding their personal, household and local association budgets, and they start demanding accountability or even changes in the process of drawing up future budgets. The main lesson to share with other NGOs is that it is important to integrate aspects of lobbying and advocacy in their service delivery. In LABE, we advocate for instructional methods that are participatory, interactive and learner controlled. While government programmes promote literacy through beginners' books, called 'primers', and ActionAid openly calls for 'abolishing primers', LABE has taken a middle course. Although there are times when, in order to be able to read with understanding, conventional texts are important to a non-literate (for example, report cards of children, signposts, government forms etc.), at other times conventional techniques of teaching fast silent reading may be more appropriate. So, in LABE we alternate between supporting the government primer approach to adult literacy and selecting certain useful ideas in the Regenerated Freirean Literacy through Empowering Community Technique (REFLECT) promoted by ActionAid. Being allies to both has not been easy though.

Getting the right balance: the tightrope LABE has walked

As an emerging small yet national NGO, life has been mainly a balancing process. We have had to balance our:

- vision and mission;
- board governance;
- management;
- products, practices and services; and
- workplace and conditions.

A hare does not stop to drink water when a dog is chasing it and one of the biggest challenges for me, as a founder and now leader, has been to take time to determine the most significant components and subcomponents that make LABE function effectively and to consider what will sustain LABE as a twenty-first-century organisation.

Often I have wondered how I can balance all the aspects of NGO life since they all seem necessary to achieve an integrated sustainable organisation. For example, the necessity of keeping within the budget released to us quarterly by WUS must be balanced against the requirement to fulfill financial commitments to partners who do not appreciate planning on a quarterly basis. When NOVIB started working with us and releasing money on an annual basis, our planning improved greatly. We could then bring forward or postpone activities according to the circumstances of our village-level partners. The problems of a mechanical approach to running organisations on a 'project' basis and quarterly planning were rectified.

As a founder of LABE, I have had to grow as the organisation has grown. I have learnt that we need to constantly improve our operational capabilities and sharpen our strategic vision. Doing this has not been easy or painless. I have been labelled in several ways: 'dictatorial' by some staff (at certain times), 'too consultative' by donors, 'arrogant' by LABE competitors, 'quarrelsome' by partners in villages and 'too relaxed' by national level partners.

I have often asked myself why people who wish to find out how heavy a bag of salt is just do not ask the one carrying it rather than keep guessing from a distance. The truth is that as a leader of a young NGO working in a country that was undertaking radical changes including decentralisation – where donors were finding government more attractive to fund and where local NGOs were looked upon with suspicion – various combinations of skills and approaches were needed rather than a conventional management style.

Governance of LABE

Below is an attempt to present the development of LABE's governance as a logical progression. However, the LABE board, like a tightrope walker, has run forward a few steps, stopped to catch its balance, sometimes continued moving forwards, sometimes retreated. The process has been one of constant re-evaluation and renewal. Amidst the ups and downs, there has been a painful attempt to put in place a functioning and effective governance structure in which the board, senior managers, funders and other governing structures (like the committees and patron) understand their respective roles and responsibilities.

Founding phase

In 1989, when the group of friends came together over the shared desire to deliver literacy services, we had little knowledge, let alone information, on NGO governance and management. In order to gain legal registration, a constitution was written as a legally binding document. Unfortunately, the document was crowded with too many details. In addition, there was confusion about appropriate roles. The management committee that existed before a board was put in place did not recognise the importance of separating policy from management roles. As a result, it became engaged in the day-to-day tasks of management, such as monitoring staff movements. The founder staff members were as much involved in policy decisions as the management committee.

A crisis occurred in 1990 when the management committee accused the secretariat (the office-based staff) of using the committee merely for 'rubber stamping'. This prompted frank discussions about the expectations and roles of board members.

In 1994 a reasonable amount of money started coming in from donors – DFID, Comic Relief and WUS – on condition that LABE put in place a 'proper governing body that oversees the organisation'. The Management Committee had to be dissolved but there were problems over how this should be done. Whereas the LABE Constitution mentioned the need to renew the 'committee', it was vague as to whether this would be done by the Secretariat, the Patron or the Committee itself. The Management Committee was just as new to NGO management as the Secretariat. The members wished to contribute more than they were doing and take on new responsibilities as part of a governing body, yet all members had very limited time. It was even difficult to organise meetings between the Chair and the Coordinator, as the Chief Executive of LABE was then known. Although the

Management Committee had solid representation from partner groups and the relevant government ministry, there was no financial, legal or resource mobilisation expert. The committee members from the local partner organisations had an additional problem, in that they came from organisations where the committees did most of the work otherwise done by a paid staff.

In 1995, when LABE was searching for legal status under Ugandan law as an NGO, it had to have a governing body. As the group of founders opted to be paid staff members rather than Board members, it was necessary to solicit other people to serve on the governing body. Those nominated were people exclusively associated with adult literacy – trainers, administrators and lecturers.

Youthful phase

In 1998 the management committee was enlarged to incorporate members from government, the University of Makerere's adult education department and partner NGOs. It was renamed the National Executive Board (NEB). On paper the NEB was bigger and more structured than the Management Committee but, in reality, the meetings were irregular and not well attended. In the meantime, I was attending various training sessions sponsored by the British Council and DFID, as LABE Coordinator. I also spent a lot of time privately studying books on NGO management. LABE itself was undergoing various changes and taking on new roles at this time. For example, it had started dialogue with government and with various funders, and had extended its programme coverage. As Coordinator I found these to be demanding tasks. The duty of taking care of governance was delegated to two new staff members, including a volunteer from Visions in Action. Initially, not much changed as the two were equally new to NGO governance and NGO management. The LABE Constitution was rewritten, but was still too detailed and included operational, management and policy issues. In 1999 a new Board was elected after reviewing the Constitution but, although Board meetings were held regularly, the governance of LABE was not strengthened.

A crisis occurred because, even though Board members said that they understood their role, they failed to adhere to their respective duties. They still demanded to be given operational tasks at LABE, implying that they would then be accountable to the Director, not the other way around as stated in the Constitution. There were also complaints from Board members about not receiving adequate remuneration while, at the same time, the Director complained about the low quality of work delivered by those same Board members.

Consolidation phase

When the Constitution was reviewed in 1999, management and policy issues were separated. New Board members constituted the majority in 1999. The Finance and Administration Committee became more active. While acknowledging an improvement over past boards, staff and Board members identified the need for a more professional and smaller board during an organisational assessment workshop attended by Board members, LABE staff and some NGO partners. The Board at that time was criticised for being too large at seventeen members, and too homogenous, with all members coming from adult education or basic education backgrounds. A further criticism was that the Board included only a few women.

Mature phase

In every single evaluation of the work of LABE, evaluators have identified the governance of LABE as a major weak area. The 2000 evaluators' report noted that 'the national executive board has not yet settled into a common understanding of its own role and LABE's work.' This issue of weak governance is not unique to LABE. In a recent workshop on legal and organisational issues for NGO leaders, a number of NGO directors voiced the opinion that they preferred a weak, barely-functioning board. They feared (not without justification) that a strong board would only try to wrest management control from the director and not contribute otherwise to the organisation. LABE has not deliberately cultivated a weak board, but has ended up with one by default.

In an organisational management and development workshop held in January 2001, Board members and staff once again re-evaluated the role and structure of the Board. There was consensus among the group that, given the changes taking place in LABE (that is, the decentralisation of activities and the more complex needs of the organisation), a more technical and professional board would be appropriate. The current structure of seventeen members (representatives from partner groups, educational institutions, government ministries and an international NGO) might not be as dynamic as needed. Although the Financial Committee had met several times in the preceding year and had reviewed the financial reports, it had been extremely difficult to assemble the entire Board and even more difficult to get Board members to put in any effort beyond simply attending meetings. In the workshop, staff and Board members agreed that a new board would have to be much smaller, more accessible, more technically proficient and have a higher profile.

LABE's Board currently stands at nine members. The Constitution was amended to clarify the Board's role in key governance issues, such as policy direction, public relations, financial monitoring and overall vision. As well as the adult education constituent, the Board now comprises members from the private sector, the legal fraternity and NGOs working in areas other than literacy.

A number of issues, however, remain unresolved. These are:

- the amount of executive power a board should have;
- the most appropriate size for the board of a national NGO;
- who ought to govern and who ought to review the board;
- who the ideal board member might be and how they can be co-opted;
- how the patron of an organisation fits into the governance system;
- what strategies might be used for building board capacity;
- how to ensure that a board maintains a policy and not a management role;
- whether the government has a role on the board; and
- the best structure for voicing the concerns of learners, instructors and partner organisations.

When discussing boards and board management, one has to consider the context, which in this case is Uganda. Evaluators and facilitators from the North base their recommendations and advice on their experience of European or American board operation where there is a long-standing custom of voluntary service. In Uganda, it is impossible to co-opt people onto a board unless there is some sort of financial compensation. Donors, until recently, refused to acknowledge this fact and so, with very limited resources, LABE had great difficulty in co-opting and maintaining Board members of any sort, particularly busy professional people with high demands and expectations. There is also an unfortunate tendency to use one's board membership to one's personal benefit (getting loans, extra work etc.). In reconstituting its Board, LABE will have to contend with these issues as well as the standard ones.

Were I to do it afresh

If you asked me what to avoid should you wish to start or run a local NGO, I would, without resorting to any textbook, list my 'commandments'. These I have learnt through making mistakes as a founder and director of LABE, and I have been in the latter role for about a decade now.

1 *You shall not start or run an NGO in a development field that you know little about.* Development is now a sophisticated industry that demands good general information and knowledge about rural micro finance, basic education, gender etc.
2 *You shall not carry your strategic plans in your head.* Writing down plans and seeking critical assessment from others is a must. It is helpful to think in the 'logical framework' model. Great ideas must be subjected to the 'if' and 'then' analysis.

3 *You shall not place sentiment above rationality.* Development is of people, by people and for people. However attached you are to your idea, if the people we call the 'target group' do not feel for the idea, then perhaps, it is not an NGO you should be thinking about.

4 *You shall be sentimental but also rational.* In running a local NGO, you will inevitably make errors, yet you should have sufficient passion to persuade others that in spite of this you are full of fire and so the organisation will run on after all.

5 *You shall admit when you have erred.* To slip is not to fall. You should say this often to yourself: 'How silly I was to do that, I must correct it so that the organisation goes on.'

6 *You shall be a chameleon while working with donors, your board, other rival NGOs, local and central government.* You will need to be flexible, but often this demands changing colours, tempo, approach and even language if you are to survive in the turbulent times that go with initiating an NGO.

7 *You shall bring in others with different skills from those that you possess.* I initially thought great trainers were all I needed to build a strong NGO. Soon I discovered I needed a finance person, a monitoring expert and, recently, an advocacy guru.

8 *You shall work with your potential competitors even more than your obvious allies.* Opening up to your competitors in a professional and confident way helps you to discover those aspects that may actually be mutually beneficial. For a long time, I was suspicious of government approaches to development. When I opened up to government officials, they realised that my initial criticism was well meant. I also discovered that my line ministry needed me to put forward the case for literacy in the face of competition for resources from the national budget.

9 *You shall always look for cheaper ways of doing the same thing.* As a local NGO grows and as more financial resources come in, the initial frugality is lost and the new arrivals will push for conventional ways of doing things – going to hotels for workshops instead of outdoor camping, buying cars instead of jumping on bicycles etc. Resist these temptations; keep frugal even when budgets on paper appear fat.

10 *You shall know when to say goodbye to your beloved NGO and serve it in a different capacity.* The 'founder syndrome' is a real problem. Yet to prove you are really great, found an NGO, move on and found something even greater – perhaps transfer the entrepreneurship, managerial and resource-mobilisation skills you have honed into a real private business enterprise.

The fruits of our work: linking literacy to wider development

One of the debates amongst adult education professionals and policy makers is this: In societies where literacy is not universal and where big sections of the population survive, if not thrive, without it, what is the use of making illiterate adults literate?

Below are the responses from various adult literacy learners and teachers when asked why they participated in literacy classes, what they hoped to gain and what, if any, benefits they got out of literacy learning/teaching. Rural and urban respondents expressed different views from each other, as did younger and older adults.

I grew up in rural Bugerere. I spent three years at school but never mastered the skills of reading, writing and numeracy. Now I am a mechanic and I want to keep records. I want to learn basic education English to read instructions in manuals and, if possible, enroll in a basic mechanics course. For this, I need to have a primary school leaving certificate. I can now read some English and, at the garage, I read my supervisor's notes, but with difficulty. (*Johnson Mukasa, 21 years, Kampala.*)

Mukasa is representative of the demand for adult basic education services to accomplish personal goals linked to economic wellbeing. He is an example of how our adult basic education services have been able to meet a learning need that formal primary schooling failed to. This proves one of our advocacy issues, namely that those who plan basic education in terms of either basic child or adult education are missing the point. They should be seen as complementary.

I lost my opportunity but why should my child not benefit from this universal primary education drive? I get so worried when I realise that I read better than my child, although I only attended adult literacy classes for one and a half years and my child is in the third year at school. I look at his exercise books and I shake my head. He does not know how to count. How will he be able to write big figures? I wish I could learn more in order to help my child. (*Anne Naigaga, 28 years, Bugiri District.*)

Anne is an example of how our learners have been able to learn basic skills, retain them and apply this knowledge in other literacy-related tasks. Some have used their knowledge to assist their children's learning. This example also illustrates that, since literacy is becoming widespread in rural areas, the skills of reading, writing and numeracy are valued in themselves. This is not necessarily the perception of those who are literate only. For Anne, the ability to use the literacy skills acquired in classes to influence the education of her child is satisfying.

Literacy is, of course, more than learning how to read and write. It should enable people to have better access to information, to become confident and gain a greater voice in decision making. This then reinforces people's capacity to link with development in other sectors which makes sense because development issues are increasingly being tackled with cross sectoral approaches. But this brings in a major LABE advocacy issue. Whereas there have been significant achievements in adult basic education in many parts of the world, including Uganda, future achievements are being jeopardised by exaggeration (or 'overclaiming') and, as a result, expectations become unrealistic. In Uganda, these unrealistic claims have come about as a result of organisational, national and international pressures, such as:

❑ the competitive relationships between NGOs and the Government of Uganda;
❑ competing pressures by funding partners; and
❑ competition for resources between 'formal' and 'non-formal' education.

LABE's close association with literacy learners and literacy instructors has revealed that there is a strong demand for reading, writing and numeracy skills. Yet often, at seminars, politicians and even NGOs tell non-literates that literacy learning is not a priority! Some non-literates have come to believe this because they find it is sometimes difficult to articulate clearly the practical uses of literacy. But they will stay on in literacy classes, for three years if necessary. Here is an example:

I have been in the class for one year now but I will stay for three or four years. I can read and write a little (then she writes three sentences with over 23 words fairly correctly). People think I am silly to want a certificate that may take me three years to get. But I will get it. Those who stand for elections think we are useless. Our local leaders think we have no clever ideas but I will read those messages at the subcounty chief's office, and I will expose them. (*Ana Luma, Ogo Club, Koboko.*)

While avoiding the trap of 'overclaiming', LABE has been able to build a basis for individuals and communities to embark on continuing and lifelong education.

> By LABE printing views expressed by non-literate learners in their local language, then producing reading materials locally written by local instructors, it has been shown that wisdom, cleverness and ideas can be locally found. Local solutions to local problems are now written in the local language on wall newspapers. Various local actions are agreed. They are read over again and again, and rewritten with various angles added. New literates volunteer to read out these actions suggested within the literacy classes at local village meetings. You see, there is pride in demonstrating that one is now literate. In many cases, these actions have been taken on as village level community actions. For example, having a maize granary at every home was an idea that started in one literacy class session – now it is a village bylaw. A little fire in the bush can burn the whole village. *(Joseph Nambago, Programme Manager, Kamuli Adult Education Association.)*

Is LABE making an impact?

When we started working with smaller NGOs and CBOs, we underestimated the preparation we ourselves needed to make as a national NGO. With hindsight, it is clear that we raised expectations and made other mistakes. The confusion surrounding the term 'functional literacy' made many rural partners imagine that we would provide literacy services alongside other 'practical vocational skills'. As LABE was a national NGO, some groups thought it was a kind of donor. One literacy learner put it like this: 'Yes, I have got new information. I can write and read but shall I eat information?' Our monitoring and evaluation section early on noted a mismatch between LABE's goal of empowering people through literacy education and people's preoccupation with sustaining their livelihoods.

After realising these initial errors, LABE staff embarked on vigorous training in participatory planning techniques, such as PRA/PLA, theatre for development and other methodologies. Between 1995 and 1997 we reassessed our work. This almost undermined our confidence but what helped us a lot was the fact that we had a clear vision of where we wanted to go, i.e. creating a literate and informed society. We asked another local NGO, Community Development Resource Network (CDRN), to assess our strategies and methodologies.

From CDRN's assessment and a mid-term review by Prof. Lalage Bown, it became clear that we needed to utilise the new capacities amongst staff to mainstream participation in our strategies, mission, methodologies and objectives. We realised that it was inevitable, that, in addition to focusing on LABE's mission, we would have to use our information and contacts to link partners to other resources so that they were able to achieve what they regarded as immediate priorities, alongside literacy education which they thought was important but not so urgent.

One example is the Multipurpose Training and Employment Association (MTEA). In addition to grassroots agricultural education, this rural group was engaged in providing literacy training. We linked them to a USAID marketing programme. MTEA started buying maize produce from the CBOs and selling it to urban centres at a profit. The need for numeracy, recording and fairly sophisticated literacy skills became even greater and the literacy groups became more active. The literacy instructors were in greater demand and were paid out of profits raised from the increased maize sales. Next, MTEA started selling simple equipment like hoes and slashers. This again required greater recording skills.

There are still some unanswered questions in our minds. When NGOs are implementing projects with donors, with a definite entry point and a finish line, how can they negotiate for time to prepare for implementation? How can an NGO demonstrate, without being tied down to the numbers, the changes that have occurred in a targeted community during the processes of dialogue and negotiation in getting that community merely to accept a project?

We must not create the impression that all became a bed of roses when we employed participatory planning. At one stage, in 1997, tension cropped up between LABE and our intermediary partner, WUS. LABE was accused of unquestioningly agreeing to the local community's agendas and of neglecting earlier WUS/LABE programme activities. There was such a great demand for local musical instruments, community theatre and exchange visits between groups that we spent quite some time and resources on these. WUS was alarmed and started expressing dissatisfaction. Yet, when a mid-term review of goals and targets was undertaken, the groups were generous in their assessment.

Our experiences with participatory planning

In taking on participatory approaches to planning, we were caught in a dilemma. LABE had a more or less fixed mission approved by our Board. Our programmes and activities had been well internalised by the staff and had already been packaged into projects with funding when our partner groups voiced different demands and priorities.

When we had first conducted rapid rural appraisals with community groups to design the initial projects, we had explained our vision and mission, and the organisation's capacities. In retrospect we learnt that this had shaped what the community groups told us. They initially presented literacy as one of their priorities because they thought that if they had not said so, perhaps LABE would have shifted to a different geographical location. Due to project schedule pressure, we had missed a number of steps when condensing our participatory planning process. We had explained LABE's vision and mission, identified partner community groups to work with and embarked on developing budgets, plans, guidelines and memoranda of understanding; this was too much in a short time and must have overwhelmed the groups. The participatory planning, in reality, aborted; instead we 'indoctrinated' the community groups and, in fact, ended up subjecting and controlling them. It would have been better to separate each of these processes. For example, instead of 'training' (which turned out to be 'drilling') community groups in developing budgets and forwarding them to LABE, it would have been better to support groups to develop resource mobilisation plans for their adult basic education so that the groups could select those elements that they wished to negotiate with LABE for funding.

While we were well-meaning and wished to target the often neglected small NGOs and CBOs in rural areas, we did not give enough attention to establishing strategic linkages with other non-NGO and non-CBO actors. The visibility of the small NGOs and CBOs only lasted as far as the state and local government authorities lacked financial and technical resources. As soon as the state developed a national functional adult literacy strategic investment plan with resources flowing through state and local government structures, our small partner NGOs and CBOs suddenly became vulnerable. Their roles were initially not recognised in the national strategic investment plan and were, it seemed, about to be bypassed. In a rather reactive response, LABE embarked upon lobbying activities for channelling donor resources under a sector-wide approach to funding through both state and non-state agencies, rather than exclusively through government as the draft functional adult literacy strategic investment plan had suggested. A lesson we learned was that we should have been proactive and started lobbying the state and local government structures even before a formal strategic plan was in place. The linking of small NGOs and CBOs to local government financial, human and physical resources use would have promoted joint local actions and the resultant synergy would, indeed, have promoted the visibility and perhaps sustainability of the small partner groups.

Participation, defined as negotiating with primary stakeholders outside LABE, was being attempted and was fairly successful although it left many questions unanswered (see below). But there was also the issue of participation within LABE in terms of who was responsible for decision making. A lot of learning took place. About half of the staff was very new to development work and three-quarters had no prior training in basic education work. While out in the communities, negotiating, there were moments when they had to make decisions. Often, they gave the impression that they needed to refer to LABE headquarters and senior staff or even to the Director before taking a decision. This inevitably undermined their authority in communities and promoted the image of LABE as a bureaucratic organisation, which was not an image that we wanted. So, we allowed staff to take decisions but exercise judgement. There were painful and expensive mistakes made on the way: poorly arranged trainings were approved, and funds released for non-strategic and non-core LABE activities. But, this was part of LABE's staff participating and owning LABE's successes and failures. Fewer errors would have been made had we ensured that LABE's vision, mission, programmes, capacities and what LABE could and could not do were clearly understood by all staff, but one wonders whether this would have killed the creativity and innovativeness of the new staff, and turned it into an indoctrination centre.

Other questions related to our experience in promoting participation are:

☐ What happens when, in a community, development priorities and needs are in dispute and what should the role of an NGO be in the planning process when it is well aware it cannot address divergent demands?

☐ There are always local élites, even in a very poor rural setting. In LABE's case, these consisted of some literate people who often influenced the development agenda. How should an NGO handle local élites whom it does not intend to target immediately but who have influence in communities and distort genuine community demands by interpreting them from an élitist angle?

☐ The pre-programme intervention phase creates many expectations in a community. An NGO comes in and its name is heard everywhere: how should it incorporate participation in activities right from the first day rather than waiting until the launch of the project?

☐ What is roughly the appropriate time for preparing and planning with the community before embarking on agreed activities?

Phasing out and exit strategies

In considering whether to phase out and exit from some communities, to stop working with certain NGO partners or to change the nature of the relationships, our guiding torch has been the monitoring and evaluation framework we have adopted. Some tension has also been experienced in this. On the one hand, there is the conventional logical framework which works as a guiding management tool, showing the indicators and means of verification and spelling out what outputs are required and what activities must be undertaken. But equally and possibly more useful are the community originated monitoring and evaluation frameworks. At various stages, as we write up proposals, it has been confusing and in a way amusing to find that what a donor arrogantly rejects as 'not an indicator', 'not measurable', 'not reliable' is what a community will insist on as a means of showing progress as we work with them. Here is an example: in our logical framework to donors, one indicator of literacy benefits was the number of new literates who enrolled their children in school. Yet, as we worked with communities in setting their indicators, there was one which seemed to indicate the opposite: the men particularly felt that, for them, a reliable measure of benefit is when they 'stop depending on children to read and write letters for them'.

'Does that mean if you can read and write letters on your own, you won't take the children to school?'

'That will depend on how much school costs. Literacy classes are free, school is expensive, and if we can learn through literacy, why pay so heavily at school? These days there is no formal employment for school graduates.'

Unwittingly, because we did not clarify the phase-out periods with communities, we created unending dependence on LABE. We should have agreed with partner groups beforehand and negotiated as to when we would part company. If we had done this, the communities could have created systems to sustain and build on what LABE had achieved and they would have been empowered beyond LABE's intervention period.

We have started correcting the dependency syndrome error without just abandoning the groups. In Bugiri district the school results are very poor – among the lowest in the country. We have initiated a new programme called Family Basic Education (FABE), which links adult literacy learning directly with school learning. School teachers teach in FABE sessions and adult literacy instructors help out in school classes as 'teaching assistants'. This means adult literacy is being accepted as part of overall local community development. The school will be in the community long after LABE and its partners have left. So, there is a greater probability of FABE-related work continuing.

A paradoxical situation occurred in planning a phase-out strategy. We started devolving powers to local organisations. Initially, after the first three years, they would openly challenge us, but as soon as they realised that we were letting them take many decisions, they stopped challenging our style of doing things. Life went into a rather monotonous stage of agreeing budgets, plans and schedules. We need to know how an NGO can devolve powers to communities and yet keep up the fire of challenging, questioning and even rejecting certain roles.

LABE has adopted two exit strategies:

1. challenging partner groups by insisting that they must demonstrate that they are working with local government authorities before LABE continues working with them; and
2. negotiating a system whereby all the partners LABE works with in a geographical area come together in a loose network and start taking up some of the roles LABE was previously fulfilling.

We must, however, admit that we are uncertain of the extent to which these strategies will promote the continuation of benefits of sustainable adult community education.

In our desire to be a professional NGO, we have taken time to find out if we are making any impact. We have asked ourselves these hard questions:

- What long-term, sustainable impact do we want to make on the literacy sector as a whole?
- Are we contributing to immediate social change?
- What do we want LABE to be remembered for?

The indicators that LABE is making an impact are:

- People, particularly women, are more literate (especially in their own language), more involved in local governance, more inclined to demand accountability and materially better off.
- The literacy infrastructure – instructors, trainers, partner groups, district focal organisations – sustains the delivery of high-quality services.
- Literacy issues are higher on the national and local (district and subcounty) agendas.
- LABE is consulted on issues of adult literacy.

There are claims which literacy learners attribute to LABE but which make us uncomfortable. All over the world, so called 'functional adult literacy' programmes are supposed to impart, in addition to the skills of literacy, new information on agriculture, health etc. They do this through primers. If literacy learning is not given alongside 'functional information', then that literacy is quickly labelled 'traditional'.

Over the years, we have learnt that it is not clear how people in rural communities obtain information on functional issues like agriculture and health. Yet rural communities have come to internalise what they think development agencies want to hear and will often tell us things which make one wonder about what is being claimed. Here are examples of benefits some learners have mentioned as a result of their newly acquired skills:

- Before, my agricultural produce was low, but after participating in functional adult literacy programmes, I have more than doubled my produce due to my improved farming methods.
- My health and that of my children is now better because of the healthy habits I formed after attending literacy classes.
- I now do not beat my wife because our instructor taught us that it is not civilised behaviour.

Even if our partner organisations are doing tremendous facilitating work, we wonder whether, when people acquire new information and knowledge, it leads to new attitudes. Do new attitudes lead to reformed behaviour? Does information automatically translate into new skills? Does intervention of one agency – a literacy agency – guarantee dramatic changes in attitude, behavior, skills, income and gender-awareness?

Our view is that occasionally 'overclaiming' our product and impact gives us, as NGOs, problems of credibility and inhibits true learning.

Of course, there is sometimes transferred learning. Our focus on helping communities and individuals to learn literacy does not mean that we do not integrate our work with other participatory development agencies. Our approach to literacy is one that enables learners to embark on various development choices – literacy for enhancing current livelihoods, or for examining possible alternative livelihood options, or for linking to civic education. That is why we have adopted the slogan, 'Promoting literacy choices'. The examples below illustrate realistic results that LABE can achieve without any pretense.

On active participation in local community associations, Balikowa Moses, literacy instructor, Nakisente Literacy Class had this to say:

> I became a literacy instructor in 1993. Since then, I have been elected chairperson of Nakisenhe Village Development Society. I think this was because more literacy learners took part in the elections in 1996. I often cannot believe what these learners have become. Our village theatre club is dominated by them; the list of leaders of the local farmers association is like calling out names from the register of the literacy classes. Go and ask at that school there (points), the parent–teacher association has four women in it and they are all from my literacy class. I hear they are very vocal.

On democratic participation in politics, this is what Anne Mutesi, a literacy learner from Luwooko said:

> You do not know how humiliating it is to tell someone the candidate of your choice before you cast a vote. And if I can learn to write faster and with fewer errors, I wish to stand next year for position of Village Councillor.

I said to Mutesi, 'But you can still stand even if elections are held now. You write well. I have seen your book.' She was sceptical. She said, for example, that people manipulated the election and sent each other notes.

'... you sit thinking, why can we not hold elections through secret ballot? The other day, I actually stood up and asked, "But Mr Chairman, let us still vote on this one candidate by secret ballot." Then I was reminded to read the association Constitution and told it does not allow that! My reading skills are not good enough to read constitutions. But yes, it will not be long now... When a leopard makes short slow strides, it is not out of weakness.'

We think that even if LABE has, like a leopard, been making slow strides, our learners have been our source of strength. In any event, what impact indicators can one use to judge whether or not an NGO has moved at a suitable pace?

Networking: how big is the 'new' space for NGOs in the 'Education for All' plans?

The Dakar Framework for Action commits governments to producing a national education plan which addresses the six Dakar goals, to be developed through a process of systematic consultation with civil society, by the end of 2002.

LABE has been at the forefront of bringing various NGOs and other members of civil society engaged in literacy and adult basic education into a loose network called the Uganda National Literacy Network (LitNet). Although the LitNet is just one year old, two main lessons have already been learnt:

1. There is much uncalled-for suspicion amongst NGOs and initially it was difficult to convince others that LABE did not have a hidden agenda in bringing them together.
2. Because networks only function effectively if they are rallying around a concrete cause, it was only when the state started making arrangements to launch a national literacy strategic investment plan affecting NGOs, that the NGOs realised they should join forces.

It is to the last lesson that we now turn, to illustrate how it has worked for LABE and the LitNet.

Up to 2000, the Ugandan government did not have a strategic national plan for adult literacy. Previous work was run along 'project' lines. There was no national adult literacy policy and the government projects worked in total isolation from the NGOs. Government officials used to ask NGOs whether their activities were 'functional', and NGOs responded by asking whether their activities and plans were 'participatory'.

Through the LitNet, the NGOs, adult education academic institutions and individuals are coming together to begin a process of refining the government's five-year functional adult literacy strategic investment plan.

Government chose the conventional approach of asking for bids and selected a private consultancy firm to write an adult literacy plan for stakeholders. At the time of writing, the LitNet had lodged a 'nothing for us without us' protest to the Ministry.

The LitNet demanded active participation in formulating the national plan, including:

- having regular meetings between NGOs and the line ministry on major aspects of the national plan with agendas being contributed to by NGOs and government;
- getting two or more seats on the proposed nine-member national Council for Adult and Non-formal Education;
- letting NGOs themselves elect their representatives on future long-term committees of the functional adult literacy programme rather than the Ministry nominating its own appointees;
- having access to forums that monitor progress, the use of resources and budgetary processes; and
- gaining commitment by the line ministry to finance NGO adult literacy innovations.

We are not sure how these demands will be received. The initial reaction from the Ministry is one of alarm. For us in LABE, this raises the usual dilemmas: For an NGO, what approaches are appropriate in holding government accountable? Is there a way of advocating for the voiceless poor without challenging those who wield power and control resources?

'Teeth that do not move in unison cannot bite a piece of meat'. This proverb calls attention to the disunity that has characterised NGOs engaged in adult education in Uganda. Prior to the coming of the LitNet, there was no properly accepted unifying organisation for adult education NGOs, although the need for them to be represented in a unified way did exist.

Initially, the purpose of the LitNet was to bring together various agencies, national NGOs, district literacy networks, the university Adult Education Department, the National Social Development Institute and a government line ministry. It was assumed that this would strengthen cooperation between the state and CSOs. Unfortunately, it was not long before the LitNet found contradictions in its membership and in its advocacy activities (specifically, the ones that challenged government decisions). The incident narrated below illustrates this practical dilemma.

A LitNet meeting was held in which members expressed unhappiness at the way government was going about the process of developing a national literacy strategic investment plan without the active participation of NGOs. An adult literacy policy was not in place either. A decision was made to go ahead and meet the relevant government officials to express LitNet's concerns. If the government refused to meet with us, we agreed that we would disassociate ourselves from the government and organise a peaceful demonstration of our unhappiness. The Chair attended the full meeting where this was discussed. As the Secretary, I prepared minutes and took them to the Chair to sign. After a week, the Chair reluctantly signed the minutes, which were then dispatched to the Ministry of Gender, Labour and Social Development. Soon afterwards he was summoned to the Ministry and told to 'reform his behavior'.

Back in the LitNet, a reshuffle had to take place. The contradiction for this individual was that he was Chair of the LitNet and a lecturer at a government institution. Government capitalised on this in order to weaken the LitNet. Later, the Chair was assigned special tasks in the Ministry and, when the LitNet representatives met government officials, he sat on the side of the government and espoused the views that one often associates with government bureaucrats and officialdom.

Consultation with local government authorities and donors is the next step the LitNet is embarking on. But there are already tensions among members of the group. The other NGOs are apprehensive about being subordinated by LABE. Their fears are valid. The original idea of the initiators of the LitNet was that it should be a loose coalition. Networking was to be electronic, where possible, and person-to-person or organisation-to-organisation, where applicable. There was a deliberate wish to avoid setting up expensive structures, for example an office and secretariat. So, LABE offered its physical facilities – telephone, vehicle and staff time – as well as contributing a part-time coordinator. To ease decision making and because I was best placed, as director of LABE, I also became the secretary of the LitNet. Frank discussions were held and LABE had to choose to either 'control' the LitNet (a concern voiced by other NGOs) or to relinquish control and opt for influencing the decisions as just another member. In choosing the latter, LABE would have to give up one of the two key positions it already held – Secretary and Coordinator. When this option was presented to the rest of the members of the LitNet, no one was willing to fill the positions. So, LABE took a difficult decision. Whilst accepting that LABE played a key role in initiating the LitNet, further coordination could no longer be the responsibility of LABE alone. A one-year plan to promote and develop the LitNet as a truly autonomous body was worked out between members. The challenge then was how to mobilise extra resources and yet keep to the key tasks of networking, sharing learning, research and partnering with government and other external agencies.

Many questions still remained unanswered as far as networking was concerned:

❑ Is it possible to set up an inexpensive reference point in one NGO and yet promote networking and sharing beyond that NGO without evoking the mistrust of other agencies in the same sector?
❑ What are the 'dos and the don'ts' in this regard?

- How does a host NGO that has its own previously defined systems and procedures promote democratic approaches in networking with other equally autonomous agencies?
- How would a group of NGOs set up an indigenous version of networking and collaboration without resorting to conventional structures of secretariat, funding, projects etc?
- How can a network interact with donors and yet remain an independent organisation?
- In the light of scarce resources, what priority actions should a strong network embark on?
- Are there participatory approaches that can be used by local communities and community organisations to network amongst themselves, and also allow them to retain their African and indigenous identity?

Advocacy

A study conducted in Uganda by the World Bank (2001) on adult literacy programmes in Uganda noted that:

> Both the government and NGO programs are achieving similar levels of effectiveness, and even in districts where both are operating, demand is such that there is no risk of duplication or competition. On the contrary, there has already been some beneficial interaction between the government and NGO programs. Clearly, then, both the government and NGOs must continue to be directly involved in providing programs. At the moment, however, the two sets of programs operate separately from each other, and might benefit from closer interdependence.

This observation sets the background for advocacy work in LABE and the LitNet. While on the surface all seems well in the relationship between NGOs and the government, there is more going on than meets the eye of those who made the above recommendation.

The number of NGOs in Uganda contributing to adult basic education is reasonably large. But the influence of these NGOs on national policies is negligible. That is why, when LABE and LitNet started making policy related demands, tensions emerged with the government.

Government was not the only body advancing a policy antagonistic to NGOs. In a draft report, the government and World Bank (1999) stated: 'The NGO programs are all being done on a very limited, quasi-experimental basis.' LABE mobilised other NGOs and countered this statement. We met the evaluation team and wrote to the World Bank in Washington challenging it. When the final report was written, NGOs were presented in a more positive way. In a revised edition of the report, a specific recommendation in favour of NGOs was made:

Recommendation 4: The Ministry of Gender, Labour and Social Development should review experience in other countries and initiate discussions on ways of enabling the growing NGO sector to contribute even more to literacy education and lifelong education.

This acknowledgement, in the final revision, was a real achievement by the LitNet.

Despite this achievement, a number of difficulties remained. Future strategies in policy analysis, lobbying and advocacy had to be worked out. After this, the design of various advocacy tools and the development of a monitoring and evaluation system for advocacy work would be undertaken jointly through the LitNet.

Like many Ugandan NGOs embarking on advocacy work, we sent two staff members to a training course in neighbouring Tanzania. However, they did not come back transformed overnight into advocacy experts. Clearly, they had learned the theories of advocacy but were still uncertain as to how to proceed. Ironically, those members of the LitNet and of LABE who had not undergone training, but were clear about the objectives of the advocacy and understood the external environment, were just as capable of producing a concrete strategy as those who were supposed to be more knowledgeable.

A practical example illustrates this point: at one stage, the LitNet hit a dead end. The line ministry was going ahead to develop a national strategic plan for adult literacy without an agreed coherent policy framework in place. LABE, on behalf of the LitNet, wrote a letter to the Ministry of Internal Affairs applying for permission to stage a peaceful demonstration. The Ministry officials then alerted our line ministry about the letter. We were pleasantly surprised to hear that the line ministry officials had become more positive about suggestions they had earlier rejected. Another lesson to learn from this is that sometimes an NGO has to be tactful in order to get results. It is also possible to capitalise on the loopholes in government structures.

There are a number of advocacy tools and strategies we have used successfully. These include:

❑ bringing together government policy makers, local government officials, parliamentarians, local NGOs and CBOs, and literacy workers in planning workshops, which have enabled them to discuss their different perspectives;

❑ the LitNet taking part in policy analysis by actively participating in formulating a draft national adult basic continuing and lifelong education policy, with the LitNet being the recognised Secretary, while the government acted as Chair of a task force;

- presenting papers to key donor agencies, sharing our views with various donor representatives in the country and using electronic mail to take part in debates on the Internet initiated by the United Nations Educational, Scientific and Cultural Organisation (UNESCO) and the Canadian International Development Agency (CIDA); and
- participating in other non-basic education campaigns, such as Women's Day celebrations, Teachers' Day celebrations and media days, at which we have been able to organise alongside allies and sell our agenda.

Our dialogue with government on issues that affect both adult basic education and general literacy still goes on. We have learnt that if an NGO moves away from the generalised issues and identifies key strategic policy details the chances of being able to influence national plans are greater. In both LABE and the LitNet, we focused on these issues and they are now being incorporated into the strategic plan and the draft national policy for adult basic education.

Some of the specific issues include:

- the lack of accreditation systems for adults who have the equivalent of primary level skills;
- a dearth of follow-up reading materials in local languages;
- a need to design programmes that interest different groups, rather than one uniform curriculum, and developing different materials for both youths and adults, and non-literates and semi-literates;
- the necessity of improving the quality of literacy instructors and facilitators; and
- the urgency of allocating resources to adult basic education.

The problem of how to monitor and evaluate advocacy-related work persists. We have used various yardsticks to track our progress but have found them unreliable. The literacy workers and other stakeholders commend us for our work but the policy makers, when asked, say they have not been influenced at all by the LitNet messages. A lot of influence is still needed to change the attitudes and practices of government officials. Policy makers still talk of 'eradicating' illiteracy as a government goal even as we who are active in adult education and literacy at the grassroots levels say the more realistic goal is to 'create a literate society'. But, when it comes to practical actions, the policy makers do tend to follow the lead of the LitNet.

At the local government level, officials have started using the terminology of LABE and LitNet. In the media, literacy and adult education issues are mentioned and written about frequently and a number of ideas are attributed to us. The difficulty is that the very target audience we want – the non-literates and semi-literates – do not seem to get this information as regularly as we would like. Nevertheless, in terms of outcome indicators, we seem to have started off well.

Policy analysis is more challenging and we have to build our capacity in order to match that of government, which often hires fairly experienced consultants.

Some emerging issues in NGO–government collaboration

❑ When should an NGO work with government? In the light of entrenched government procedures, standing orders and plans, what role should an NGO play in getting government departments or sections to use participatory approaches? When the decision has been made to interact with a government ministry, the question of who to work with remains. Should it be the extension workers who are delivering services or the policy makers and planners who wield so much influence but are not directly in contact with the users of the services?

❑ How does a national NGO relate to small local civil organisations? While national level NGOs and district level NGOs are legitimately recognised and the government regulates and, to some extent, understands them, there is very little appreciation and understanding of small community-based groups. Most have no paid staff, and lack formal organisational structures. Where does one start empowering them?

❑ How does an NGO retain good public relations with government officials, yet challenge and, at times, confront them on fundamental issues that relate to empowering people or questioning major decisions?

❑ How can an NGO remain 'non political' in the face of the politicised nature of participatory development that leads towards empowerment?

❑ How can the volunteer spirit amongst NGOs and CBOs be maintained while government officials are paid allowances for almost everything, including 'sitting' allowances for attending meetings?

❑ How should an NGO market its innovations to government officials, without giving financial resources to accompany the ideas? In other words, how can technical capital be packaged so that it is as attractive as the financial capital that NGOs are often associated with when they interact with government structures?

❑ Can genuine trust be built between an NGO and the government? What are the 'no compromise' issues an NGO should stand firm on?

❑ Is the contractual funding relationship between NGOs and the government problematic? How should NGOs go about addressing this?

It is self-deceiving for NGOs to describe themselves as non-political institutions. True, they are not political parties – those are partisan. But I am convinced that formidable NGOs should be where conflicting interests are at play. For example, to balance pro-poor interests against business interests and remind business of its corporate citizenship obligations, to promote people's associations or to challenge 'standing orders' in often outdated policies. All these are political issues and an NGO must be ready for the turbulent waters of this type of non-partisan politics.

Conclusion

Considering where LABE has come from, the time wasted and tensions generated, I think the phases of setting up an NGO should include an activity-oriented pre-NGO formation stage. During this time, the founders should make decisions on the nature of the NGO that they wish to set up. There is vagueness about what constitutes a strong NGO. Is it the one with 'proper' systems in place or is it the one that experiments with various alternatives? The experience of LABE suggests that, even when an NGO is set up, it should not be based on rigid structures and systems. The ability to combine the standard approaches, which can incorporate informal, even ad hoc systems, eventually produces a strong hybrid structure. Rigid systems in a newly formed NGO stifle the leaders and the staff.

There is no definite starting point in the formation of an NGO. I trace the origin of LABE to my childhood admiration of my father's dedication to teaching, his religious inclinations and my dissatisfaction with what I was subjected to in my teaching career and my quest for higher education.

A marriage between NGOs and governments is inevitably cultivated but it must be a daring relationship. If possible, the NGO should initiate the marriage. But NGOs should not bring all areas of their activities and objectives into the NGO-government relationship. Why should you use both your feet to test how deep a river is? A national NGO can take the lead in initiating the relationship with central government and mobilise other NGOs and CBOs, at every level, to do so as well. NGOs should ensure that they are not, in these relationships, used as cheap (hidden in words like 'cost effective') robots to fulfill government agendas. When such a relationship starts, part of the NGO networks' responsibilities should be to lobby for legislation of NGO-government collaboration at both central and local levels.

An overriding priority for a national level NGO should be to engage line ministries and local government in policy dialogue. Unfortunately, NGOs are often weak in policy work or unable to acquire up to date information on development policies that are pro-poor. Even if results do not come immediately, just the continuous dialogue, the pushing, the threatening, is good enough. It is only in these cases that an NGO should open up its plans and tactics fully to donors of grants (not the lenders), for they are great allies. What donors may not say aloud due to diplomatic niceties, a local NGO can shout out and their shouting can be timed to coincide with elections.

NGOs cannot bring about miracles merely by using high-sounding jargon, such as 'beneficiaries', 'capacity building', 'participation', 'empowerment', and 'civil society'. What NGOs should constantly strive for are alternative ways of doing things. There are no fixed systems in today's world of globalisation, market forces and information accessibility. There is a limit to closing ourselves in and talking our jargon to and at each other. We need to initiate the changes ourselves. No healthy person takes medicine on behalf of the sick. The answers lie in opening up to collaboration with the business sector and the government. Remember, no matter how thirsty you are you cannot quench your thirst with your saliva. And if the rhythm of the drumbeat changes, the dance steps must also change.

Bibliography

Archer, D. 2000, 'Words and action: the implications of Dakar for adult literacy and REFLECT' in *Education Action* 13: 25–26.

Bown, L. and Mayatsa, G. W. W. 1998, 'Training for literacy choices: A mid-term review and evaluation of the work of LABE (Uganda)' in *Training of Literacy Trainers, Women's Literacy and Continuing Literacy Support*, WUS(UK) & LABE, Kampala.

Bown, L., Kwesiga, J. B. H., Baryayebwa, H and Mace, J. 2000, *LABE 2000: An Evaluation of the Work of LABE (Uganda) from 1995 to the Present*, WUS(UK) and LABE, Kampala.

Mace, J. and Keihangwe, S. 2000, 'We are together, we are many: Adult literacy in rural Uganda', report, WUS(UK), London.

Ministry of Finance, Planning and Economic Development 2000, 'Uganda Participatory Poverty Assessment Report: Learning from the Poor', Kampala.

Ministry of Gender, Labour and Social Development & World Bank 1999, 'Evaluation of the functional adult literacy programmes in Uganda', draft report.

Müller, J. 2000, 'From Jomtien to Dakar: Meeting Basic Learning Needs of Whom?' in *Adult Education and Development* 55: 22-59.

UNESCO, *Dakar Framework for Action, Education for All: Meeting Our Collective Commitments*. Available at: www.unesco.org/education

United Nations Development Programme 2000, *Human Development Report 2000*, New York.

World Bank 2001, *Adult Literacy Programs in Uganda*, Africa Region Human Development Series, Washington, D.C.

ORAP AND THE SPIRIT OF ZENZELE

Tomson Dube

Introduction

Zimbabwe's Organisation of Rural Associations for Progress (ORAP) is now twenty years old. Its constituency consists of approximately one and a half million people in family groups in some 12,800 areas. ORAP's vision is to create empowered grassroots communities, free from hunger and poverty. These communities should draw up their own development plans based on their own intellect, resources and cultural context to uplift themselves. This story of ORAP aims to show the processes in empowerment among the grassroots people of the provinces of Matabeleland North and South, and the Midlands.

ORAP has been internationally recognised and has received a number of awards. From 1988 to 1990, Sithembiso Nyoni, then Executive Coordinator, was named Zimbabwe's candidate for the Africa Prize for Leadership for the Sustainable End of Hunger. In 1993, ORAP won the 'alternative Nobel Prize', the Right Livelihood Award, sponsored by the Swedish Parliament. This was in recognition of ORAP's leadership in working with communities and allowing the grassroots people of Zimbabwe to choose their own path of development using culture as a tool to work toward self-reliance and sustainability. The award is for 'vision and work forming an essential contribution to making life more whole, healing our planet and uplifting humanity'. In 1996, ORAP was awarded the We-the-50-Communities Award, sponsored by the United Nations Development Programme (UNDP), in recognition of its contribution to creating common unity. The following year, We-the-50-Communities Award again recognised ORAP, this time in the category of Food, Agriculture, Fisheries and Forests.

It is the work of ORAP and its members, the majority of whom are women and children, that is shared in this paper. The grassroots people tell the story themselves, as do the managers and some donor representatives in Zimbabwe. Allow me to walk you through the twenty-year history of ORAP. Though it does not portray all that ORAP has done, the people have spoken and these are their voices.

Alice Zulu has been working with ORAP for sixteen years and has served as Board Secretary for seven years. She speaks about her community's proudest achievements. These include a dam that was constructed for the community, a library that was built at Simwango School and a loan facility that has been extended to farmers at Silalabuhwa. The Usizo Credit and Savings Scheme, an ORAP programme headed by Florence Mafeking, extended this loan facility. Mafeking says that there are eighteen groups being supported, forming a total clientele base of 378. These clients are involved in trading, savings, vending and manufacturing. Mafeking says that she is proud of the achievements of this programme.

The origins of ORAP and its unique approach to development

ORAP was formed in 1980, soon after Zimbabwe's war of liberation. For about a year, a small group of people, mainly teachers, social workers and church people, had been meeting and discussing possible new rural development strategies in the light of the independence struggle and its effects in the rural areas. They operated as a Rural Development Coordination Council (RDCC) and their objective was to facilitate self-reliance through skills training and sharing of expertise, information and resources at village level. Sithembiso Nyoni, a member of the group, was completing her Master's thesis in rural development at the time. Her supervisor recommended that her work should be tried out and should not just lie and gather dust in a library. Nyoni says, 'I never intended to form an NGO. It is a process that happened because I followed my passion.'

Funds were obtained from international voluntary organisations to employ two local development workers who, together with a British couple working as volunteers, began making contacts with groups, raising funds for small projects and working towards the creation of ORAP. They offered training in rural development to the future Executive Coordinator of ORAP and one future staff member.

ORAP was created out of the need to help improve the quality of life of the rural masses and to establish support for communities which would enable them to develop according to their own priorities. The transformation from the RDCC to ORAP was a practical recognition that the power base within an organisation should lie with the rural people themselves and not with the promoters of the ORAP concept, or with any permanent staff. The role of the latter is to assist in the implementation of priorities determined by the rural groups.

Nyoni says that hopes were high at the start and there was a sense of stability from 1980 to the end of 1982. In March 1983, when the Zimbabwe government imposed curfews intended to minimise dissident activities that were prevalent in the areas of ORAP's operation, ORAP decided to organise small. This meant that people could get on with what needed to be done without being noticed. One way of organising was through development centres, where networking could take place without arousing any suspicion.

During this period, ORAP had more than its fair share of problems, even to the point of being banned at one stage by the then Governors of Matabeleland South and the Midlands. Nevertheless, the organisation struggled on and grew from strength to strength. In 1985, ORAP found itself suddenly burdened in terms of management and budgetary needs after the village people had joined with others to do research into why development was not taking off at village level. Many suggestions as to what to do came from the villagers themselves and the programmes expanded greatly. It was during this time of institutionalising its work that ORAP decided to start operating with family units in the villages and grouping these into regional associations.

The methodology used was dialogue, which was something people felt strongly about. In the past they had been told what to do and plans had been made for them; they were not consulted and were not given the opportunity to think things through for themselves. Because of its innovative methodology, ORAP attracted the attention of the international community. From early on, ORAP didn't have to go out and ask for funds. Right from the beginning, funds were given to it, with the first donor to assist being the Norwegian Save the Children Fund. Nyoni remembers having talked with donors as early as 1979. She says:

> They were drawn to the idea of people participating in their own development. So when things started happening within ORAP, we wrote to them giving a report of what we were doing. They sent us funds to support our activities and the relationship existed for a long time thereafter. Then Oxfam UK gave us funding that made it possible for me to travel and meet people in the rural areas. When my research report came out, other organisations, like War on Want, came in with supporting funds. In those earlier years, we really never ran short of support because people were always impressed by what was going on within ORAP.

In its first years of operation, ORAP learned the importance of traditional culture and knowledge to the African rural population. In spite of decades of missionary teaching and colonialism, the people had maintained their traditional knowledge of agriculture, environmental sustainability, medicine and the democratic articulation of their interests.

Phineas Sibanda, from the Tsholotsho association, says that he is grateful to ORAP for its work that ranges from water and food security to the construction of granaries. He observes that today people are engaged in development because of ORAP's transparent methods. James Nyathi from Inyathi says, 'ORAP has developed in us a love for our communities.'

The ORAP philosophy

The methodology that has evolved in ORAP is one by which members of the organisation, at all levels, go through the process of analysing their situations, problems and challenges and jointly make plans to take care of their needs – plans which they can implement through self-management. In this way, ORAP's participatory development is truly a process of people's empowerment, which is an objective often talked about in governmental, organisational and educational circles in glowing rhetoric but not often realised.

ORAP has always worked on the basis that rural people are underdeveloped because they have been dispossessed of their culture, traditional knowledge, language, way of life and voice in the structures that control and determine their lives. Development, therefore, consists of reversing the process of underdevelopment. ORAP stresses that development is not simply a material goal, but rather processes which begin and end with people.

In Zhombe, J. Nkomo says that he has helped to spread ORAP's activities and most people appreciate ORAP's development methods. Nkomo says that his most memorable experience with ORAP is when, in 1984, three schools in his area were assisted with roofing materials. He also brags of the Vusisizwe Development Centre that has become the source of life for the community. He says that the whole community gets their drinking water and buys their vegetables from the centre. Other NGOs in the area use the centre as well. Jerry Muleya says that ORAP's philosophy has become so popular that even other NGOs and the government emulate how ORAP works. 'For me that is positive development.'

The Zs and Q concept

ORAP's success may be attributed to its core organisational philosophy, the 'Zs and Q' concept. The philosophy centres on the notion of *'zenzele'* (do it yourself in the Ndebele language) that underpins everything ORAP does and is evident wherever ORAP operates.

ORAP's belief is that the human being is the prime instrument for development and should be empowered, through consciousness raising, to self-determination.

The fulcrum of such a process is perceived to be the family, hence ORAP's unique family approach to development. The approach starts with the self-examination of an individual who belongs to a family. The concepts used are components of the Ndebele language and culture and are rooted in their traditional structures. They are therefore dynamic, originating from people's own practices and experience. The concepts are 'zihluze' (examine yourself), 'ziqoqe' (mobilise yourself), 'zenzele' (do it yourself), 'zimisele' (commit yourself), 'ziqhatshe' (be self-employed), 'zimele' (be self-reliant, independent), 'ziqhenye' (be proud of yourself and your achievements), and 'qogelela' (little by little, one day at a time, save and invest or mobilise resources).

The overall idea is for people to stand on their own and to develop their own resources. Dependency and begging is looked down upon. Zenzele recognises that in every human being there is something good and positive which can be used as a basis for development. Through zenzele, people put into practice what they are and what they think. This encourages self-expression, self-esteem and self-confidence, and enables people to learn from experience and to develop their practical skills and expertise. They also channel their energies towards self-help. Only interdependence is encouraged. Dependence is frowned upon. Rural communities are encouraged to identify and define their problems and constraints and, using their culture, try to find solutions. As soon as this is done, ORAP, through its management structure, tries to provide educational, technical and financial support.

Dumiso Vundla, ORAP's Board Chairperson, says that he has worked tirelessly to help people to understand the zenzele concept. 'Some members talk about the Zs and Q concept but do not have a real understanding.' He thinks that the greatest achievement he has made as chairperson is to unite people for a cause.

> To fight poverty with an organisation like ORAP has been the greatest of challenges. Modern development and aid has created a beggar mentality and dependence on outside aid. Knowledge, skills and management systems that are part of donor conditionally become prerequisites for funding. To avoid this, we have started the qogelela process upon which we shall build a self-sustaining ORAP.

Edith Ncube, from the Tsholotsho association, has been involved with ORAP for nine years and says that ORAP is for the people and the Zs and Q concept is central to people's lives. 'I am a widow. My husband died four years ago, but I am able to provide for my family due to ORAP's education and philosophy.' Betty Manyathela, a secretary of the association and member of ORAP for ten years, is proud of the knowledge imparted to the people in tie and dye, garment making, and the construction of dams. She says, 'I no longer rely on anyone. I pay school fees for my three children without problems. I sell vegetables from my small garden. I got the skills and assistance from ORAP. It has taught us to do it ourselves.'

A closer look at the ORAP concept of Zenzele

The concept of *zenzele* was developed after a realisation that most development projects, including those within ORAP itself, by-passed the very poor in the communities or even marginalised them further. If ORAP were to live true to its philosophy of being a people's movement whose primary goal is to empower the poor, it could not continue with such an approach. The evaluation exercise of 1984-85, conducted by rural people themselves, recommended that ORAP become a cultural movement of '*amalima*' (meaning people working together to help themselves) in which the development of family and community becomes the thrust towards *zenzele*.

Zenzele stems from an Ndebele saying, '*Akusimuntu ongasimuntu walutho*' (there is nobody who has no purpose). *Zenzele* is thus a process of self-discovery, self-mobilisation, management and application for one's own development and that of others that leads to social power. It begins with a statement of affirmation that in every human being there is a force of good, love, self-respect, dignity, caring and sharing which can be used to enhance life. These qualities can then be used for social mobilisation and development. *Amalima* should be understood in the family context. In ORAP's early days, when small project grants were made to individual groups, the motivation for joining and forming groups was often linked to receiving material and financial benefits. However, over time, groups have come to be seen by their members more in the spirit of traditional self-help groups.

African families do not live in isolation. Families might be both nuclear and extended. In some cases, they include friends and neighbours. Individual families define who is family to them. In this context, *zenzele* has the following objectives:

❑ identification of individual talents;
❑ identification of African values upon which to build relationships and development goals;
❑ production of food and other necessities to meet basic family needs;
❑ development and utilisation of local resources and processes;
❑ sharing of responsibilities as well as benefits in the development process;
❑ promotion of initiative, creativity, knowledge and family skills which might have been handed down through generations; and
❑ promotion of African values of community which, in turn, promote and support *amalima* and the cohesive ORAP structure.

The goals of *zenzele* through *amalima* are to:

❑ receive and strengthen the good African cultural community values of caring, hard work, cooperation, sharing and self-help;
❑ develop people's cultural, political and economic potential;
❑ have a high degree of autonomy in decision making at all levels of the ORAP structure;

- foster self-sustaining activities, especially at the family level;
- ensure that the projects which ORAP members embark on are not only self-sustaining but also self-generating;
- foster a strong unity of purpose;
- build a strong cultural base and instill a clear African identity in a people-centred development process;
- strive for partnership;
- relate to outsiders as equals;
- avoid aid which creates mere accountable receivers out of the poor; and
- identify, harness and develop local resources for development to build a strong foundation for the future.

> Alice Zulu says, 'I appreciate the way ORAP works. It is very relevant, though there are some adjustments that need to be made.' She gives the *amalima* concept as an example. 'This works well in the context of Ndebele culture, but we still need to be businesslike when it comes to the getting or receiving of loans.' Elizabeth Moyo has worked with ORAP for eight years. She says, 'I have *zenzele*. The Zs have enabled me to be what I am today. I have a herd of cattle. ORAP taught me to keep cattle. ORAP does not only assist in projects, they make a thorough follow-up on the projects to see that people are really doing something sustainable.'

ORAP's structure

ORAP works through a self-empowering development structure based on a traditional communal methodology of assisting one another. The pillar of this structure is the empowerment of the rural people through community mobilisation and the holding of development dialogue, especially on topical issues. The structure seeks to address the problems of the rural people who have hardly any access to basic resources and are, to a large extent, excluded from decision making processes, although they are the majority in the country and are very much affected by these decisions.

Many of the village groups, averaging 25 families per group, which now make up the ORAP network have their origins in the village committees of the liberation war era and the women's clubs. Others have been set up after coming into contact with ORAP, through meeting either ORAP staff or other ORAP groups. As much as possible, ORAP encourages membership of a group to be on a family rather than individual basis. This is because ORAP believes that the development of a person takes place not only as an individual but also within the family and the community. In this way, particular groups in the community, such as women or youth, are not excluded from the discussion and activity processes.

Traditional family unit structures have been gradually eroded through the colonial period and through the demands of the modern economy, which sends the men to look for jobs outside the village and leaves the women and the old behind to look after the children. People have found new strength in the restoration of family unit structures through ORAP's programmes.

The family unit is basic to ORAP's multi-tier structure, which evolved over time in response to specific organisational and democratic demands emanating from the grassroots. It is the most basic level at which problems are discussed and solutions found, and is the primary level of the organisation into which neighbouring households organise themselves. The family units debate development issues affecting them and propose solutions as they come together to share resources, knowledge, labour and ideas, and work collectively to solve day-to-day problems. Programmes at this level include food production, household chores, homestead improvement, education and training. The families also engage in small scale businesses in an effort to supplement their income. These activities are mainly poultry and pig raising, vegetable gardening, sewing, baking, traditional craft making, brewing of traditional beer, saving schemes etc. In ORAP's experience, family units have proven to be the most effective means of the sharing of work and resources in a way that benefits every member directly. This process has developed trust and solidarity among different families.

ORAP's five-level structure enables all of its members to participate in planning development programmes. The five levels are:

1 Family Units.
2 Village Groups, made up of between ten and 25 family units, where representatives of family units meet to examine their problems in a wider context. At this level, small scale community objectives are implemented such as the construction of dams, weirs, boreholes, wells, irrigation schemes, and the preservation and multiplication of indigenous seeds and trees. In 1990 ORAP comprised approximately 800 such groups.
3 Umbrellas, made up of five or more groups in each locality to facilitate communication and channel decision making amongst different groups. Each group appoints representatives to the umbrella to present programmes they would like to implement. Such programmes consist mainly of grinding mills, irrigation schemes, water management and development education.
4 Associations, at district level, which embrace all the umbrellas in that area. The role of an association is to examine and discuss all problems and issues presented by the umbrella members. During these meetings, participants learn what is happening in different groups. ORAP's programmes at association level (development centres) include blacksmithing, sewing, carpentry, cattle fattening, grinding mills, vegetable gardening, pre-schooling and study groups. The development centres also cater for the training needs of the people.

5   The formal ORAP structure comprising Advisory Board, Board of Trustees and staff.

Conrad Ndebele, from Bubi, believes ORAP taught him *zenzele* and now he lives on his carpentry project. Enock Khabo says ORAP helped him to be proud of his heritage. Rebecca Masuku, from Nkayi association, has worked for five years with ORAP. She speaks highly of the home-based care that came into being through ORAP's assistance. She runs a small gardening project that helps the home-based care group to get fresh vegetables for the sick. She feels that ORAP has assisted them a lot.

Some of ORAP's programmes

ORAP's primary goal is to see rural communities of women, men and youth empowered to plan, implement and manage poverty alleviation strategies on a sustainable basis. In an effort to be more relevant to the communities it serves, ORAP is engaged in several developmental programmes:

- Food Security, Rural Livelihoods and Water Development, promotes crop and livestock production as well as irrigation schemes;
- Conservation and Management of the Environment, promotes environmentally sound farming methods, the use of solar energy, the use of coal burning stoves, land rehabilitation and gully reclamation, forestation and reforestation;
- Education, Training and Capacity Building, improves education, knowledge and skills pertaining to various critical disciplines;
- Microenterprise Development, creates sources of funding and facilitates potential and existing entrepreneurs; and
- Education Services, includes secondary school and bursary portfolios for school children.

Zenzele College administers a six and a half month diploma programme in Grassroots Development and NGO Management (GDNM), which is offered in partnership with the Bangladesh Rural Advancement Committee (BRAC), an NGO based in Dhaka, and the School for International Training based in Vermont, USA. ORAP believes that formal education both at secondary and tertiary level is the key to development. The activities of Zenzele College are my prime occupation. For the last six years several ORAP managers and I have developed the GDNM programme. The programme has strengthened the capacity of many African NGOs by training their middle managers in the management of grassroots communities. The programme is very popular with USA college students who have an interest in learning about NGO work and development in general. The programme is self-financing as it relies on student fees.

Resources

ORAP's resources are numerous. Apart from the investments and the human resources, ORAP as an organisation is a valuable resource. ORAP has been supported by a variety of donors and does not receive any government assistance. In fact, there is a need to improve relations between the government and the many NGOs in Zimbabwe.

In Bulawayo, in 2000, a meeting was held between the government and representatives of the NGOs. It was here that Sithembiso Nyoni said the NGO community felt the government did not like NGOs and that there was not a healthy rapport between the government and NGOs. Some NGOs had been deregistered because they failed to submit their annual reports and others found it difficult to register. The mistrust has resulted in many NGOs feeling anxious about their future. This is not a healthy environment for Zimbabwean NGOs and it has affected the capacity of many.

In response, July Moyo, the Minister of Public Service, Labour and Social Welfare, agreed that there was a need to harmonise relations between the state and the NGOs. 'We want you to have healthy relationships with the communities, government departments, the governor's office and councils because you are an integral part of society.' He added that it is a legal requirement that NGOs produce annual reports and audited financial statements. 'If these reports are not submitted to the government, you will be deregistered. This is clearly spelt out in the Private Voluntary Organisations Act of 1997.' He said that, in Matabeleland, 27 NGOs had produced audited reports while fifteen had not done so in the last three years. About 121 NGOs countrywide had never produced updated statements. ORAP, although it is one of the 27 NGOs, continues to fight other forms of intimidation from government with regard to its autonomy.

Overall, ORAP has had good relationships with its funders. These are based on each party understanding that there has to be give and take. According to ORAP Executive Coordinator, Thandiwe Nkomo, 'ORAP's relationship with donors varies from contractual and strategic alliances, to formal and informal networking, and relationships based on friendship.' One such contractual relationship is with the Canadian International Development Agency (CIDA). Jim Mackinnon, the country representative of CIDA, says that CIDA's relationship with ORAP is at two levels: that of a donor and that of a partner.

Nkomo says that ORAP has come a long way in its relationships with donors. Learning to deal with donors' own values and ethics is essential in building good rapport. ORAP has continuously devised systems that promote transparency and accountability, both for its communities and its funders.

ORAP's funders include Oxfam USA, Oxfam Canada, Christian Aid, Kellogg Foundation, Belgium's Federatie voor Open Scouting (FOS), NOVIB (Netherlands

Organisation for International Development Cooperation), GTZ (Deutsche Gesellschaft für Technische Zusammenarbeit), Norwegian People's Aid (NPA), and Tudor Trust (UK).

The context of culture as a development tool for ORAP

To better understand the ORAP framework, we should turn for a moment to the various developmentalist thinkers of the 1990s. These developmentalists, championing the cause of what is now referred to as 'post-modernism', argue that culture is the key to development. Post-modernism denotes development that is culture specific and focuses on the local community's initiatives and how they articulate their needs. It is hoped that this new paradigm will chart the course for development that is neither Eurocentric nor Western, in the interests of sustainable development and protecting the biodiversities of the developing world.

In the South, writers such as Lovemore Mbigi and Jenny Maree (1995), in their book *Ubuntu: The Spirit of African Transformation*, have begun to pioneer some original perspectives. The authors claim that a culture-centred management style in the new South Africa was part of that country's process for healing civil conflicts. *Ubuntu* culture encourages people not to lose sight of their social responsibility, individual self-respect and human dignity.

In the North, Thierry G. Verhelst (1990) criticises modernism, which leads the poor of the developing world to view development 'as a Trojan horse of Westernisation'. Verhelst puts forward the view that a 'strong local culture identity and spiritual inspiration can be the reservoir for people's creative resistance to alienation and oppression'. He pleads for a 'non-instrumentalist view of cultural diversity in development'.

ORAP has struggled to articulate and facilitate a development model which recognises that culture organises life and is influenced by life, and that there is a dialectical relationship between culture and the so-called 'hard' facts of life. Superficially, the poor may seem uncultured or totally uprooted from their culture but the opposite is true. What we see as failures in development are often indications of resistance by local cultures that are fighting extinction. Most social problems and social conflicts reflect the extent of erosion of the local cultural values and internal or spiritual contradictions within individuals and society as a whole. External and material matter constitute the contemporary development emphasis and that part of culture which makes people a people is not part of the development agenda.

ORAP believes that development, as a process of social change, cannot be imposed upon people by external factors such as the state, developers or projects, but has to come from the people. ORAP recognises that external interventions have failed to reverse the processes of marginalisation and exclusion. Development needs to begin with the people's understanding of their situation as a whole. But even more, it needs to help people understand the causes and the need for them to disengage themselves from these causes and find solutions first from within themselves, no matter how humble. It is only by building on these solutions that people-centred development can be achieved.

ORAP's concept of indigenous knowledge and culture in development

In an unpublished preliminary study for ORAP from 1997, entitled 'Return to the Roots: The place of indigenous knowledge and culture in development', Sithembiso Nyoni interviews 140 respondents in the different regions of Matabeleland and Midlands. She documents people's perceptions of the relevance of culture in development.

Nyoni's study examines the concept of *'ukusiselana'* (helping one another). This concept is key to ORAP because it builds the basis of *'amalima'*. Using the tradition of *ukusiselana*, which literally means exchanging a commodity with another person in a spirit of love and kindness (*isisa* or *umusa*) people were able to invest in or borrow livestock from others with interest. The value of *'amathole'* (calves) was attached to the borrower's name; the more *amathole*, the greater the respect given to the borrower. This encouraged good management. *Ukusiselana* served to equalise community relations. For example, in lending cattle to a needy person, the lender benefited from the borrower's labour and input in the care of his cattle. The borrower, in turn, was able to derive all the benefits of cattle. After a period of about five years, the owner took back his cattle, which included economic interest of a few calves. In focus group discussions, people said that though this traditional economy still exists, people no longer have *umusa* for other people's poverty.

When the colonialists arrived, with their ideas of a cash economy, the people failed to see the purpose of transforming their tangible resources into money. There was some degree of resistance to the cash economy. To break this resistance and the spirit of communal self-reliance, the colonialists shot Ndebele cattle, claiming that this was part of disease control. The people were also moved from their prime cattle land onto poor unproductive land (regions 4 and 5, which were classified as unsuitable for agriculture) and the good rich lands were given to white commercial farmers who concentrated on cattle ranching as a major economic activity. People were pushed into smaller and drier parts, then called 'Tribal Trust Lands'. The Ndebele people's economy was thus destroyed and poverty engulfed them.

Traditional culture and food security

Norbert Dube, the regional manager of the Food Security, Rural Livelihoods and Water Development department, says that ORAP sees food security as a major component of human and economic development. One of the major development indicators is the ability of a family or community to feed itself. In the past, wealth creation and accumulation was despised if the people around the rich went hungry. Besides keeping peace and harmony, leaders were responsible for ensuring that their people had enough to eat.

ORAP strives to ensure that food self-sufficiency is central to communal life and is the focus of production activities. Crops, livestock, farm implements, land use, environmental protection strategies and the number of children in a household all have a bearing on food availability. ORAP works with the communities to see that the culture of sharing food, as well as having sufficient grain storage to last until the next harvest, is always upheld. Even those who have no livestock, crops or resources to share with their neighbours use the only resource they have, their labour, to participate in food security. ORAP members know that it is a communal and national shame for some people to go hungry while others have too much to eat. Thus, to avoid food dependency, draught power, land and farming implements are made affordable to all.

Irene Ncube speaks highly of ORAP's various programmes. She says that the ORAP Food Security, Rural Livelihoods and Water Development department extended loans to the people to purchase dairy cows. The villagers also have small vegetable gardens. Ncube referred to the Dema Family Water Project, which was jointly constructed by the community and ORAP's department of Water Development. Here there is a water tank which can hold 9,000 cubic metres. The water is used for homes, small vegetable gardens and medium scale irrigation schemes.

According to the 1999 Annual Report, the objectives of the Food Security, Rural Livelihoods and Water Development department are to:

❑ support communities in working towards household food security by providing assistance for crop and livestock production;
❑ support drought mitigation programmes through the provision of drought-tolerant seed, like small grains, to communal farmers;
❑ provide emergency drought relief aid to vulnerable people to prevent disasters in rural areas;
❑ encourage seed production of small grains;
❑ establish seed banks;
❑ establish family 'kitchen' gardens;

- establish food-processing centres; and
- promote nutrition and health.

Members of the department insist that it is necessary to return to the small grains for rural communities to curtail food insecurity. ORAP board members are encouraged to grow small grains because of their nutritional value.

Governance

The idea of 'governance', as used here, differs slightly from how it is widely understood today. I am not trying to explain what is demanded by the 'world leaders' of today as good governance or responsible government. Rather, I am speaking of the concept as understood by the Ndebele people that form 85 per cent of ORAP's membership.

Institutions of governance existed in Zimbabwe prior to the arrival of the colonial masters. The physical, socioeconomic, legal and political structures of communities were designed to benefit all members of society, not just the privileged. Everybody had a right to land, food, security and shelter through their chiefs and leaders. The environment had to be protected by all for all. An effort was made to develop citizens who understood that the interests of the individual and those of the community were inextricably linked. It was believed that work was both a means of livelihood for the individual and a way of contributing to the prosperity of the community as a whole. By contrast, in Zimbabwe today, institutions of governance have been removed from people's development and daily lives. Power and leadership is seen as separate from the people. Leaders exercise power. They do not share power.

The Ndebele people have a saying: '*Induna ibikhethwa ematholeni njalo ibibusa njenge thole*'. This means that the king or *induna* (chief) was selected from among the calves when he was young. The king or chief was supposed to rule with grace, patience and wisdom. He also had to listen to, and learn from, his people and his advisers. In so doing, democracy was ensured. In the Ndebele state, leadership served to promote justice, peace and the protection of human rights.

ORAP has built its development process around some of the key concepts of traditional Ndebele society. One of the most important of these is how its field officers approach communities through their existing communal district leadership. This has had a tremendous impact on both the community and the projects.

Networking

From 1992 to 1993 there was a devastating drought that motivated ORAP staff and members to sit down and map out a permanent solution to alleviate suffering during drought years. After input from the communities, the ORAP management put together a project proposal that was submitted to the Harare office of the UNDP. At the same time, the Bulawayo office of World Vision (Zimbabwe) had submitted a similar proposal to UNDP. A meeting was convened at ORAP in August 1994 with UNDP, Africa 2000, ORAP and World Vision (Zimbabwe). At that meeting, the organisations agreed to involve the other actors in the province of Matabeleland South. A second meeting was held in Gwanda, this time including provincial government representatives. At a final meeting in Kezi, which included international agencies such as the United Nations Children's Fund (UNICEF) and Africare, the Give-a-Dam Campaign (GADC) was born.

The project aims to provide long-term solutions to drought-related poverty by raising funds for the construction of 55 (the original target was 47) small to medium sized dams and gravity-fed irrigation schemes to ensure sustainable food security.

The objectives of the campaign are to:

❑ raise funds to construct 55 small and medium sized dams and develop more than 155 hectares of land for irrigation by gravity;
❑ strengthen the organisational structures within communities equipping them with the capacity to take control of the planning, implementation and management of dam projects;
❑ prevent further environmental degradation by promoting sustainable development and by training communities in the protection and management of dam catchment areas; and
❑ create opportunities for income generating and food producing activities.

Five years on, the campaign has yielded positive results. To date 36 dams have been completed, and eleven more are under construction. In addition, a total of five irrigation schemes have been completed, with eighteen more under construction. The remaining dams and irrigation schemes are to be completed within the next three years.

A cornerstone of the GADC has been community involvement. Villagers, with the assistance of Rural District Councils, play a crucial role in selecting, planning, implementing and managing the projects. As with the ORAP approach, GADC members agree that it is the community's responsibility to identify its development needs and also to evaluate its input in development projects. In this case, locally elected dam committees are involved in all stages of the project cycle. Women and young people also play a critical role by contributing labour and other required resources. The Rural District Councils, being the planning authority at district level, play an important role by approving and giving top priority to the dam projects when drafting the community's development plans.

NGOs are involved in mobilising resources for dam construction and irrigation development. Some of the NGOs who are partners in the campaign also implement the projects on the ground. This is a good example of ORAP's networking process.

There are many other examples of ORAP initiatives, but I would like to refer particularly to the networking between ORAP and the Philisisizwe Association for Development (PAD), which is an NGO based in Durban, South Africa. In early 1985, the Director of PAD and her team visited ORAP. They studied how ORAP worked and how, through the use of culture, it had mobilised the rural grassroots. They returned to South Africa and started using the ORAP strategy. PAD officers have confirmed that the ORAP approach to development is the best thing ever to have happened to the people they work with.

> Jerry Muleya remembers how ORAP's Rural Health Outreach project provided malaria kits to fight malaria in Binga and how two and three boreholes were drilled in Pashu and Siyadindi respectively. All in all, ORAP has constructed eighteen dams and 33 boreholes. He recounts how life improved after the community got a thresher for maize. There is no more need for the villagers to separate the maize seed from the cob by hand. 'Our children no longer faint in school because of hunger.'

Development challenges

An interview with Sithembiso Nyoni, first Executive Coordinator of ORAP

Sithembiso Nyoni believes that empowerment is a very important word. She says that no one can empower someone else. People have to empower themselves. She believes that when one empowers somebody else, at some stage, one can take that power away. But when people empower themselves, that empowerment process belongs to them. It is part of their struggle.

If one is to facilitate people's empowerment, one has to understand what power means. Power is a life force needed by human beings. If one does not understand that, then the concept is academic only. Nyoni says:

> I would like to define what power is and how it is used, how it is organised and how it is maintained. Power is neutral and remains such until it is used. When power is used, it stops being neutral. When people are going through a process of empowering, they need to know that there is positive and negative power. Being in government has helped me to understand the use of power. Power in the negative sense is destructive. It can kill.

> Positive power enables, nurtures and loves. I believe that a nation that is not empowered cannot succeed. It doesn't matter how glamorous the project or projects, it will not succeed. Most grassroots people are powerless. In some research I have carried out, the prevailing notion is that people at

grassroots level cannot make decisions and others have to make decisions on their behalf. ORAP's philosophy and structure works to empower people; in so doing, you cannot have power over them. You can only empower a people when you disempower yourself so that you feel what it means to be powerless. Then, with those who feel powerless, one works out a strategy to get somewhere. Power exercised is power lost. Power shared is power gained. In ORAP we have tried to share structures that create leaders who are part of the people, and feel and talk with the people. This is different from leaders that plan for the people.

We discussed how ORAP had used the people's culture to build itself as an organisation. Nyoni stated that a people's culture is not just about dress or food. It is about how people connect to each other. Culture is a deep phenomenon that makes a people unique. If one excludes culture from development, one is excluding the people and their distinctiveness. It is important to make people proud of their culture, thus of themselves. If one is proud of one's culture, one is proud of who one is.

I asked Nyoni to comment on ORAP's continued donor support in the era of globalisation. Nyoni says the ground has to be levelled and we need to share resources. At the moment, resources are in the hands of a few people only. When she looks at donors, she sees people of goodwill who want to share resources with others. In this case, donor money is good money. Nevertheless, she has problems when donor money is used to manipulate or translate people's agendas. When donor conditionality stops people from being themselves, it becomes a problem. ORAP has been careful and has still to be careful as to what donor money it receives. It has to be money that is liberating, not money which generates dependency.

Nyoni and I discussed what measures ORAP has taken to become sustainable. She sees sustainability occurring at different levels. Firstly, how people think about themselves and about the work they are doing in development. Secondly, there is no sustainable development without sustainable relationships. Underdevelopment occurs when relationships have broken down between the people and the NGO or development workers, between those who are powerful and those who are powerless. Sustainability occurs when people start thinking together positively about their situation and each other, and strategise development action using their own resources first. Thirdly, sustainability occurs when there are resources to go towards a development path that people have chosen. In 1991, ORAP started organising its own financial sustainability in a businesslike manner through the Community Foundation of the Western Region of Zimbabwe (CFWRZ), the Usizo Credit and Savings Scheme, and the Zimbabwe Progress Fund, which is a venture capital company formed with other NGOs and financial institutions. At village level, the *qogelela* concept has to continue. If one does not save, one does not have anything to fall back on during hard times.

I asked Nyoni what she saw as ORAP's strengths and weaknesses. She believes that its major strength is the ORAP philosophy of development which addresses intellectual, cultural and material poverty. Another strength is that its structure ensures that grassroots people participate in formulating strategies for all ORAP's programmes and projects.

Nyoni knows that ORAP has weaknesses too. Donor dependency can become a problem. As long as one continues to depend on other people, one's development agenda cannot be completely independent. In spite of this, ORAP now has both small and large programmes that are well established and will last for a long time. When ORAP started, it did not have qualified staff at village level to deal with real mobilisation and the effective implementation of plans of action. The other problem is how to close the gap between the fast moving train of globalisation, and underdevelopment and poverty.

From 1995 to 2000 Nyoni was working fulltime for the government of Zimbabwe as a Member of Parliament for an urban constituency. She rose within a short space of time to be a Deputy Minister and finally a Minister of State in the Vice-President's office, responsible for economic projects in the country.

Asked what led her to take a five-year break from the work that she is so passionate about, Nyoni says:

> I did not choose to take a break from ORAP at that particular point. I was invited to represent the people of Makokoba in Parliament, which I accepted. When my party did not win the parliamentary elections of 2000, I was not worried. It did not bother me at all, because that is people's power. I understood that this power could be taken from me at any time. I was already preparing to go back to my studies to do my PhD. This is the reason I encouraged Thandiwe Nkomo to go to university to attain a master's degree. I hoped that when she came back, I could take a break. A break is important in life. It facilitates reflection. I was tired. Fifteen years of acting, thinking, implementing and initiating is not a joke. I thought it was time for me to step aside and reflect. My belief is that if the visionary leader steps aside and the vision crumbles, then the vision was not shared.

I asked her to explain the difference between running an NGO and being in government and whether she had gained any new insights about the role of NGOs in development.

Nyoni says that her experience in government was difficult. As an activist, she likes getting things done. She loathes procrastination. In government, she says, she did not manage to get to do the things she had envisioned. She had to fight red tape. She confesses to having really learned the functions of bureaucracy. This experience confirmed her reservation and fears of bureaucracy in government. Bureaucracy, according to Nyoni, can make or break those that are below it. She believes that she came out of the government believing that the system is only as good as those who created it. She came back convinced that whatever development workers do, it must be done in a system that facilitates togetherness and participation. Nyoni says, 'Now nobody can tell me how government works. I know. When I talk to people during workshops on empowerment, I know what I am talking about.'

We talked about her return to ORAP and whether that was easy. She says:

I never left ORAP. My spirit, soul, intellect and passion never left ORAP. Every now and then, I got frustrated in government or sad because of some of the things that were happening. I resorted to thinking about ORAP, particularly on what a great organisation it has become. My coming back was not a problem at all.

I asked Nyoni about her focus now. Nyoni still has hopes for the education system of Zimbabwe, although she says a lot has to be done. She thinks that both the government and the NGOs have neglected the youth. The problems that we are facing as a nation right now are because we have the wrong kind of education – education that sees the government as a god that has to deliver and not as a facilitator that should enable people to acquire power. Nyoni says that people think of empowerment as the power to rule or to control others. She thinks the government should help unleash the energy and power in people so that they live a fuller life. Her focus now will be on education because she believes that when one educates children properly, one equips them for eradicating poverty.

Nyoni says that in spite of 'not being at ORAP' she is familiar with everything that goes on. Nevertheless, she does not want to go back and be the Executive Coordinator of ORAP.

I am a thinker, reflector and initiator. I do not like the nitty gritties of management. I want to be a wise woman. I want to keep my job of being a thinker, and keep reflecting with those that want to think with me. I want to learn more from other thinkers too through Zenzele College.

Nyoni says the most frustrating moments in her efforts to address poverty have been those when she sees someone using development to climb the ladder to wealth. If resources are meant for the poor, let them go to the poor. It is as simple as that. Some leaders use their power to exercise control over others and divide people. Once this is done, we create poverty. We need to bridge the gap between the haves and the have nots.

Asked when she intends to call it a day in development work, Nyoni says that, if someone were employing her, then she would think of retirement but, in her kind of work, normal retirement is not possible. 'But let me assure you, as long as poverty, injustice, greed and selfishness exist, I will not retire. As long as we have children in the streets, women sleeping outside and being raped, I will not retire.'

Nyoni says that she is proud of ORAP. She believes ORAP has worked as a holistic organisation. She is proud that the world can look and say ORAP grassroots women produced a leader, a Councillor, an MP and a Minister. For her, ORAP is an organisation that recognises people's power. People's power is a force that enables one to act, to change a situation. Empowerment is about life and helping people to take charge of life themselves.

An interview with Thandiwe Cornelia Nkomo, current Executive Coordinator of ORAP

Thandiwe Cornelia Nkomo is passionate about her involvement in development. Nkomo says that development is a process whereby one deals with questions such as who am I, where am I coming from and where am I going? It has to do with destiny. On the one hand, it looks at how one can deal with external issues and, on the other, acknowledges that people need people and can help each other. 'I believe development has to do with making decisions. When one is able to make a decision one is empowered.'

Nkomo grew up in both urban and rural areas, but went to school in the rural areas. When she went to visit her old school, she was dismayed to find it in the same condition as it had been when she was a student. Nkomo is disgusted by the stagnancy of development in rural areas. 'There is a rural to urban brain drain. I wanted to work with ORAP so that I could give back to the community that made me what I am.' Nkomo remembers how her mother used to till the land in order to supplement her father's income as a teacher. Her mother's efforts allowed Nkomo to complete her basic education.

> At independence I taught briefly and initially wanted to go and train as a teacher. However, I had second thoughts and decided that I would not be able to help the communities as I wished to. Some of the children that I taught are in the cities fighting hard to make a living. Those that I work with in the rural areas have achieved some level of respect in what they have done to uplift themselves. This inspires me and gives me pride in my work.

Nkomo observes that grassroots people have been labelled lazy people who do not think. But they are the salt of the earth. The so-called educated élite does not want to look broadly and unlearn whatever assumptions they hold about the poor.

> I get frustrated seated behind the desk. When I go out into the field, I learn so much. Many of these grassroots people do not have certificates or diplomas, but they have what it takes to survive. They survive on meagre resources – if you or I were in the same circumstances, we could not survive. I respect them because they are capable of dealing with their tough lives.

I asked Nkomo if she could describe her leadership contribution to ORAP. She believes that leadership takes many forms. She was with ORAP from the very beginning and started with the actual mobilisation of communities. Nkomo remembers that, at independence, communities felt disempowered and the regime of that time made them believe that they could not think for themselves or solve their own problems. Nkomo says that she was part of the process that linked these people to each other and the outside world. She was also part of the process that facilitated the formulation of ORAP's structure and philosophy. 'I thoroughly enjoyed the mobilisation process and the concept of mobilisers. Now I know that the best people to mobilise rural people are the people themselves.'

Nkomo was closely involved with ORAP's programme of development centres. These centres developed out of the need to have a place to discuss ideas and strategies.

When Nkomo took over as the Executive Coordinator, she saw her greatest challenge as strengthening ORAP as an institution. She did this by systematising the finances, personnel policies and project proposal writing. Nkomo also had to ensure that the development centres were well equipped and had trained staff. The greatest challenge was to professionalise and, at the same time, continue to mobilise and ensure that the people's processes remained intact and continued to evolve.

I asked Nkomo what empowerment meant to her, what ORAP's perspective was and what ORAP had done for the people of the Matabeleland and Midlands provinces. 'I believe people are empowered when they have access to resources that enable them to make informed decisions. These are financial, human and material resources.' In ORAP, the empowerment processes have not been easy. Nkomo remembers the Vusisizwe community case. Vusisizwe was one of the first centres to have a good infrastructure. Management had helped to raise funds for a one-year building and bricklaying training session. Under normal circumstances, the association is supposed to contribute food for the trainers and the different umbrellas provide food for the trainees. Unfortunately, three months before the course was due to end, the food ran out and there was no more money. The managers decided that the training had to be stopped. 'This was a big mistake because we did not consult the association leadership at that community level,' says Nkomo. The local association leadership decided to recall the trainees after they had agreed to contribute buckets of maize meal from the rations they were given by the government as drought relief. This enabled the trainees to complete their course.

At the next general Board meeting there was an agenda item that was listed only as: 'Who has power, the staff or the association? Where does the power lie?' Nkomo remembers wondering where this came from. On the meeting day, the management was challenged: 'Because of the staff's inefficiency, you ordered a course to stop without consulting the local leaders!' The managers were supposed to warn them of the impending budgetary constraints so that they could find a solution together without having to stop the course. 'That for me was the highest level of empowerment, where one disempowers oneself in order to empower others,' says Nkomo. In this case, it was the poor, who were supposed not to be able to think, who were challenging the management as to who they thought they were.

The other form of empowerment is that people in ORAP have been trained in practical courses, which I like to call 'training for living'. For example, we have a group in Dema-Gwanda where people were trained in livestock keeping. Owing to the continued drought, their livestock had been wiped out but they got loans from ORAP to purchase cows. The elderly people enrolled for training in disease control and feeding. These people were able to restock their herd and got a new lease on life. Nevertheless, the loans were taken on an individual basis though the collateral was the group. One member lost her beast and the other members contributed not only towards its replacement but to paying off the initial loan.

Nkomo cites another example of empowerment. In Binga, a remote and marginalised community, is a young woman whose name is Laiza. Laiza joined ORAP at the age of fourteen. She is passionate about her community's development. When things were tough and some of her group members were giving up, she battled on. ORAP used to operate grinding mills that were owned by 'everybody' in the community but that did not work. After much thought, a decision about who owned the grinding mills was made. It was done in such a way that the project should benefit women. This was so because, from the onset, women were taken for granted and merely perceived as labourers. At the same time, the question of ownership remained. It was during this time that Laiza and a friend successfully sought a loan from ORAP to purchase a grinding mill. When you meet Laiza now, she walks tall. She boasts of being a businesswoman. Nkomo sees this as a lesson in empowerment. Laiza now has confidence. She can draw up a business plan, make projections, successfully apply for and pay off loans, and manage her business.

Sustainability is a big issue for ORAP. Nkomo says that it is related to self-reliance. But she is quick to point out that self-reliance has to be put in context. ORAP understands that sustainability and self-reliance have to be linked to ORAP's belief of interdependence. ORAP looks at investing in communities as opposed to just implementing a project. Nkomo believes that investing in communities means investing in people through the provision of informed dialogue, skills and indigenous knowledge.

As an organisation, ORAP believes that investment is the key to sustainability. In 1991 the communities invested Z$80,000 to start the CFWRZ, which is really a community foundation that was endowed by the people's funds. The communities know that their returns are not immediate. They liken it to a dairy cow that you can milk as opposed to an ox which, when slaughtered, is eaten and then forgotten about. The CFWRZ has become a stand-alone institution that offers grants to people and organisations, not only ORAP members.

ORAP also has investments in the form of a farm, a service station, a workshop and a hardware shop. ORAP believes that these businesses will grow and generate enough revenue to be ploughed back into ORAP and finally to the communities. 'We have recently pulled down the old service station and invested Z$24 million in renovations. We expect this service station to be the milch cow of the organisation.'

Leading an organisation like ORAP is taxing. I asked Nkomo what challenges she faced as Executive Coordinator. She stated that it is important to keep momentum going in the organisation and to keep relationships alive with donors. 'If I had my way, I would do field trips every week. But I have to take care of the communication with the outside world. I have to coordinate with donor agencies and the other development actors.'

In order not to forget the contributions made by Sithembiso Nyoni during her term of office, the ORAP Board executive created the post of ORAP President and offered it to Nyoni in 1997. When asked about her opinion and perception about the role of the presidency at ORAP, Nkomo says:

As the founding member of ORAP, Nyoni is the one who had the dream and shared it. As one shares the dream with others, the others help in shaping the dream into a reality. As for Nyoni, I expect her to take responsibility and keep dreaming and listening also to others. When we started ORAP, we were a small group, but a lot of people have given valuable input. I expect her to be a figure that keeps carrying the torch. I believe the role of the President is not to be hands-on but to continue dreaming and sharing the dream.

I asked Nkomo about her views on NGO leaders going into politics on a fulltime basis. Nkomo believes that politics and development are inseparable. She says that she had been sceptical about having an NGO activist involved in politics but then came to the conclusion that development is politics. One is dealing with people's economic wishes, and sociocultural and political issues. She thinks that by virtue of their work, NGO leaders are in touch with the people in their communities. When a political path is taken, the leader should make an effort to keep in touch with the people they have been working with. This enables the NGO community to be informed of what is happening in politics, particularly in regard to changes in government policies. This person in the end will be an ally through whom the people can lobby.

ORAP does not exist in a vacuum. It is part of the national, regional and international community of the NGO sector. It is part of the nation of Zimbabwe. The economic and political crises Zimbabwe is going through have not spared ORAP as an institution. The future looks bleak in some ways. What is also sad is the misery created by HIV/AIDS and the economic hardships on the communities that ORAP works with. However, Nkomo sees that, given the resilience of the people, ORAP can make headway amidst all these hurdles and uncertainties.

The investments that ORAP has made in businesses will contribute much to the future of ORAP although they are threatened by the economic instability of the country. If funding is cut to Zimbabwe as a nation, it affects the NGOs working in Zimbabwe. Nkomo believes that the responsibility of her work is to understand that the pressure on the funders is from their own governments, especially as Zimbabwe has been declared not creditworthy by the Bretton Woods institutions.

My interview with Nkomo would not have been complete without a discussion on the impact of the International Monetary Fund (IMF), the World Bank, and globalisation on ORAP. Nkomo is upset with the activities of the Bretton Woods institutions. Nevertheless, she says that the reforms are a necessary evil. She says that Structural Adjustment Programmes (SAPs) negatively affect the NGOs working on the ground. SAPs have reversed all the gains that had been made, particularly with regard to raising the standard of living among the people. Health and education used to be free for the poor. Now they have to pay for every service. The government hospitals no longer have basic essential drugs. Qualified doctors are leaving for so-called 'greener pastures'. The schools are dilapidated. Nkomo's concerns are supported by the *Zimbabwe Human Development Report* (UNDP 1999).

Nkomo wants the world to look at ORAP as a people's movement, now grown, with diverse institutions.

> I know that worldwide a lot of institutions similar to ORAP have called it a day. They have folded up. I am not saying ORAP is not faced by those challenges that have led to other organisations' closure. It is! If ORAP were to close down today, the family units and the umbrellas will live and move on. They may move in a different or at a slower pace but there is no way that they can be destroyed. That is the way of life. It is their way of life. They can continue to solve their own problems in their own way.

I asked Nkomo what would happen if donor funds dried up, as they have already started to dwindle.

> ORAP, the movement, is key to every facet of the organisation. The board meetings, where associations chart their way forward, are what matters to ORAP. The dialoguing of people at unit, umbrella and association level is not funded externally. It is the people who pool their resources and finance these meetings. The unavailability of donor funds cannot stop the people from meeting. The magnitude of the funded projects may be affected but not the formulative strategic meetings and working together. Also, the *amalima* concept is an indigenous concept, part of the people's culture. So nothing will die.

Conclusion

Nothing is sustainable without a holistic system being in place. With the advent of colonialism, new systems of governance, development, economic relations and cultural practices emerged. The cohesion of our culture and social fabric was weakened. Our urban areas are run on the Western style of development and governance but, in rural areas, there are still elements of traditional cultural practices. It would appear that the two systems continue to fight for space and control, rather than work together. Western culture, with its knowledge, skills and technology, has co-opted part of the population without giving them the Western cultural tools and the thinking behind the development paradigms and technologies used. Neither did they build on the local culture to help local people grow and develop in their own way. The result is cultures at war.

Real contradictions and challenges confront our development processes. Our decision makers and developers need to face them head on if sustainable development is to be achieved. Some of these challenges and contradictions are, firstly, that the Western model of development is not yet rooted in our people and culture. It is not inclusive and leaves the majority of our people on the periphery, rather than in the development driving seat. The élite may appear to be in control but their sustainability depends on the extent to which they are rooted in the African reality, culture and resources yet linked to like minds in the global space, and also on how long the West will continue to support them. Secondly, the ORAP model has demonstrated some successes and has thrown light on a few possibilities. For example, marginalised groups of people can find empowerment through new ways of expressing their spirituality and cultural values. Development education and cultural analysis may lead people to say 'no' to concealment, hidden histories and oppressive relationships. It can also lead people to find practical solutions to problems as has been demonstrated in this paper.

To move forward from where it is, ORAP's cultural approach needs:

□ the political will to make decisions in its favour;
□ an economic base of its own;
□ a social, economic or institutional support system; and
□ to be grounded in strong African values of community, caring, sharing, honesty and integrity.

This paper has shown that ORAP has a lot of strengths. Its members can be proud of what they have achieved so far. However, there are dangerous signs and threats which ORAP needs to deal with urgently.

In examining the current ORAP programmes, such as big and small business units and the savings and credit programme, it is encouraging to see how rooted they are in our cultural and organisational structures. I recommend that this be strengthened to ensure sustainable linkages with the global economy. One of the challenges that remains is whether the mobilisation programmes have the strength and capacity to spearhead the eradication of intellectual poverty. In reading most of ORAP's literature, nothing new seems to be emerging. If ORAP is to remain a cultural movement, it is recommended that each unit or division be examined and evaluated against its capacity to strengthen people's developmental cultural norms, values and practices without losing its ability to collaborate with international individuals, organisations and institutions with similar values and goals.

ORAP has to develop capacities among its membership and staff to enable them to successfully manage the interaction between people's roots (their culture and identity) and the global environment. This paper has shown that the spirit of our culture is resilient. Like the taproot of a tree, it has lived on. The environment and models of development are like branches. They change. Management of a dynamic culture requires a learning society and a learning organisation which constantly develops systems, thinking capacities and new mental models. It also needs to encourage personal mastery of new and team learning.

As development aid is declining, and has been doing so since 1990, I believe that ORAP can assist itself by strengthening its self-financing mechanisms – the Qogelela Foundation and the venture capital company.

ORAP's partners such as NOVIB, Oxfam UK, Oxfam Canada, Synergos Institute, NPA, Christian Aid (UK) and South North Development Initiatives have been very committed to people's economic empowerment. ORAP should build on its support by being clear about what inspires its visions of development. A commitment to recapturing the central role of culture in development is what defines ORAP.

The ORAP story of empowerment can be summed up by one of the many songs that the ORAP mobilisers use when they go about doing their work.

Kusese duze kuseseduze laphe siyakhona
Kude kukhatshana laphe siyakhona

Chorus: *Amagixigo amagixigo entuthuko*
Kukhona ameva matshe lamagodi

Translated, the song says: 'It's nearer, getting nearer where we are going. It's far, very far, where we are going. There are thorns, stones and potholes.' The chorus expresses the ups and downs one has to go through to achieve development.

Women and children sing such songs at development gatherings. They dance and *toi-toi* in rejoicing. The songs are sentimental. They invoke the inner 'personhood'. They console. The people feel good and are refreshed. Their voices keep echoing in the villages and through the big trees, valleys and mountains. These are the sounds of empowered women and children. Long live ORAP!

Bibliography

Kempadoo, P. and ORAP 1991, *Zenzele the ORAP Way*, ORAP, Bulawayo.

Mbigi, L. and Maree, J. 1995, *Ubuntu: The Spirit of African Transformation*, Knowledge Resources, Johannesburg.

Nyoni, S. 1997, 'Return to the roots: The place of indigenous knowledge and culture in development', unpublished study, Harare.

United Nations Development Programme 1999, *Zimbabwe Human Development Report 1999*, Harare.

Verhelst, T. G. 1990, *No Life Without Roots: Culture and Development*, Zed Books, London.

TAMWA: LEVINA'S SONG – SUPPORTING WOMEN IN TANZANIA

Leila Sheikh

I am a traveller through time. I'm not going to attach big names like 'odyssey' or 'voyage' to my travels because all I'm doing is going backwards in history to tell the stories of people, some of whom I have never met, but whose voices clamour to be heard; stories which are a constant ache in my heart. I just have to tell their stories. So many voices, some loud, some merely echoes but strange – their voices, though different, don't clang nor clash. They simply cry out to be heard.

TAMWA's beginnings

The Tanzania Media Women's Association (TAMWA) was formed in the wake of the Third World Conference on Women held in Nairobi, Kenya, in 1985. In its key recommendations, the Conference emphasised the importance of women organising to enable themselves to confront the multitude of issues and problems which perpetuate women's low status in society and to spearhead the struggle for their emancipation. In 1986 a number of motivated media women in Tanzania had the idea of forming a media women's association, and TAMWA was born a year later. Its mission was to use the media to sensitise society on gender issues, and advocate and lobby for policy and legal changes which would promote the human rights of women and children.

There were twelve of us initially, women journalists from different backgrounds with different social orientations and, I suspect, with different expectations. But we shared a common agenda, that of uplifting the status of women in the Tanzanian media. There were not all that many women in the media at that time, just a handful, and not all that many media organs either.

Eight women attended the first meeting in Nelly Kidela's house in Upanga, Dar es Salaam. We were an assorted lot. There was Fatma Alloo just back from Uganda with a lot of skills and energy; Jamiila Chipo, a diaspora woman who was trying to find a niche for herself in Tanzanian society; Pili Mtambalike, Halima Shariff and Elizabeth Marealle trying to work out challenges that media women face in male-dominated newsrooms; Edda Sanga and Nelly lamenting the lack of upward mobility for women in media organisations; and myself, a young bride, recently arrived from England, just waiting for the right platform to unleash my mental energy.

We took stock of each other at the first meeting. Some of us knew each other; others met for the first time. Some of us had grown up in newsrooms and we were still naive about gender politics. I remember sneering when one of the members talked about sisterhood.

The twelve founder members were soon joined by sixteen others and we used to meet in the *Daily News* boardroom on Tuesday afternoons. Joseph Mapunda, the Managing Editor of the *Daily News* at that time, kindly allowed us access to the boardroom, tea and a bit of stationery. A hat (scarf actually) was passed around at the end of each meeting for donations that went to the kitty for additional stationery. Fatma used to chair the meetings. Jamiila took us through the paces of group therapy where we discussed anecdotes from our lives. I used to show off my culinary skills by baking biscuits for members. Three members were assigned the task of registering the association while Jamiila and I became the editors of the group's photocopied and stapled newsletter, *Titbits*.

The men in the newsroom used to tease us: '*TAMWA tamu*' meaning 'TAMWA is sweet' and we decided we were not going to get angry. There were also allegations that we were a bunch of frustrated women, desperate for a sense of direction in our personal lives.

We used to be a collective then and, since there was no funding, with most of the work done on a voluntary basis, there was no resentment and the feeling of sisterhood was highly visible, even though a couple of us had sneered at it initially.

We came from assorted backgrounds but somehow we became activists with our first 'official' function, a seminar on the portrayal of women in the media. It was a success and what came out of the seminar was the need to have a feminist magazine that would provide an alternative to the patriarchal sexist images of women then being portrayed in the media.

Sauti ya Siti was launched and I became its editor, simply because I was not in fulltime employment but was doing freelance work and, therefore, could devote time to its publication, which was on a quarterly basis. We published in both English and Swahili and we used poems, illustrations, focus features and short stories to impart images that would counteract the sexist literature being churned out at that time. We launched *Sauti ya Siti* on 8 March 1988 and we set the ball rolling by doing skits, songs and dances. It was a festive atmosphere, full of bantering and optimism.

By 1989 we had moved to the offices of Canadian University Service Overseas (CUSO) where we were allowed to use a room for two hours every day, Monday to Friday. We shared this space with several other non-governmental organisations (NGOs) on a rotational basis. Although the office was tiny, holding only a desk and two chairs, it gave us anchorage and more enthusiasm for our work. At last, we had a focal point and we could invite visitors for discussions.

We decided to refocus from being a 'trade union' for media women to being a platform for changes for all women. We felt that if we worked on improving the lot of women in our society, our own status would inevitably go up.

Though we had started implementing activities through short term projects, we lacked formal structures like policies, financial management systems and criteria for consultancies. A member would be motivated by an issue, mostly through the media, and come up with a short term project proposal which would be sent out to funders for endorsement. Creative members obviously got the bulk of the implementation work as the person who had had the idea would invariably also become the coordinator of the project.

After some time, we moved into our own office, a tiny room where we set up a computer, a round table for discussion and a documentation centre. We did not have an official secretariat but members volunteered to put in some hours at the office. We had also gained popularity among donors and continued building a small constituency, mainly among NGOs and gender rights activists. We were still not popular with the media.

Cracks began to appear by 1992, with some members getting paid for consultancies while others were considered 'volunteers'. Some members started feeling marginalised and there was a lot of resentment leading to the departure of some members. Because we had not been trained in NGO management, the cracks became crevices and, in 1993, TAMWA split into three distinct groups: the 'dead' members, who eventually lost interest and left; the 'bruised' group – those who were marginalised to the extent that they were forced to leave; and the 'gang of ten' who remained behind for one reason or another. I was one of those who remained behind. With hindsight, I think I remained because I was ambitious and needed a platform from which I could put the gender-based violence agenda onto the Tanzanian map. TAMWA seemed the best platform for the fulfillment of my ambition. I was also vain, wanting to show off the skills I had acquired in England where I had been a student.

We went through an evaluation exercise in 1994 and the report illustrated the level of fragmentation that TAMWA had come to. There were fourteen units which, according to the evaluation report, were either tools or tasks, rather than programmes. There was a lack of transparency in the financial management structures and transactions. Most of all, the 'gang of ten' was itself becoming fragmented.

Those of us who had remained had become isolated, insecure and disorganised, but we controlled TAMWA's finances, were custodians of the office and TAMWA's vehicle, and could still call on some of the remaining constituency for support, mainly because we pretended that everything was alright. In reality, however, activities were not consolidated and, on analysis, we all functioned as separate entities under one umbrella. There were discrepancies in payment of coordination fees; there were separate bank accounts for each unit; and members were not told what was happening in other units.

We did not accept the evaluation report and protested vehemently to the funding partners, Humanist Institute for Cooperation with Developing Countries (HIVOS) and the Netherlands Organisation for International Development Cooperation (NOVIB), the two Dutch organisations that had funded the exercise.

Then, we heard about organisational development (OD). We were advised to request an OD partly because some of the 'gang of ten' members had become tired of the stressful environment brought on by insecurity and suppressed anger but, mainly, because funders had by then withdrawn support and only three units were getting funding. By mid-1995 we had come to an agreement with HIVOS and NOVIB on the proposed OD, the facilitators for the OD, and the terms of reference.

After the Women's Conference in Beijing in September 1995, Fatma Alloo stepped down and Edda Sanga took over as acting Chairperson. Pili Mtambalike was appointed to coordinate the process and I was to assist her. An internal coordinator was appointed and two Zimbabwe-based consultants were brought on board to oversee the OD and to assist in putting together the pieces of the fragmented TAMWA. We held several meetings with one of the consultants and agreed to draw up a timetable with a number of activities, such as workshops for members, a review of the Constitution etc.

However, the consultants, on the basis of the reports from these meetings, came to the conclusion that a lot of information was missing. They wrote saying that they would not continue with the OD unless we agreed to be honest. They also said that the OD process had to be owned by all members and, therefore, we had to try and become inclusive by going out and talking to all the members that we could get hold of and trying to bring them back into the fold.

It was no mean feat, but we managed to persuade members to come to a Dialogue and Reconciliation workshop. There were tears, fights and recriminations, but we made up. The glue that held it together was a mix of the revised vision and mission statement of TAMWA, the Constitution and the fact that we had become tired of fighting among ourselves. We decided to use all this latent energy to consolidate TAMWA through restructuring with a formalised secretariat, financial systems and other accoutrements that make an association viable and dynamic. Our activities were streamlined under two main programmes – Information, Lobbying and Advocacy, and Training and Outreach.

Implementing committees were set up and, by 1996, we had the first democratic elections in years. Once the secretariat had been set up with a Director, programme officers and other support staff, TAMWA designed a consolidated programme on the eradication of gender-based violence in Tanzania. The media was going to be the main tool and what TAMWA had to do was to get the support of the proprietors of the media organs – editors, producers and others. This was done through information kits especially prepared for them and through consultative meetings.

By mid-1997 TAMWA had come of age, having gained the confidence of sister NGOs in the Feminist Action Coalition (FemAct) and credibility in media organs for coming up with correct data and information on pertinent issues. Was it worthwhile? Of course!

But I often have to try to lift myself out of sadness, the type of sadness brought by having witnessed a lot of pain in life. I have witnessed so much pain and suffering that it makes me feel old at times.

I remember the times my husband sat stone cold having a solitary dinner when I came home late from the Crisis Centre.

I remember the look in his eyes and the unspoken words hanging between us, 'Don't you realise I too need you?'

I try to divert attention from my late arrival with incessant chatter about clothes, about the neighbours, anything to lift him out of 'that mood'. He tries to perk up, but words, though unspoken, keep hanging between us.

He turns on the television and watches the news. I look at his stiff neck, his unsmiling countenance and go to bed.

The nature and magnitude of the problem of gender-based violence in Tanzania

The magnitude of the problem can illustrated in the story of Levina Mukasa, as told here by Chemi Che Mponda, TAMWA member.

In 1990 the issue of sexual harassment facing Tanzanian women came to a head when a first-year education student at the University of Dar es Salaam, Levina Mukasa, killed herself by taking an overdose of chloroquine tablets.

Levina had been severely harassed over a long period by a group of male engineering students and a clandestine satire group called 'Mzee Punch' which specialised in producing pornographic wall literature about selected female student victims. Their aim was to make female students give in to the sexual demands of Mzee Punch members, or to make the women students who did well in their studies perform badly. Their efforts, according to several ex-students, were highly successful.

'My grades suffered terribly, I was really demoralised,' says one female student who underwent the torture of Mzee Punch. She is now a successful businesswoman in the city but when asked if she could be identified in the press, she said, 'For heaven's sake, no! My name has been tarnished enough. Don't you know that once "punched", you're "punched" for life?'

Mzee Punch was one of the reasons Levina took her life. The real culprits were a group of male engineering students but hardly anything was done to them.

Mzee Punch has existed on the university campus for over twenty years and was originally a political instrument to ridicule government policy. Over the years, however, it has evolved into a major instrument of sexual harassment and repression of women. Because its victims were women, no one has ever thought seriously of banning it.

Even when Levina killed herself on 7 February 1990, there was still reluctance to ban it. Despite the uproar by women leaders and women's groups to put an end to Mzee Punch, their cries fell on deaf ears. It was finally banned later that year when it 'punched' President Ali Hassan Mwinyi and other top government leaders. At the same time, the university was closed down and all the students, men and women, were expelled.

After Levina's death, a team was formed to investigate the cause. It recommended that the then second-year engineering student, Omari Sarota, be expelled for harassing Levina two days before she committed suicide. It also recommended that two others involved be suspended. Sarota was expelled, but was reinstated in 1991 following an appeal through the male-dominated court system. The other two have completed their studies.

Levina killed herself because, when she pleaded for help to stop the harassment, no one listened to her. Mzee Punch had threatened to 'punch' any female student who was seen walking with Levina. The terrified women heeded the call and Levina was left to walk alone and was shunned. She was haunted by knocks on her door at night. Obscene messages and threats were stuck on her room door. She was to be the next person to be 'punched' on walls throughout the campus.

An emergency meeting of women, which was called after Levina's death, accused the then student government (MUWATA) of silently watching sexual harassment and sometimes collaborating with the perpetrators. They said that female victims who attempted to get assistance from MUWATA found themselves in deeper trouble as, instead of help, they were lectured on the superiority and invincibility of Mzee Punch.

Gender-based violence is a global phenomenon. In Tanzania, the magnitude of the problem can be illustrated by surveys conducted by TAMWA and statistics from the Ministry of Home Affairs. A survey conducted by TAMWA in 1989 revealed that six out of ten women in the city of Dar es Salaam had experienced domestic violence in the form of threats, battery, insulting language or pushing and shoving from their partners or spouses. Another recent survey in Mara Region, north-eastern Tanzania, shows that of 238 respondents, 116 or 90.2 per cent confirmed the existence of battery in the region and 89.7 per cent of the male respondents admitted to having battered their wives or partners. According to the statistics, between January 1990 and December 1996, there were over 5,000 rape and defilement cases reported to the police, 3,443 of which were rape cases. Research conducted at the Tanzanian High Court in 1996 also reveals that 70 (known) women were killed by husbands, boyfriends and close relatives in Tanzania between 1972 and 1996.

In rape there is another fear among women's rights activists, that of HIV/AIDS. A victim who is sexually abused by an HIV-infected assailant may well have contracted HIV as well. Yet it is only recently that people have thought of HIV/AIDS in relation to sexual violence.

Statistics from the Ministry of Home Affairs highlight violence against the aged, particularly in regions where old women have been victims of superstition. In regions such as Mwanza, Shinyanga and Tabora, old women have been brutally put to death after being accused of practising witchcraft.

So far, we have not been able to determine whether the increase of reported cases of violence in Tanzania is due to an increase of incidents or due to more awareness by the public reporting the cases. Either way, these statistics do not show the true picture and TAMWA believes that there are many more cases and incidences which are not reported to the police.

A survey conducted by TAMWA in 1988 for a seminar on 'The Portrayal of Women in the Media', shows that the media played a major role in undermining women's images of themselves. This goes for language too. Many abusive terms are female-oriented and mention parts of a woman's anatomy explicitly and in a derogatory way. Dr. Ruth Besha, in her paper for the seminar, said that whenever society wants to abuse a person (man or woman), his or her mother's anatomy is brought into focus, not his or her father's anatomy. She notes that,

This serves to perpetuate the notion that women are just sexual objects and that they are objects of ridicule who don't merit societal respect. Even women's reproductive functions are undermined when a victim is abused and insulted by mentioning his or her mother's genitals and the fact that she gave birth to him or her!

'For years it has been kept under wraps, most women didn't dare talk about it…' sums up the whole notion of sexual harassment. It is not a new problem but most women have either been too embarrassed to bring it out in the open or have accepted it as the norm.

In fact, sexual harassment is one of the oldest forms of 'power play', with women being the victims and men the perpetrators or intimidators. In its most basic form, when it is 'direct assault', sexual harassment brings into focus the helplessness of women because they are physically weaker and do not hold positions of authority at places of work or in the home. When a man talks, a woman is not supposed to answer back. All that the victims (women) can feel is anger and impotent rage. Very few have taken the step to fight back against this vile practice.

It is only in recent years that the term 'sexual harassment' has been used formally in Tanzania. This is as a result of the work of women's pressure groups in fighting all forms of discrimination – sexual harassment being one of the most common. Tanzania did not have a Swahili term for sexual harassment until 1989 when TAMWA conferred with Bakita, the Tanzanian Council for Swahili Language, and decided on the phrase '*Unyanyasaji wa Kijinsia*'.

Violence against women and children in Tanzania, as elsewhere, is a violation of human rights and its prevention can only be achieved through advocacy and protection of those rights. This is what TAMWA has been doing since its inception through advocacy of women and children's rights using the media as the mobilising tool in its campaigns.

There are positive signs that women are now willing to take legal action against gender-based violence; until five years ago, women were afraid to speak up for fear of stigma, isolation and the subsequent trauma. Society often does not take kindly to a woman who dares to speak up.

Awareness raising

Levina died of a broken heart, not of cowardice, as some would believe. Suicide? Of course not. Society killed her. A judgmental society that always passes sentence on a woman who dares to speak up.

'You are a slut.' 'You must have asked for it.' 'It's the way you dress and those "come hither" eyes.' 'What did you expect?' Sentence proclaimed!

'I'm not dead,' Levina says, 'why do you keep saying I'm dead? I still live through the lives of people like you,' she insists.

'Go away, Levina,' I tell her.

'I won't – not until you tell the story. Tell the story of crime and violence against women and children. Give faces and names to those statistics that people like you, storytellers who tell stories that are not theirs, keep churning out in print and on the airwaves. You have to give face and speech to those numbers.'

Over the last ten years TAMWA, in coalition with sister NGOs, has worked to improve the status of women in Tanzania by highlighting the issues and problems that act as barriers to their development. This has been done through research to determine the magnitude and the form of the discrimination that takes place, meetings and seminars, news reports and features, and radio and television programmes. TAMWA's magazine, *Sauti ya Siti*, is a means of sensitising and informing women and others in society about the issues and concerns of women, and shows how there can be a positive portrayal of women in the media. *Sauti ya Siti* has been augmented by popular education materials, including booklets, pamphlets and posters.

Through media advocacy to raise public awareness, TAMWA has published booklets on domestic violence and rape to educate the public on what the law says on domestic and sexual violence, how to avoid violence, and what to do if it has taken place. Radio and television programmes, and the print media have also been used to educate the public on relevant aspects of the law so that the law becomes demystified and accessible to the public. This has been possible because 95 per cent of TAMWA members work in the mainstream media.

The NGO movement in Tanzania believes that raising public awareness on gender-based violence will help prevent the crimes from occurring. TAMWA, through its programmes, has gradually raised the issue of accountability for all Tanzanians as part of collective community action against gender-based violence.

'Please tell my story,' says the voice of little Tumaini who died aged six after being defiled by her uncle.

Little Tumaini, a beautiful name meaning 'hope', though there wasn't much of that in her life, died in hospital. We used to visit her and read her stories, and she would look at us with the eyes of an old woman. She once asked, 'Will I die?' That was when the infection had spread to her blood and there wasn't much hope for her.

Tumaini was brave. Not once did she complain about the pain, but would lie in the hospital cot, looking at us with wizened eyes and sometimes ask for a soda.

A consolidated programme on lobbying and advocacy against gender-based violence

Between April 1997 and December 2000, TAMWA implemented a four-year programme to reduce gender-based violence through advocacy, victim services and consciousness raising. The programme, entitled Sensitisation, Lobbying and Advocacy to Break Free of Gender-based Violence, evolved out of the work of the Crisis Centre and was a comprehensive campaign aimed at eliminating domestic and sexual violence. The aim was to make Tanzania a society free from gender-based violence. The programme, funded by HIVOS and NOVIB, focused on lobbying for the repeal of discriminatory laws as a strategy for intervention, and also on creating a human rights culture as a strategy for prevention.

A substantial part of the programme was outreach work in order to spread legal literacy through the media and to stimulate collective community action against the problem. Hand in hand with outreach was the media advocacy component in a 'bang style' campaign through which an item is reported and covered simultaneously by all media organs to raise its impact. TAMWA feels the media is an important tool for legal literacy and human rights education in Tanzania.

To support the media campaign, TAMWA established links with legislators, policy makers, law enforcers, members of the judiciary, and community and religious leaders. TAMWA organised workshops with these groups because they are influential members of society and, more often than not, they preach and defend the human rights of women and children. They have also been critics of domestic and sexual violence in the country.

Dialogue and seminars are other tools that TAMWA uses. For example, one of the most important lobbying undertakings by TAMWA was a *Kongamano/* Symposium organised for MPs. The objective of the symposium, held in Dodoma on 26 July 1997, was to inform MPs of the multitude of problems faced by Tanzanian women and to lobby for the support of the legislators to take measures to repeal or amend laws which discriminate against women and children.

One glaring example is that the recommendations made in 1995 by the Tanzania Law Reform Commission to repeal several laws that are gender discriminatory, including the customary law on inheritance, are still languishing in files, and debates have not been conducted in Parliament over them. TAMWA hoped that, as a result of dialogue, MPs would push for those recommendations to be enacted as laws. MPs, being representatives of their constituents, would also be the watchdogs of the legal and human rights of women and children and would push for the reinforcement of the laws. MPs have a moral obligation to ensure that human rights charters, such as the Convention on the Elimination of all Forms of Discrimination Against Women (CEDAW) and the Convention on the Rights of the Child (CRC), are implemented in Tanzania. This calls for the incorporation of these charters in our Constitution and legal system.

The symposium was a success as it raised awareness of the issue of gender-based violence in both MPs and other groups within the civil society. The signs of support extended by the MPs to TAMWA over its endeavors against gender-based violence is a clear indication of the impact TAMWA's messages have had in Tanzania.

During the symposium, the MPs unanimously supported TAMWA's proposals for the formation of a human rights commission, the establishment of special hearings in law courts for victims of gender-based violence, and the devising of a new police form for victims of gender-based violence instead of the current form, commonly known as PF 3, which is used for all crimes. The fact that the symposium was broadcast live by Radio Tanzania meant that the message was delivered to millions of people who had tuned in.

The parliamentary symposium was part of a series of Days of Action which has been organised by TAMWA over the last nine years to focus on a particular issue which affects the welfare of women and children, and to initiate collective community action over the issue.

TAMWA organised a mock tribunal during the International Day of Action against Gender-based Violence on 16 December 1995 in Dar es Salaam. This tribunal included testimonials from women who are survivors of violence like rape, battery, sexual harassment and discrimination at work places. This too was broadcast live over the radio. The testimonials given by women in their own voices were similar to those given in Vienna, Austria (1992); Cairo, Egypt (1994); and Copenhagen, Denmark, and Beijing, China (1995).

Since 1996, on the last day of the 16 Days of Activism Against Gender-based Violence, TAMWA has also been holding a vigil to remember women who died at the hands of their husbands, lovers and relatives.

Experience has shown that in many courts, magistrates, prosecutors, defence lawyers and court clerks have not been supportive of the victims of domestic and sexual violence. They are often guilty of being biased against the woman victim and of favouring the male accused. In addition, sexual assault cases were, without exception, tried in open court. This, undoubtedly, added to the victim's trauma. The cross-examination that goes with such trials tends to instill in the woman a sense of great shame and a loss of dignity, and the woman is often made to feel she is at fault.

There was essentially no difference between being raped and giving evidence as a key witness at the trial of her rape except that, this time, it takes place in front of a mostly male crowd. The accused was present when such evidence as the description of the woman's or girl's genitals, the colour and size of the bruises on her body and the presence of semen on her legs or clothes is given. This clearly demonstrates how gravely tormenting the moment must be when a woman victim of a rape offence is called to testify about such an incident in an open court.

Proposals to establish special courts or special hearings to protect the dignity of women were heard from gender rights activists. After all, if there were special courts for labour and housing disputes why not special courts for victims of gender-based violence?

The Crisis Centre

In 1990 TAMWA started a Crisis Centre in Dar es Salaam to provide legal aid and counselling services to women and children who are victims of gender-based violence. The Centre also conducts outreach programmes with the aim of sensitising communities on gender-based violence and providing legal literacy.

We started the Crisis Centre with US$50. We started a Crisis Centre because Levina had died. Though we didn't have the expertise needed for running such centres, we just went ahead and started one because we felt there was a gap in our society – places of refuge where distressed women and children could seek help.

At first we were regarded with suspicion by many people in Dar es Salaam who had heard, through radio or from friends, that such a centre existed. Gradually, we gained credibility. It wasn't easy. Some said we were taking advantage of women who told us their stories which we 'sold' to outsiders. Others said we just wanted to get access to donor funds, and a few said we were running a brothel for married women who would otherwise be recognised if they 'walked' the streets.

I was a young woman when we started the centre, barely 28. I remember the sessions where we used to cry each time a 'client' came in seeking help. Their stories were so terrible that we consumed large amounts of tea and coffee to keep ourselves from giving up.

It certainly wasn't true about being a brothel, but a few men believed it was, and some even ventured in, looking for 'services'. I remember the day the first one came in to solicit such 'services.' I cried and cried asking anyone who would care to listen 'why?'

Then it occurred to us that communication was the best antidote for getting rid of such speculations. We started giving out leaflets which we photocopied over and over explaining the aim, objectives and services of the Centre.

We started conducting outreach activities in Dar es Salaam in 1993 by visiting many secondary and primary schools to inform pupils about child sexual abuse, how it can take place, when and where, and how to deal with it when it does take place. We had separate sessions with teachers to help them spot abused children and discussed ways of helping such children.

By then, we had acquired some skills in outreach techniques. We had also undergone paralegal and counselling training which was an added advantage in our work. Research and data collection of reported cases from police stations provided us with information which strengthened our resolve. We also started becoming friends with the law enforcers and the judiciary.

In 1995, we started training police officers in dealing with gender-based violence cases. We were also training community-based organisations (CBOs) and parish workers on paralegal and counselling skills which, we had realised earlier on, would give women and children in need access to support, even if the reach was limited as we did not have the capacity to conduct such services throughout the country. The University of Dar es Salaam provided us with lecturers in law who designed training programmes on paralegal skills for CBOs while the Social Welfare Institute assisted us with social welfare and counselling training.

By 1995, interns from the university and from the Institute were volunteering at the centre as part of their training. Now we have at least five students doing three-month internships with us every year and the centre has become recognised by the education authorities in Tanzania. The police training colleges in Dar es Salaam and Moshi often send students to do research at the centre and consult us on matters of protocol in dealing with, for example, gender-based violence. Our recommendations have been included in their curricula.

The Crisis Centre gave birth to TAMWA's first consolidated core programme – Sensitisation, Lobbying and Advocacy to Break Free of Gender-based Violence (1997 to 2000).

Georgina's husband battered her for eleven years because they couldn't have children. Her father in law finally threw her out because she had 'disgraced her family'. Being unable to have children is considered a crime.

She came to the centre because she had nowhere to go and we put her up at a hostel run by our friends from religious organisations. She attended counselling sessions, found a job, later got a boyfriend and, wonders, she became pregnant! She came with her baby to the centre to tell us that though the baby was baptised Maria, she called her Tamwa.

To spread legal literacy, TAMWA runs training workshops for women's groups on paralegal and counselling skills and, so far, several community-based centres have been opened in different parts of the country. The community-based centres, like the Crisis Centre in Dar es Salaam, give support to victims of gender-based violence and raise public awareness on women's and children's human rights. At the moment, there are 30 community-based support centres in the country, some working under the umbrella of TAMWA, while others work under religious organisations.

A profile of the Crisis Centre in 1999

In 1999 the Crisis Centre continued to support victims of gender-based violence. The victims, regardless of their sex, received legal aid and counselling services.

Common cases that were dealt with included matrimonial and domestic violence, sexual harassment, rape and sexual abuse (defilement), child custody and maintenance, inheritance, school pregnancy, and domestic workers' disputes.

The centre received 893 new clients, this being an average of 84 new clients every month. There was a 15.5 per cent increase in the number of clients compared to 1998. Of the clients, 773 were women, 43 girls, ten boys below eighteen years of age, and 67 were men.

Over 47 per cent of all cases that were handled at the centre were matrimonial or domestic violence complaints, which included spousal battery, denial of financial support for basic needs, and sexual harassment or women being thrown out of their matrimonial homes for one reason or another. There were 141 more complaints than in 1998.

The other cases handled were as follows:

- Some 114 clients came with child maintenance problems, 22 more clients than in 1998. Child maintenance problems involved women, mostly young and single mothers, whose boyfriends, after making them pregnant, had abandoned them. However, others were married women who were totally dependent on their husbands economically, but had been abandoned with the children.
- There were 110 widows whose in-laws had wanted to deprive them of the right to acquire and possess property left by their deceased husbands. Some of these widows were thrown out of their matrimonial homes, leaving behind their children, property, and even their personal clothing, soon after the deaths of their husbands. There were 85 more widows than in the previous year.
- Twenty-seven cases were of defilement or rape. The victims were mostly girls and boys, some as young as two years old. The perpetrators included the children's fathers, brothers, uncles, neighbours, co-tenants, teachers, and people known and trusted by the victims.
- Some 153 clients came seeking legal aid. They included people who had cases in court and wanted to appeal, or had won cases in court but the judgement had not been executed, or those whose matrimonial disputes had failed to be reconciled and were petitioning for divorce. Others were clients who needed child maintenance, or widows who needed guidance in their probate and property administration cases.

In 1999, 22 cases were concluded while 68 cases were still pending in court. A further 343 cases were referred to various institutions, such as the Marriage Conciliatory Board, the police, the courts, NGOs and the Muslim Council of Tanzania (BAKWATA). Staff at the centre made 370 visits to police and courts to get more of an insight into the cases and documents. There were 50 more visits than in 1998.

The centre gave shelter to seven clients. As there are no shelter facilities at the centre, the clients had to stay with 'good Samaritans' or at the annexe of the centre.

Travelling back over the road that has been my life for the last ten years, I realise I gave so much of myself away to alleviate sadness in others that I didn't find the time to bring joy into my own life, and by the time I realised it, I had forgotten the word 'joy'.

His eyes tell me, 'I married you and not a Crisis Centre.' I pretend I don't understand but I make it worse by telling him about little Suma whose father had repeatedly abused him and was now in a 'safe house' being harboured by Catholic nuns while the case was being processed in court.

'Are you looking for glory?'

'No,' I reply, shocked. 'There is no glory in suffering.' He didn't understand.

I often reflect – maybe I tried to replace the baby we had lost with the Crisis Centre. Then I reassure myself – no.

'Don't you have more joyful stories to tell? Do you have to talk about sexual abuse and wife battery all the time? You do it on television, over the radio, in the print media, on public platforms. Do you have to bring it to our dinner table?'

I had forgotten that the Crisis Centre was a separate entity, living its own life, and my presence was just one cog in the wheel.

'What is this woman looking for?' The question kept hanging between us.

'Don't bring the Crisis Centre into the house, leave it at the gate,' he often said. I gave no quarter – love me, love 'my' centre. By then I had become acquisitive, referring to it as my centre. So vain of me.

The overall strategy that TAMWA uses to achieve impact

In coalition with gender rights NGOs, TAMWA is working on the elimination of gender-based violence within a strategy to expand the availability of services for victims by setting up more crisis centres nationally, and increase counselling services and support groups. So far, this is what TAMWA has achieved:

- working with other NGOs and government agencies to implement a coordinated campaign against gender-based violence;
- informing women, through media and outreach, of the need for economic empowerment as a means of providing alternatives to staying in abusive relationships;
- launching a national media campaign which challenges social norms concerning violence against women;
- training community-based organisations in counselling and paralegal skills to enable them to start support centres elsewhere in the country;
- incorporating themes related to all forms of gender-based violence and gender role stereotyping into radio shows, soap operas and other popular education materials;
- conducting sensitivity training workshops for doctors on violence against women and on how to collect and document evidence of assault, sexual abuse and rape;
- documenting how laws related to gender-based violence are (or are not) enforced, detailing arrest rates, judgements and sentences;
- lobbying for amendment of regulations to allow any licensed healthcare provider to examine and collect evidence of physical and sexual assault to enable victims to press charges early, especially in the rural areas where there are no doctors;
- lobbying for improved medical and legal services provided by the state for victims of gender-based violence in urban and rural areas;
- supporting legal aid NGOs by advertising their services in the media;
- conducting training programmes on gender-based violence for the police, prosecutors and judges;
- lobbying for the removal of gender stereotyping from the press, school teaching materials and popular songs;
- working with mass media personnel to portray positive images of relationships based on equity; and
- training teachers on gender awareness to equip them to spot signs of abuse.

Doto was abused by her uncle and needed six reconstructive surgical operations. Her pelvis had broken and she was incontinent. She died.

I remember her warm pudgy hands that she always offered as a greeting when we visited her in hospital. I once took flowers for her and she couldn't stop marvelling. 'Flowers? For me?' she kept asking. Only then did I remember that Africans traditionally don't take flowers to visit sick people. We take soup and words of comfort, but we have become so immersed in other people's cultures that we have forgotten our own traditions.

A local government leader brought Doto in. He also assisted the traumatised parents and later gave evidence in court.

Strategies and tools used in implementing of the programme against gender-based violence

Violence against women is deeply rooted in gender-based power relations and any strategy to eliminate gender-based violence must confront the underlying cultural beliefs and social structures that perpetuate it.

To be effective, such a strategy has to draw on a wide range of expertise and resources; underlying all this, is the need to refine our understanding of the exact causes of gender violence.

In a survey that TAMWA did on domestic violence in 1989 and another on sexual violence in 1990, it was learnt that there are seven main factors from which gender violence can be predicted. These are:

1 economic inequality between men and women;
2 male authority, control and decision making in the home;
3 social stigma and isolation of a woman who speaks up or tries to break free of gender-based violence;
4 lack of awareness of the law;
5 lack of access to the legal process when, for example, women have to travel for miles before they can get to a law court;
6 lack of sympathy from law enforcers; and
7 women being made to feel it is their fault – 'She must have asked for it'.

The media strategy

An increasing number of cases of domestic and sexual violence, including child abuse, are now being reported. This is an indication that there has been an increase in public awareness on matters pertaining to domestic and sexual violence, and that victims are more willing to speak up.

What is needed is to maintain the tempo by increasing public awareness about domestic and sexual violence, particularly through the media. TAMWA can help this effort by supporting projects aimed at fighting discrimination against women. Efforts can also be made to establish centres, such as those started by TAMWA, to provide counselling, legal aid and outreach.

A sample of print media coverage of social issues from January to December 1999 shows the following:

- stories on rape, 198;
- stories covering land issues, 237;
- HIV/AIDS stories, 355;
- stories on the killing of elderly people, 576; and
- domestic violence stories, 640.

Gender-based violence as a health and a human rights issue

Although violence against women is universal, the patterns and its causes should be understood in specific social and cultural contexts. In the context of Tanzania, the deeply entrenched traditional and patriarchal structures have, to a large extent, perpetuated gender-based violence in the country.

Improving women's access to power and resources so as to give them alternatives to staying in abusive relationships is one strategy. This meant that a media campaign was needed on the following:

- public education on legal literacy and human rights education;
- empowerment of women, through lobbying for higher education and, therefore, higher incomes for women;
- providing assertiveness skills and empowerment training for women to boost their self-esteem; and
- changing cultural beliefs and social mores on the role of women in society.

This strategy includes the promotion of non-violent means to resolve domestic conflict by encouraging families to speak openly about their fears and prejudices. This has been done in the form of chat shows on radio and television.

Strategic media production

TAMWA has ensured that the media in Tanzania is used effectively to create awareness on issues concerning women and children. The media is mobilised through a method called Strategic Media Production. This entails sending to the regions a team of journalists from radio, television and newspapers to report the same issue at the same time, from a gender-sensitive angle.

TAMWA has held workshops to show media personnel how the media can be used to raise human and legal rights awareness in the following ways:

- in stories or features, journalists can reveal rights violations, including the specific rights that have been infringed and laws that have been flouted;
- through radio broadcasts and feature articles;
- in popular education materials (pamphlets, booklets) where the information is translated into simple Swahili with a lot of illustrations to make the text comprehensible to even semi-literate readers;
- in the form of radio magazines where the journalist or broadcaster can insert snippets into the script;
- through popular theatre where the script is deliberately written to include rights information;

- in the form of panel discussions on radio or television where lawyers and human rights activists are interviewed about specific laws and the repercussions of flouting them;
- through outreach programmes where the outreach team selects an audience and gives lectures;
- by reproducing NGO reports on human rights and the legal process in the form of feature articles and radio and television magazines that indicate human rights violations; and
- through community theatre.

Training and induction in implementing the core programmes

Before any TAMWA member or consultant could implement our core programmes, they attended workshops on the following topics:

- the local and gender perspective of law and human rights;
- media and legal and human rights issues;
- reporting on legal and human rights issues;
- media ethics and legal and human rights issues;
- outreach techniques;
- the role of the media in ensuring the implementation of legal and human rights;
- education of media workers and their contribution to the improvement of the status of women and children in Tanzania; and
- how women can be made aware that peace, equality and justice are neither a luxury, nor a foreign concept but a right that can and should be attained.

The case of *RV Kitila* v. *Tintina*

In this case, the accused was convicted of doing grievous harm and was sentenced to fifteen months imprisonment by the lower court. During a quarrel with his wife, when he had taken offence at the way she helped herself to a portion of meat, the accused had struck her with a stick on the hand, fracturing a joint of one of her fingers. On appeal the court held that the offence was 'a domestic one...that by imposing a long term of imprisonment, he was, in fact, causing the complainant to suffer more, by depriving her of her bread winner'. The sentence was altered and the convict was given immediate release. This indicates that the courts condone wife abuse. It is our contention that, in such cases, once domestic violence has been established, the courts should be empowered to order payment of compensation and hold the husband criminally liable in a civil suit.

The case of *Sanga* v. *Sanga*

In *Sanga* v. *Sanga*, the appellant and the deceased were wife and husband. The appellant killed her husband by hitting him with an axe. The dispute arose from the fact that the appellant had made a complaint to the ten cell leader against the deceased. This angered the deceased and he locked their bedroom saying he was going to eliminate her. He further said that the appellant was wasting her time as he would not bring back her deceased child whom he had killed through witchcraft. She said, 'He grabbed my throat. I pushed him back and he fell against a bed. I looked around and saw an axe. I was convinced he was going to kill me. I picked up the axe and cut him with it. He fell by the bed. I opened the door and ran into the maize *shamba* (field)...' The High Court convicted her of murder. The defence of provocation or self defence was not available to her.

In the court of appeal, the conviction was reduced to that of manslaughter. The court held: 'We think that the appellant had killed under provocation. However, the deceased was not armed and, when he was pushed and fell back against the bed, the appellant could have opened the door and run off. In any event, using an axe to cut the deceased in the circumstances was excessive.'

But from the facts of the case it is evident that when the deceased fell on the bed, he could have up and beaten the woman to the door. Thus, the argument that the appellant could have opened the door and run off after pushing him would not necessarily stand. Even if she had managed to open the door, the deceased could have caught up with her and there is no telling what could have happened. Another factor is the danger that the appellant felt. The force used, we think, was equivalent to the provocation received.

Magdalena Sanga's defence was based on the single episode of the immediate quarrel. Inadmissible as defence was the history of the couple, whether the deceased was in the habit of beating the accused, the torment she underwent on the death of her child and the anguish of learning from the deceased that he was responsible for it. In sum, the case met the standard of provocation as required by the law. Suppose the accused managed to run off, and she later killed her husband in his sleep, what would the ruling have been? In the hypothetical case, there would be a history of domestic violence. But we believe the ruling would be murder and the court would not even touch on the defence.

Outreach through radio

Tanzania is a vast country with an area of more than 945,000 square kilometres and, because of poor infrastructure, it is difficult to reach the people. To overcome the problem in delivering its message, TAMWA has adopted outreach through radio. In addition to using normal programmes, TAMWA also has its own special radio programme – *KIOO* (mirror) – which is broadcast over Radio Tanzania every Wednesday at prime time from 8:15 to 8:30 pm. Themes of the programmes include the rights of women and children, the need to eradicate wife battery and female genital mutilation, and human rights education.

General assessment indicates that the media advocacy has had a tremendous impact in raising public awareness. As a result of media advocacy, some people have sent letters to radio stations directly and others through Readers Forums in the newspapers to give their views on the issues.

Eliza from Sina

Eliza is a 29-year-old woman working for a private company. She is a bit on the plump side and has big breasts which she is conscious of and tries to camouflage under loose dresses, but to no avail. Every time her male colleagues want to make a joke, Eliza's breasts are brought in. They go to the extent of fondling the breasts when they want to make a point.

Eliza has not taken any steps to report the incidents to the management, but she is very depressed about it and is thinking of moving from her present job. Her friends have advised her against it saying that wherever she goes she will get similar treatment. Short of having plastic surgery to reduce her breasts, Eliza feels she has no option but to put up with the harassment. In the meantime, her work suffers and she dreads office parties where one of the managers will invariably make a joke about her breasts before her office colleagues and they will all laugh, the women included.

TAMWA's campaign against gender-based violence has had a significant impact. For example, some sections of the public have become aware of gender issues and are calling on the government to take action against gender-based violence. Others have taken the initiative to give strong comments against gender-based violence through public debates, phone-in radio and television programmes, and letters to the editors. Policy makers and government leaders have become vocal against gender-based violence and attend seminars and workshops organised by TAMWA and sister NGOs – a new trend because, a few years ago, they tended not to take NGOs seriously.

Magistrates have become more sensitive in dealing with such cases. The media has acted as a watchdog and the government has taken a firmer stance on gender-based violence. In effect, TAMWA has been able to put gender and development on the Tanzanian map via the media.

Asha from Kariakoo

My boss, who is from Italy, always makes passes at me. Once he asked me to stay behind in the afternoon and, after everyone had left, tried to assault me. He kept chasing me around his desk and I couldn't get out of the room as he had locked the door. I told him I would scream, and he didn't believe me. I did scream and the watchman came to the door. I told him what was happening and he told the boss to open the door. The boss opened the door and I rushed out and went home. When I told my husband about it, he said that I must have been behaving like a prostitute. It was a very bad experience for me and I had hoped to get sympathy from my husband but he only blamed me. Now I am so depressed. If only I could afford to stop working but we need the extra income. My husband has now become very suspicious and watches my movements all the time. The boss is still there, I wish he would get recalled to Italy. He still propositions me and has even offered me money. I told him I am a respectable married woman, but he wouldn't listen

Annie from Upanga

My ex-husband, from whom I am separated, keeps coming to the house where I live with my children and demands sex from me. I always tell him to get lost, but he often gets violent and threatens to take the children away from me if I don't comply with his wishes. I reported the matter to the police who told me to 'give in' after all 'you are not formally divorced'! I have a boyfriend and once my ex-husband saw us together at a function. He made a scene and tried to beat me up. The strange thing is that people, my relatives included, later blamed me. They said I shouldn't have flaunted my new relationship so soon after my separation. My God! It is two years now since I moved out of my marital home and people blame me!

He used to hit and abuse me in public. I just had to leave him. Now he demands his conjugal rights. It's a joke. I'm planning to get a court injunction to keep him away.

He phones my office at all times and says all sorts of obscene things on the phone. He even comes there and shouts for all to hear that I am still his wife. My boss has called me and said that this has got to stop. I am very angry but there is nothing I can do.

Activities leading to the enactment of the Sexual Offences Special Provisions Act (SOSPA) 1998

TAMWA's focus on child sexual abuse, sexual harassment, rape and female genital mutilation gave birth to SOSPA.

In summary, the programme was implemented as follows:

- In April 1997 the core programme was launched with a press conference. One hundred journalists attended. They were given data going back five years to establish the magnitude of the problem. The launch received extensive coverage in the mainstream media and acquired legitimacy from the public through its focus on making every section of society feel accountable.
- In the same month, TAMWA conducted a two-week training and induction workshop for its members on legal literacy, research techniques and media strategy.
- From May to July, TAMWA held a series of consultative meetings with different stakeholders, starting with heads of mass media organs – editors, news editors, columnists and senior journalists, and radio and television programme producers. This was followed by a meeting with the clergy where religious leaders of all denominations were co-opted into the programme; sister NGOs and CBOs were next, followed by traditional healers, the police and members of the judiciary.
- In July, TAMWA held the *Kongamano*/Symposium with 275 MPs in Dodoma. They were told about the magnitude of the problem, made to feel accountable, and asked what they were going to do about it.
- From August to October, TAMWA commissioned features in the mainstream print media and special programmes on radio and television, and printed 30,000 copies of a supplement which was disseminated through the mainstream print media.
- In February 1998, a bill addressing sexual offences was sent to Parliament. It took the NGO movement totally by surprise. We were expecting law reform on sexual offences to take about two years, so when we heard that it had been sent to Parliament, we were elated.
- In March, TAMWA conducted a five-day training seminar for law enforcers and NGOs in Dar es Salaam. Participants in the seminar came from all regions on the mainland. TAMWA used the seminar as a peg to lobby for the enactment of the Bill, through both media advocacy and physical lobbying. The Minister of Home Affairs sent a representative to open the seminar, and the Minister of Justice and Constitutional Affairs closed it.
- The following month, April 1998, the Bill was enacted as the Sexual Offences Special Provisions Act (SOSPA) 1998.

Mwamvua from Temeke

My stepfather always paws me when my mother is on duty. She is a nurse and sometimes works the night shift. He buys me presents and gives me money to spend which I always give back to him. He says I shouldn't be afraid of getting pregnant, that he knows how to prevent pregnancy. I hate him. I am too scared to tell my mother, I don't think she would believe me. My father died when I was small and three years ago my mother remarried.

He gets angry when I speak to boys and once slapped me as I walked home from school with a male classmate. He tells my mother that I am cheap and she shouts at me.

Habiba from Msasani

I was groped by a man in the bus as I was going home from a friend's house. At first I thought it was accidental. But when it persisted, I looked behind and saw this man trying to put his hand in my skirt. He pulled until the zip broke. The bus was full and, as I shouted at him to stop, the passengers laughed. The conductor told me to stop behaving like a child. I got off the bus at the next stop although I was far from home. I felt so dirty after that incident. I told my neighbour who said she had had a similar experience in a bus.

The Sexual Offences Special Provisions Act has been described as revolutionary. It is unambiguous and wide in scope and application. Also, it offers victims greater legal protection. Besides increasing sentences, the Act offers compensation to victims of most offences, apart from the fine which is paid to the state. The Act has also broadened the definition of rape and the corroboration of evidence. It has allowed for a case involving a minor to be held in camera and has addressed the issue of female genital mutilation as a sexual offence. Further, it is visionary, addressing issues that are increasingly becoming or have the potential to become major threats to women, youths and children, such as gang-rape, procurement for prostitution and trafficking in persons.

The law has also addressed persons in authority, such as medical doctors, traditional healers and religious leaders, who could otherwise exploit their positions to commit sexual offences.

Maria from Kipaw

I went for an interview in a parastatal to get a job as an accountant. I'm fairly well qualified, having studied at the College of Business Education in Dar es Salaam. The manager looked me up and down and I felt he was undressing me. After the interview, he called me aside and offered to buy me drinks after office hours. When I sounded reluctant, he told me pointedly that I might not get the job. I questioned him further and he said other people had been interviewed before me and they were men and more qualified, but he liked my looks and thought that we could become more intimate. I refused and he told me not to go near his office again. Needless to say, I didn't get the job.

In the Penal Code, a number of provisions were amended, others repealed and some new sections added with the overall effect of making the act women-friendly. Unlike previous provisions, the amendments are more compassionate towards the victims. Whereas previously only the state could impose fines against an offender, the amendments offer compensation to victims of violence as retribution for the harm done to them.

In sum, the Act has addressed most of the concerns raised by activists regarding weaknesses in the existing laws relating to sexual offences. Mainly:

❑ It provides a more comprehensive definition of rape and attempted rape, and clearly outlines the circumstances in which rape can be said to have occurred.
❑ It recognises intimidations thereby reflecting recent research findings that show most rape victims to have been raped by someone they know.
❑ It imposes fines and provides compensation for victims, dispensed in conjunction with other punishments including imprisonment, fine and corporal punishment, which is quite revolutionary in that it recognises the real victim in the crime.
❑ A significant portion of the Act attempts to protect children from sexual exploitation and abuse.
❑ It provides more stringent sentences.
❑ It creates a number of new offences, for example, gang-rape, trafficking of persons, and cruelty to children.
❑ The age of the victims and the accused have been revisited and considered in designating crimes and determining sentences.
❑ The requirement for independent corroboration in sexual crimes is done away with and courts are directed to accept the evidence of minors and victims of sexual offences without independent corroboration.
❑ It protects the anonymity of children and victims of sexual violence in court records and during legal proceedings.

However, there are still some inadequacies in the Act. It only talks of rape between a husband and wife who are legally separated. Thus, a wife who is still married cannot be raped whether or not she has consented to having intercourse with her husband or she has been forced to have sex in circumstances amounting to rape. Underlying this position is the perception that a man cannot be said to rape his legal wife.

The Act does not address the issue of bail in these crimes. The experience of most legal aid centres has shown that granting bail to an accused jeopardises the outcome of the case. The accused may escape, or more seriously, may threaten the victim. This is especially true where the accused and the victim live in the same abode or neighbourhood. Activists insist that bail should be denied to people who sexually exploit children, youths and women, in order to protect the victims.

Despite the political and the legal interventions on violence against women and children, the basic way of preventing such violence from occurring is to initiate a culture of human rights in our country which would make every Tanzanian feel accountable. This is the long term strategy which TAMWA adopted in 1999. A human rights culture can be established with the introduction of human rights education on a national scale. The agents for this education should be the government, policy makers, community and religious leaders, and the media. The personal and collective responsibility of human rights protection and promotion should be inculcated into our culture so that it becomes a norm for every Tanzanian to adhere to human rights precepts.

TAMWA continues with its campaign to eradicate sexual and domestic violence through public education and services for victims. Public education on sexual offences has been given adequate attention through the mass media, training and community outreach. The main thrust is to popularise the SOSPA – a survey showed that, in 1999, twelve regions out of 25 on the mainland had not received copies of SOSPA. TAMWA has also learnt that law enforcers, members of the judiciary and social workers have not been given training in using SOSPA.

Hours have been spent on television and radio to inform and sensitise the public on the Act. Hundreds of articles were written on sexual offences. TAMWA printed and distributed a total of 25,000 fact sheets and posters. Photocopies of the Act were produced and given to journalists and other interested parties who included researchers, and NGOs and CBOs.

TAMWA members and staff talked about the Act as resource people at different forums and have engaged in information sharing on the lobbying process for the Act. Despite all these efforts, TAMWA has noted that more needs to be done to ensure that the law is administered fairly and correctly.

In one incident, a magistrate sentenced a ten-year-old boy to life imprisonment for raping a twelve-year-old girl. TAMWA and other children's rights activists had to intervene to ensure that the judgement was overruled because, according to the SOSPA, a boy under the age of twelve cannot commit the offence of rape. Also, as a first offender, a minor can only be given corporal punishment. The magistrate misused the new piece of legislation.

For the time being, it is difficult to comment on whether or not sexual offences have increased. More reporting of them in the media could be because of greater awareness among the people and breaking of silence, or the increase in gender sensitivity among law enforcers.

TAMWA has also learnt that, for fear of the law, some communities living along the Tanzania–Kenya border take their children to Kenya for female genital mutilation. Others do it secretly, without the usual festivals associated with circumcision.

'Do you feel like a heroine?' I ask Levina, 'with your story having contributed to such historic events in Tanzania society?'

'No,' she answers, 'I don't feel like a heroine, merely a traveller whose sojourn was plucked from the great road that is life, too early. Maybe a person whose story is touching the lives of people living in another time, a different space.'

Tumejifunza nini? What have we learnt?

In mid-1996, after the first democratic elections in years, TAMWA underwent structural changes that to a great extent assisted programme implementation and created a better financial system. However, the changes brought a marked degree of bureaucratisation which took away from the members the spirit of collectivism.

The implications are that though efficiency, accountability and, therefore, impact, have been enhanced, activism on the other hand – the activism that comes along spontaneously because an event has taken place and, therefore, needs to be addressed – is being gradually undermined.

With workplans, indicators, activity and programme design, spontaneity becomes an anachronism and those members who are inherently activist tend to become frustrated when they recommend that TAMWA take up a cause, albeit one not included in the year's workplan, with the inevitable refusal by the secretariat to reroute funds away from an activity already prescribed. Fireworks are bound to erupt with activist members saying the secretariat is acting as a deterrent to their activist work.

The solution here would be to persuade donors to give a set amount of funds each year for activist work. This could work as long as members limit themselves to a prescribed number of activist initiatives. If, for example, something comes up every week, and invariably it does, activist oriented members would still complain.

'Of course, I should have taken the custodianship of my own story more seriously,'
I tell Levina.
I dream of scales, not as in reptile but as in weighing scales, and, because it is my dream, the dishes on each side are balanced. The deep voice echoes,
'I married you not a crisis centre. Couldn't you have used your scales to balance life?'
'The scales belonged to both of us,' I answer back, 'and with your support and understanding, we could have used them to balance life.'
Because I have travelled this road through this story and because I will be able to recognise the landmarks, I'm going to insist they balance next time.

Challenges

TAMWA has, for the last four years, been facing the challenge of balancing the power of the secretariat, the Board and the members. The anomaly is that members are both the owners of the association and implementers of the programmes. This creates uneasiness within the secretariat because during Annual General Meetings the members have the most power, but when it comes to programme implementation *vis-à-vis* consultancies, the secretariat becomes the boss, being coordinator of programmes and the custodian of information, accounts and equipment.

A policy was instigated in early 1998 which ensures that Board members do not take on other roles, such as convenors of implementing committees, or implementors of programmes. This has worked but it has also acted as a deterrent for members to take up Board membership as the consultancies often have a substantial honorarium which they would miss if they were on the Board. Another challenge is from a section of members who feel that members ought to be the main beneficiaries of TAMWA with the public taking second place. In this context, they would like TAMWA to create opportunities for members to study abroad and be paid handsomely for consultancies, and lobby for upward mobility for them in the media organisations where they are employed.

TAMWA has created study opportunities for members, but donors prefer to fund studies within the country rather than abroad. Criteria for consultancies have been set up within the policy framework and those members who qualify, both in terms of skills and accessibility, are awarded consultancies within their implementing committees which are Print Media, Radio, Television, Lobby and Advocacy, and the Crisis Centre.

Therefore, although TAMWA has tried over the last four years to create opportunities for its members in education, consultancies and gender training, these opportunities are perceived differently by different people. For example, economic empowerment or poverty alleviation of its members is not on TAMWA's agenda and members have been made conscious of the fact that the Association should not be a source of employment, income or prestige for its members. It is merely a platform for lobbying for changes in society.

Strategies that have worked

TAMWA is known for taking advantage of the opportunities that come along. In fact, TAMWA is known as '*King'ang'anizi*' meaning 'persistent' and women have been known to be castigated by husbands who tell them '*usilete u-TAMWA wako huku*' meaning 'Don't bring your TAMWA-ness into the house'. These women are not TAMWA members; they are ordinary women who have gained a level of assertiveness from the gender rights awareness advocated by NGOs.

The biggest opportunity that TAMWA has taken advantage of is the liberalisation of the media with the ensuing proliferation of media houses which have provided a platform for the expression of TAMWA's vision and mission.

The only media organ that TAMWA owns is the magazine *Sauti ya Siti*, but it has been able to take advantage of space and airtime created by media proprietors, editors and producers. Considering that the media houses have varied business interests and political sympathies and are, on the whole, male dominated, TAMWA's acceptance by the media has given it muscle and moral support. This is particularly the case in the Association's campaign for human rights in Tanzania, in which the media considers itself an important stakeholder. For example, the privately owned media houses like IPP have allowed TAMWA to use airtime on subsidy and sometimes without paying. Dar es Salaam Television (DTV) allows TAMWA to use its programmes to cover issues of human rights, gender and development. Habra Corporation, with three dailies and two weeklies, has been most supportive, as has Business Care with three dailies, four weeklies and a radio station, and Coastal Television Network. This has been a source of strength to the Association. Religious radio stations, government radio stations, like Radio Tanzania, television stations like Television Tanzania (TVT), newspapers like the *Daily News*, as well as those owned by political parties, none have stinted in their support for TAMWA.

The media has been a major conduit for TAMWA's initiative in transforming Tanzanian society through awareness-raising and public education programmes. It has also been a powerful tool for lobbying and advocacy in law and policy reform. Co-opting male journalists has also helped as the public, on seeing that men have joined the bandwagon, becomes more receptive to change.

Coalitions and alliances

TAMWA has built strong links with NGO networks in Tanzania, such as FemAct, which comprises 25 national NGOs, the Intermediary Gender Network (IGN), linking the Crisis Centre with 120 CBOs, and the linkage provided by the Tanzania Association of Non-Governmental Organisations (TANGO), one of three umbrella organisations for NGOs in Tanzania.

TAMWA members sit on various boards, committees and action groups initiated by sister NGOs, the government and CBOs. It derives strength not only from its alliance with media houses, but also from the support given it by sister NGOs and CBOs. For example, in the lobby for SOSPA, TAMWA was joined in Dodoma by supporters from the Tanzania Gender Networking Programme (TGNP), Tanzania Women Lawyers' Association (TAWLA), CHAWATIATA (the Traditional Healers Association of Tanzania), activists from the community-based crisis centres, and male media practitioners.

Over the last three years, NGOs in Tanzania have forged alliances with the government over issues that are of concern to the two sides. When the Bill for SOSPA was tabled before Parliament in February 1998, several parliamentary committees met with NGO activists to analyse the Bill collectively and to point out areas for improvement.

Officials in the Attorney General's chambers, the Ministry of Community Development, Women's Affairs and Children, the Ministry of Justice and Constitutional Affairs, and the Ministry of Home Affairs have been accessible to NGO activists. They have made information accessible and NGOs have been included in the formulation of policies, giving rise to the spirit of collective decision making.

TAMWA and sister NGOs are conscious of their autonomy and, as long as this is not compromised, alliances between the government and civil societies are important because they illustrate a degree of maturity in the democratisation process and they allow decision making powers to be shared in society. Furthermore, such alliances provide a forum for dialogue. This shows a positive trend in Tanzania. Only ten years ago, the government used to be suspicious of NGOs, thinking they were agents for foreign governments. The respect accorded to NGOs by the government is shown by the invitation of NGO members to run training workshops for MPs and government officials on burning issues in society.

I remember the last week in July 1997 when 200 activists converged on Dodoma to dialogue with MPs, to instill in them a culture of breaking the silence. They refused to listen to testimonies, and the camp of activists was divided. Should we bow to their pressure or should we walk out? In the end we decided to stand firm. We told them if you won't listen to the stories as they exist, then we won't have dialogue with you.

We reached a compromise, the result of which was SOSPA.

Some MPs whispered in conclaves, 'Don't they feel ashamed, discussing sexual matters in public?' Mary Rusimbi of TGNP retorted angrily, 'It is not sexual, we are talking about crime here.'

Edda Sanga pointed her finger at them during the dialogue and said, 'The situation has got to change otherwise we shall meet in the year 2000.' The years have passed and we have voted new MPs into office, though many more years may be needed to overcome the centuries of sorrow and crimes against women and children.

Conclusion

Levina was twenty when she departed from her allotted space to join the world of spirits. 'I'm not dead,' she tells me in my dreams, 'I've merely moved to another place where they can't touch me.'

'They?' I ask, 'who are they?'

'They,' she insists, 'they who called me a prostitute. I had to leave because they hounded me. So much talk, sniggers, averted faces from the holier than thou, so much hatred. When I left my parents' house to go to university, I never imagined it would come to this. Somehow I had believed that the university campus would be a safe haven, a place to learn, make friends, become a person of distinction. Instead, they hounded me. They "punched" me on the wall newsletter. Even the teachers whom I cried to for help turned away from me. You have to tell my story.'

'But there are so many stories to be told,' I say.

'I know,' says Levina, 'but my story, my experience gave birth to the movement against gender-based violence in Tanzania. My story gave birth to the first crisis centre in the country. My story gave birth to the Sexual Offences Special Provisions Act.'

True!

Some time ago, at a conference on HIV/AIDS, I met a *sangoma* (traditional healer) from Zimbabwe who said to me, 'Lady, you are young, but you have the face of an 80-year-old woman.'

'Eighty!' I shrieked, 'I don't want to look 80!'

He looked at me with understanding in his wise *sangoma* eyes and said, 'You are looking at me with the face of your female ancestor. There is unfinished business somewhere, unsettled debts, and you are the one chosen to settle those debts.'

'But Baba,' I said, 'How can I pay debts that have not been put on chits? How can I pay debts that I was never party to?'

'You are party to those debts merely by being alive,' he told me.

I travel back the path I have trodden in the last ten years. I look at the lives of women and men I have worked with in the campaign against gender-based violence in Tanzania and I come to the conclusion that each case we have dealt with, each battered or raped woman, each sexually abused child, remains etched in our hearts.

Hundreds of them have sought help at the Crisis Centre. Each in their own way has touched our lives, and we have touched theirs.

As I travel back on the road I took ten years ago, I feel an overwhelming sense of sadness but I also feel an overwhelming sense of achievement.

I keep searching for some particular voices, those of my ancestors, to ask the faces on those voices whether, now that SOSPA exists, now that women can speak up without fear, now that assailants can be taken to court and jailed, whether the debts have been settled?

There is silence from the other side and I assume that the settlement of debts is a long process.

I keep asking myself, 'Has it all been worthwhile?' Sometimes I feel Yes! Yes! At times I feel like an intruder, getting into the homes and lives of strangers. Making them more comfortable so they would disclose their secrets.

Breaking the silence is our popular motto and broken it we have.

I also hear the *sangoma*'s wise voice, 'Your eyes are sad,' it says, 'but you were one of the people fate elected to help settle old debts.'

'What do you dream of?' the *sangoma* asks.

'I dream of a snake,' I answer.

'What do you do with the snake?' he asks.

'I fight it and I recently killed it,' I say.

'You killed your ancestor. That spirit is your ancestor, a male one,' he said. 'He was bad and killing him in your dreams is part settlement of the debt.'

I broke down and cried as if my heart were breaking.

He patted my hand, offered me some snuff from his horn and said, 'You are a brave girl. You will be fine.'

Bibliography

Alloo, F. 1990, 'Domestic violence', paper for seminar on Sexual Violence, Dar es Salaam.

Besha, R. 1988, 'Portrayal of women in the media', seminar paper, Dar es Salaam.

Kinyenje, B. 1998, 'Research on women killings and other related incidences', report, TAMWA, Dar es Salaam.

Sheikh, L. 1990, 'A survey of sexual harassment in Dar es Salaam', TAMWA, Dar es Salaam.

Sheikh, L. 1992, 'Breaking free of violence (a kit on gender-based violence)', TAMWA, Dar es Salaam.

Sheikh, L. 1992, 'Striving for women's rights within the framework of human rights charters', paper, TAMWA, Dar es Salaam.

Sheikh, L, and Gabba, A. 1990, '*Mwanamke Afanyeje Akibakwa?* (What should a woman do after rape?)', TAMWA, Dar es Salaam.

Sheikh, L. and Gabba, A. 1990, '*Ukatili Dhidi ya Wanawake* (Violence against women)', TAMWA, Dar es Salaam.

TAMWA 1988, 'The portrayal of women in the media', seminar report, Dar es Salaam.

TAMWA 1990, 'Domestic and sexual violence', seminar report, Dar es Salaam.

TAMWA 1997, '*Kongamano*/Symposium with MPs July 1997', report, Dar es Salaam.

WOMEN FOR CHANGE: WORKING WITH RURAL COMMUNITIES

Emily Sikazwe

Introduction

Women for Change (WFC) is a Zambian non-governmental organisation (NGO) committed to working with and empowering remote rural communities, especially women, through gender analysis, popular education methodologies and advocacy to contribute towards sustainable human development and the eradication of all forms of poverty. WFC exists on the principle of non-partisan collaboration with civic, political and other organisations on matters concerning the development of rural communities.

Recognising the importance of good governance, respect for human rights and democracy as necessary conditions for human development, WFC has strong advocacy and human rights education components in its programmes and activities. These complement other programmes in gender analysis and awareness-raising, overall child development and economic empowerment. The human rights education programmes aim to increase the participation of rural people in local governance. WFC considers this participation an indispensable ingredient to sustainable human development.

The national context

In 1991, Zambia experienced a peaceful political transition from a one-party system of government to a multiparty system. Zambia is one of the few countries in Africa that has never experienced civil war. However, the system is still, *de facto*, one-party. The political and governance environment in the country has continued to deteriorate and the government has proved unwilling to have meaningful dialogue with any political stakeholders to address various contentious issues. The Movement for Multiparty Democracy (MMD) government has been inclined to rely solely on its majority in Parliament and has shown no inclination to respond to the various demands from its citizens through representation by opposition parties and other CSOs, including WFC.

At independence in 1964, Zambia was a prosperous country. During the period immediately after independence Zambia managed to expand the provision of basic services, including quality education, to most of its citizens. Zambia's literacy levels were ranked amongst the highest in Africa. The economy, however, continued to be solely dependent on copper production and exports. The poor performance of the copper industry, coupled with other factors, created unprecedented social and economic difficulties which continue to this day.

Social Watch has estimated that, currently, over 72 per cent of Zambia's population is poor. This country, which once had one of the highest standards of living in Africa, is now categorised as a Least Developed Country (LDC) with more than eight million people living in extreme poverty (Social Watch, 1999).

In world rankings, Zambia is sixth among states with the highest crude death rate in the world. For every 1,000 people, 20.1 die every day. People die from malaria, in road traffic accidents, at the hand of armed robbers, and from preventable diseases including HIV/AIDS. Zambians have to contend with some of the highest rates of infant, under-five and maternal mortality in the world. Life expectancy declined from 52 years in 1980 to 49.9 in 1990, 43.5 in 1996 and 30 in 2000.

Zambian women continue to be almost invisible in decision making and other areas of human endeavour. This remains the case even though women, because they are more likely than men to spend money on household requirements, are the most important human resource required to eliminate poverty.

The rural context

Although the entire nation is poor, the phenomenon is more pronounced in rural areas and among women than it is in urban areas and among men. In addition, people in rural areas face a number of particular problems. They lack health services, safe drinking water, food security, schools and money to pay user fees at schools and health centres where these are available. They also suffer from higher than national average levels of child and maternal mortality.

The rural people have been further impoverished and disempowered by the collapse of the agricultural sector, which used to serve as the main source of their income. The current agricultural policy has greatly disadvantaged rural areas where people continue to work very hard, tilling the land but not finding a market for their produce. In the end, the produce is often sold at, or below, cost price.

The evolution of WFC

WFC is an evolving organisation. It has gone through a number of expansion and developmental stages since 1992 and has to go through many more.

WFC was born out of the Women's Development Programme under CUSO. The programme used to run income generating projects for women in remote rural areas of the country as they were considered the most disadvantaged and vulnerable.

WFC was registered in August 1992 as a Zambian NGO after CUSO left the country. The new organisation continued with the same activities undertaken by the Women's Development Programme. What changed, though, was the governance of the programme. WFC established itself as a Zambian NGO working with rural communities to achieve social change. The Programme Advisers of the Women's Development Programme constituted the Advisory Board of WFC.

WFC was born, one might say, prematurely and under risky conditions. The programme did not have a bank account and no one knew how much money was being carried over from CUSO. The Administrative Secretary was not trained to handle the finances of the organisation in terms of producing full financial reports. However, she could raise vouchers and make out cheques which were approved by CUSO. Thus, before the departure of CUSO, WFC did not have any financial autonomy.

I remember being interviewed by the then Executive Committee of the Advisory Board, who informed me that they were interviewing three people for the post of Executive Director and that they were looking for a person with good fundraising skills and with a clear vision of the task at hand. They also told me that there was funding for six months only. The task at hand was enormous and the successful candidate was supposed to win donor confidence, secure the organisation's finances and see to it that the programmes responded to the needs of the people that we were serving.

I was offered the job with virtually no handover notes or roadmap of any kind. The former Executive Director gave me an hour's rundown. At first, I did not know where to start. I needed to consult urgently but it was not easy. Fundraising had never been done locally and the organisation had little experience in this. There was one Field Officer who had suffered a stroke due to stress. I had no choice but to send her away on sick leave. The Information Officer had been with the organisation for one year but it was also her first job. The Administrative Secretary was marvellous. She knew where all the letters were filed. So it was easy to obtain files to read through, but nothing else.

I felt it was best for me to begin with project visits. One thing I was confident of was that I would not be lost in the field. Having worked as an agronomist in the rural areas for over nine years, I was very familiar with the rural setting. So I embarked on field visits to acquaint myself with how the Women's Development Programme was assisting the rural people to find solutions to the many challenges that they encountered in their day to day lives.

From income generating activities to gender analysis and awareness raising

Reflecting on the notes taken during the field visits and reading through the evaluation reports, I found that the Women's Development Programme was based solely on income generating activities. Unfortunately, these did not empower women but, instead, added to their already heavy workload. It was clear that the programme needed to change. There was a need to put women at the centre of their own development. In addition, it was time to look at the gender relations between them and their partners. This was concluded from the observation that, although women made money from their activities, they handed over the money to their spouses who spent it on beer, bought themselves radios or bicycles, or gave it to their female friends. Women did not benefit from their sweat because of the general situation of social injustice. They just worked for their husbands and families in ways that left them dominated and exploited. The Women's Development Programme had to add gender analysis and awareness-raising to all its programmes.

At this time, programmes were being carried out in Western and Southern Provinces. In 1993 we added Central Province. Although gender analysis and awareness-raising were successful programmes in terms of reducing women's workload, enhancing their participation in meetings and decision making at household level, and reducing domestic violence, WFC decided to embark on an analysis of what else could be done by interviewing women. It was revealed that women were empowered in a lot of ways but they needed an income of their own to be able to participate fully in making decisions that affected their daily lives in their own homes. For example, they needed to be empowered so that they could make a decision about buying a new dress or cooking pot or sending their girl children to school if their husbands decided to marry them off by the age of thirteen. Thus it was found necessary to revisit the programmes being run to bring in other realistic and more effective interventions.

But how could we do this when we did not have any resources? Unlike the Women's Development Programme, WFC was not known to most funders. It was only six months old and had not yet done any fundraising. This meant that we had to begin by advertising the organisation more vigorously by producing brochures explaining who we were, what we were and where we intended to go. We also had to start holding meetings with a wide range of donors after developing proposals, getting in touch with former funders and so on. There were not many people on the staff and there was much to be done.

After preparing all the documentation we called meetings with donors. To our surprise, two donors, both of them based overseas, agreed to visit us. Another donor, after hearing about our activities from a partner organisation, decided to drop by as well. This particular donor was encouraged by our commitment and passion, and promised to get back to us in a short while. This marked the beginning of our fundraising crusade.

Within a month, the United Church of Canada sent us US$15,000. With this, we were able to ask other donors to contribute too. The Netherlands Organisation for International Development Cooperation (NOVIB), being a co-funding agency, agreed to co-fund with United Church of Canada and, within a short space of time, Development and Peace of Canada also agreed to give us US$20,000. NOVIB pledged US$80,000, on top of which some of their personnel came for a field visit to the most remote part of Sinazeze in Southern Province, slept in a hut and spent three days listening and observing. I remember Ellen Springer, then the NOVIB gender advisor, asking how we managed. The money that came in following this was a lifeline. We opened a bank account, got two phone lines and bought a photocopier. CUSO had left us some old furniture and vehicles which we used for field activities. There was no vehicle for administrative use. Pestallozi Children's Foundation, another cooperating partner, also assisted us.

All the donors mentioned above have continued to fund WFC to date and we have learnt a number of lessons in people's empowerment together.

As a core focus area, gender analysis and awareness-raising have continued to occupy a significant place in WFC programming. The organisation has continued to ensure that all group members, especially those in new operational areas, undergo training in gender analysis and awareness-raising to enable them to identify gender issues in their environment, analyse them, and challenge and encourage community members to address them effectively at household, community and national level. Advanced gender analysis and awareness training, or training of trainers, is also being provided to area association members to enable them to train others. Thereafter, extended training is given to all group members. The area associations are expected to continue training their members from then on. The training sessions are open to all members of the community in the operational areas. In this way, WFC expects a multiplier effect of gender awareness after the training sessions.

Specifically, the following activities are undertaken in gender awareness and training:

❑ providing continuous training in gender awareness and analysis to WFC members of staff so as to ensure that quality training of trainers is provided to area association members who, in turn, will carry out training of the larger communities;

❑ carrying out gender sensitisation workshops on the division of labour between men and women, and boys and girls, at household, community and national levels;

❑ carrying out gender sensitisation workshops on violence against women, reproductive health and reproductive rights;

- identifying and carrying out sensitisation workshops on cultural beliefs and practices that hinder the full participation of women and deny them equity and equality; and
- encouraging and supporting initiatives to abolish gender-biased practices such as sexual cleansing, the denial of inheritance rights to women and girl children, discrimination against girl children when educational opportunities are limited, and early marriages.

> Our area has people from many different ethnic groups: Ilas, Salas, Kaondes, Zezurus, Tongas, Ndebeles and several others. Members of these communities are very hard-working and cultivate large tracts of land every year. Because the farms are not mechanised, men get round the problem of labour by marrying two to ten women. These women are not married because the man loves them. They are cheap labour for him. You see them working in the fields with their older children, all bending down like cattle grazing. (*Woman from Moona Area Association.*)

From gender analysis and awareness-raising to economic empowerment

Once WFC had a financial base, we began examining the programmes and staffing needs of the organisation. I managed to speak with the women and men in the groups. They were happy with the gender analysis and awareness-raising work but were not happy with their lack of economic empowerment. This seemed to be the consensus of most of the 30 groups we were working with at the time. We decided to try to learn from the experience by providing very small amounts of money for vegetable growing, chicken trading, poultry keeping, carpentry and other domestic economic activities. We agreed that they should double these amounts within three months. When we went back after this period, we were overwhelmed by what had happened. All those who had received loans had met their targets.

WFC uses animators to assist communities identify their problems, analyse their causes and effects, and find solutions. We needed two more field animators so Elizabeth Mubiana and Gertrude Nkunta joined Patrick Chambisha. The animator has to live with the people for two or three weeks a month and only comes to the office to strategise for more action. WFC believes that you can only know and effectively animate people for development work if you live with them and understand their customs and traditions. Since both the gender analysis and awareness-raising, and income generation involves the changing of attitudes, it is necessary for animators to live in the communities.

> Poverty is still there, but we have learnt the important lesson that we must identify our problems ourselves and use our own efforts to overcome them. WFC gives us technical advice and is ready to loan us money if they're satisfied that our plans for investment are sound. (*Woman from Moona Area Association.*)

Things began to work in our favour as fund raising seemed to stabilise. Soon, we bought our own offices, employed a finance officer and, in 1994, produced our first set of audited accounts, accounting for the money we had raised ourselves. It was an exciting period.

Since its inception, WFC has continued with economic empowerment as a core area of activity. WFC, in conjunction with the area associations and the groups, undertakes small income generating activities. These activities have in the past benefited the area association and the groups as well as the community at large. WFC has gone a step further to ensure that these activities are beneficial to individual group members. In terms of capacity building, training is being provided in relevant skills such as agribusiness and assertiveness. As far as possible, community members with relevant experience and expertise are used as facilitators.

From economic empowerment to human rights education and advocacy

People's demands increased after gender-awareness workshops. They began to ask why we emphasised children's education when schools were so far away; why we emphasised health and hygiene when they had no access to clean drinking water, and the clinics were miles away and often had no drugs. They wanted to know how, in a liberalised market economy, they could access markets for their produce in their effort to eradicate poverty. We were forced to go back to the drawing board. That is how we began the human rights education component of our work. We also added advocacy. The reason was simple. As WFC, we could not provide basic infrastructure but we could educate the people on their constitutional rights and obligations. Therefore, we needed to demystify the right to life, food security, education and health, among others. We needed to bring the discourse to the attention of the 'powers that be' at all levels to see if something could be done to change the status quo and make the right to development meaningful.

We knew that we would be accused by politicians of being a political party. However, this did not scare us because we would root our advocacy work in the everyday lives of the people, and if challenged we would say 'let us go and see what we are talking about'. Then they would see for themselves the lack of roads, which spelt poverty for the people as they couldn't get their produce to the markets to be sold; that if anyone fell sick or a woman was in labour, there would be no transport except a sledge on which to drag the person to the nearest health centre some 40 km away; that children could not start school early because schools were very far away and parents had to wait until the children were over ten years old before allowing them to walk the long distances; that even a thirteen-year-old girl could be married off, thereby denying her the right to education.

> Then WFC came to our area and told us that God does not wish to see people suffer. We were told that poverty could be fought off, but we had to do more to change our lifestyles. Workshops in gender awareness, children's rights and human rights began. The way they carry out their work fires you. You are driven to act. Within a short time, we had formed groups that went out to teach what the core group had learnt. More groups were formed and we soon had an area association. (*Woman from Nkenga Association.*)

We needed to have these issues very clear in our minds. Therefore, we embarked on the programme using both electronic and print media. It was necessary for us to do this even though it was costly. At the same time, we needed to build the skills of our staff to understand and articulate these issues well when called upon. The staff would also be able to train the communities that we worked with using participatory education methodologies (PEM) to enable them to speak on their own behalf. This was critical because we realised that even if we lived with the communities for long periods we were an advantaged lot and could not fully and effectively speak for them. The personal life experiences of our group members were key to the advocacy and human rights work. They needed to speak on their own behalf. We did not realise then that we were opening a Pandora's box. The people began demanding services such as clean water, accessible clinics, food security, transportation for themselves and their produce, markets for their produce and accessible education for their children.

Since then, advocacy, based on issues that emanate from the core programming areas, has continued to be an important area of operation for WFC. Advocacy initiatives on economic issues are designed to contribute to the analysis, critique and dissemination of information on the effects of the Structural Adjustment Programme (SAP) and other policy matters that impact negatively on the lives of the rural people in particular and the Zambian citizenry in general. Specific areas include the analysis of economic policies and national budgetary allocations in relation to the Copenhagen Declaration as well as to the Beijing Platform for Action, dealing with issues of poverty eradication; access to education in relation to provision of basic education for all; access to health, especially child and maternal health; access to water and sanitation; and access to shelter and food security. Other major advocacy issues are women's rights, such as the right to participate in decision making at all levels (family, household, community, institutional and national); property ownership and inheritance; sexual, physical and other forms of abuse; promotion of the Convention for the Elimination of All Forms of Discrimination against Women (CEDAW); reproductive rights of women, including issues of HIV/AIDS; and women's rights to negotiate safer sex with their partners.

> Through WFC, we have regained our dignity; we know our rights. Through WFC, women and men now work together. Women have gained self-confidence. Women in Moona area find themselves serving on committees. The area association is represented on the district development committee, on the health committee and on the parent-teacher association. Only five years ago no woman could imagine sitting on such committees and being listened to respectfully by men. (*Woman from Moona Area Association.*)

From human rights education and advocacy to overall child development

As a result of the continued success of the human rights and advocacy programme, some communities began to demand a number of rights for their children. In other cases, the communities needed more information on children's rights. It became necessary for WFC to incorporate child development in its programmes.

> Perhaps the main reason why girls dropped out after the first four years of schooling is that schools that offer the next level of education are far, far away. Even the boys had to rent houses close to the school to continue their education. As an association, we decided to build a block of rooms that are now being used as dormitories. We were gratified when 26 girls who had dropped out of school took up their education again, with the blessing of their parents. That is a welcome change. (*Woman from Mangango Area Association.*)

In this area of activity, WFC focuses on promoting increased access to basic education for both the girl and boy child, and contributes to policy change in a way that increases the effective involvement of all stakeholders, including parents and teachers. WFC also helps to identify and share strategies that help keep children in school. In addition, the organisation facilitates initiatives to provide increased opportunities for children in difficult circumstances such as orphaned children or those who might otherwise be marginalised from quality education due to poverty. WFC also harnesses the energy of in-school and out-of-school youth by helping them channel their energies into productive activities. WFC has widely disseminated information about the Convention on the Rights of the Child (CRC).

In 1995, WFC conducted human rights workshops that were attended by twelve people from my area. We were urged to form groups and spread what we had learnt. We did just that, and we went round the villages educating people about their rights. Some people value education and take their children to school. Others do not value education and do not see the need to take their daughters to school. They marry them off as soon as they reach puberty. So we started teaching about children's rights too. (*Woman from Mangango Area Association.*)

To incorporate overall child development meant that the organisation would require far more resources than it was receiving from donors. In addition, the organisation knew that one day the donors might not be in a position to support our programmes and so we had to begin preparing for that rainy day by embarking on activities that would enable us to generate our own income. We decided to establish the revenue generation department, whose mission is to generate revenue through consultancy services, to make WFC programming sustainable. We defined the following as the objectives of the department:

- generate revenue through facilitating gender strategic planning and capacity building workshops, and carrying out needs assessments for other organisations;
- generate revenue through rentals from the flats and the guest house we had purchased;
- acquire increased consultancy work by advertising our consultancy services;
- produce a training manual;
- advocate and facilitate the eradication of poverty in Zambia; and
- monitor implementation by the government of the ten commitments made during the World Summit for Social Development (WSSD) in Copenhagen in 1995.

Vision, mission, objectives and values

WFC's vision is to contribute to the creation of sustainable economic and social systems which are controlled by rural communities and which respond to their needs.

WFC's mission is to work with and empower remote rural communities, especially women, through gender analysis, popular education methodologies and advocacy to contribute towards the eradication of all forms of poverty.

WFC's strategic objectives are to:

- promote and support gender sensitivity and human rights activism at community, institutional and national levels;

- build the livelihood capacities of rural communities in a gender-balanced manner;
- advocate for policies and practices that are gender sensitive and just, and that effectively respond to the plight of the poor;
- initiate and enhance overall youth development interventions in all WFC operational areas;
- document and communicate WFC's experiences in its core activities; and
- enhance the organisational capacity of WFC.

WFC strongly believes and is guided in its operations by the following principles:

- gender awareness and sensitivity;
- equal participation and opportunities for men and women in development;
- empowerment of vulnerable groups in societies;
- working and living with the people in remote rural communities;
- the dynamism of society and the achievement of change through the use of popular education methodologies and advocacy, using women as entry points into communities;
- encouraging more women in decision making roles;
- remaining a non-membership organisation; and
- working as a team to achieve our objectives.

Organisational structure and process

The organisational structure of WFC consists of an Annual General Meeting, a Board of Trustees, a Board of Directors and staff. At grassroots level, group members come from remote rural areas.

Members of the rural groups are the recipients of the WFC services. Each group is made up of men and women living in the same community and sharing a common vision – breaking the cycle of poverty. Each group has between 30 and 40 members.

Several groups in the same area come together to form the area association which is a self-governing, community-based organisation. The area association provides a forum for the exchange of ideas and experiences between groups. Its leadership comprises two representatives from each group. Its role is to oversee the work of the groups and supplement the work of the field animator. It also provides a mechanism for self-rule even after WFC pulls out of the area and weans the groups.

We're happy to see other areas beginning to form groups and area associations. Now we even have a cooperative. There is cooperation among area associations, and between men and women now. In this way, resources are pooled and we get more work done. (*Woman from Nkenga Area Association.*)

To carry out its mission, WFC uses a multi-step process which begins with the identification of remote rural areas of the country where few, if any, other development organisations are present. Typically, such areas have no basic infrastructure, and no road networks and this is where the poorest of the poor live. This is done to avoid duplication of efforts and contradictions in approaches. Where other organisations may wish to give out handouts, WFC wants to empower people to identify their own problems and find their own solutions to these problems. Once an area has been selected, WFC uses gender analysis as the starting point for animating communities towards development work and to ensure the full participation of men and women as equal partners.

The rest of the process involves area assessment to identify what is available for development as well as assessment of the level of development of the people in the area. The most burning issues are then identified and prioritised with the community, groups are formed and leaders are identified. Thereafter, the economic status of the community is assessed and participatory education methodologies are used to explain WFC's work and how communities can manage, with available resources, to generate more resources. The process of gender analysis is also used at this stage to identify and discuss issues that oppress women and hinder them from effectively participating in and benefiting from development work. Finally, once all the burning issues have been identified, discussed and agreed upon, the communities begin planning by identifying how they can strategise to improve their situation. All this is done under the guidance or facilitation of WFC animators who live in the communities most of the time.

The canal that we dig every year has improved our yields greatly. Because water is channelled away from our fields, we no longer suffer from flooding. Even those outside the area association join us when the time to work on the canal comes. The implements we use came from WFC. We have eight strong groups that continue to teach about gender equality, civic and human rights. (*Woman from Lyamutinga Area Association.*)

WFC tools for animating development

WFC believes that sustainable development can only be realised through full and meaningful participation of rural women and men in solving the problems that limit their development. For WFC, empowerment is a continuous process of planning and animating women and men towards development work. This process is undertaken using a number of tools. These are:

❑ the River Code;
❑ the Development Tree;

- critical Analysis:
- the Blind Game; and
- the Five Friends of Planning Strategy.

WFC also employs human rights education and literacy education as additional means of empowering women and men with the necessary and appropriate knowledge to effectively participate in development work. Each of the tools is discussed below.

The River Code

WFC believes in getting communities to embrace the principle of self-reliance right from the beginning. This is introduced through a role-play called the 'river code'. This activity is used to explore issues surrounding dependency and self-reliance. The river represents an obstacle to be overcome for development to be realised. The role-play shows two approaches to overcoming the obstacle, in this case, the river.

In the first approach, two people come to the river and look for a place to cross. The current is very strong and they appear afraid to cross. A third person comes up to them, sees their difficulty, and offers to take one person across on her back. The person needing help climbs on the back of the one who has offered to help. She begins to carry her across the river on the stones. Halfway through the journey, the person carrying the other becomes tired and stops to rest. The person being carried sees the third person remaining at the bank of the river and goes back to help her. She offers to carry her but the person refuses and asks to hold her hand as they try to cross the river together. Together, in this second approach, they move stone by stone, helping and supporting each other until they arrive at the other shore. Both seem very happy and proud of themselves for making it across the river, so much so that they almost forget the other person, who is still standing stranded where she was left and is waving frantically for the others to help her.

At the end of the play, the people are asked to relate the role-play to a real life situation and state what they think the river might represent, what the people represent, why such situations happen, which of the two they consider to be the better approach and why.

In all cases, the people state that the first approach indicates dependency while the second represents self-reliance. And in all cases they opt for the second approach. This is the approach that WFC uses in animating communities for development work.

The river code is a life-and-death issue for WFC in its quest to eradicate all forms of poverty. We believe that people are not socialised into being beggars. In fact, before colonialism destroyed our traditional social systems, begging was not tolerated. The river code takes the communities back to their roots, where we lived in a manner that supported sustainable human development. Through the role-play of the river code, communities are better able to appreciate our contract of walking with them as partners; they see that we are not there to dish out free food or second hand clothes. We help them to understand that we are promoting sustainability because we cannot accompany the communities forever. The time will come for us to leave the community and move on to a more needy area. The community, through the area association, will definitely move on. This is also what the groups say once they have gone through the critical analysis stage of the process.

The Development Tree

Often, on our first encounters with the rural communities, we find that the villagers have completely given up on life and are merely existing. Under such circumstances, it is futile to begin talking about development in abstract terms. WFC strongly believes that, for people to move from one stage to another, they must have a clear and shared vision to which each one subscribes in their individual capacity. This is usually not the case with the communities that we work with. So, the first stage in our development animation process is to get the communities to create and share a vision. This development process, as it is known and understood by WFC, is depicted in the development tree. This model was created by WFC and is used to help groups identify their level of development – the 'present' reality – and help them to create in their minds a higher level – the 'future' reality. This future reality becomes their 'vision'. In this regard, WFC is in total agreement with what Martin Luther King Junior once said, 'If you want to move people, it has to be toward a vision that is positive for them, that taps important values, that gets them something they desire and it has to be presented in a compelling way that they feel inspired to follow.'

> Nkenga, like many other places in the Western Province, has high levels of poverty. People struggled to better their lives but they become poorer every year. They finally accepted that there was nothing they could do about their situation. God had decreed it. Once a girl had gone through the traditional rites of passage from girlhood to womanhood, she was married off. Some of the girls were only twelve years old. (*Woman from Nkenga Area Association.*)

The development tree enables women and men to compare their level of progress in development, from being totally unaware through the seven levels of growth and awareness to the point where they begin to realise that it is possible to change things for the better. At this point, they feel capable of doing things for themselves and for others. The seven levels represent how a group can grow and prosper to the highest level in their development process. The highest level constitutes the vision for the group as well as for the individual members of the group. The levels are explained below:

Level 1   Women and men are completely unaware of what is happening to them and how these things limit them. Because of cultural beliefs and conventional development practices, even if development initiatives are planned, often only men are invited. Women are left out and their situation either remains the same or gets worse.

Level 2   Women have heard about the development activities of others and have decided to work together, but are unsure of how to go about it. They realise they want things to improve. They begin by talking to each other about what they can do and how they can organise themselves. Then they invite a WFC animator to come to talk about what they can do to help themselves.

Level 3   The women have formed a group and have started climbing the development tree after a visit from another group or from a WFC animator. They may have started small income generating activities, such as selling vegetables or poultry rearing, to earn money for the group. They are convinced that their dream for a better reality can only be achieved by working together.

Level 4   The group is quite well up the trunk of the development tree and the members are working together very well. They have small income generating activities. They contribute money from these activities to the group and are working towards the same goal.

Level 5   This level represents a group falling away from their goal. Everything was moving along well when, due to situations beyond their control, they began falling. If they stick together as a group, they can revise their original plan and decide together to choose something more viable. For example, one group may have planted sorghum and millet and may have been expecting a bumper harvest when insects attacked. The group can then revisit their plan and decided to do something else. This level is a real test of commitment for the group. Some groups may not pass through this level while others may not stick together as a group but may still remain on the tree.

Level 6   The group is now enjoying the fruits of the development tree. The fruits are very sweet because the projects have been successful and they have achieved their goals and are working well together. There is harmony in their homes and in the community. Their children are going to school and are happy. They feel very satisfied because both their survival and strategic needs are being met.

Level 7   The group is at the very top of the development tree. They are enjoying the fruits of their successes as well as sitting high up in the tree where they can look out and see everything around them. They can see other communities where people need to work together but are still sitting under the development tree, unaware of their potential to help themselves. They share their experiences, skills, energy and knowledge with others. It is as though they have given birth to another group that will grow from their experience and enjoy the fruits of development associated with facilitating the development process of others.

The development tree is a very strong tool for communities to use in assessing their own level of development. It is also a simple monitoring and evaluation tool for self-assessment by groups and individual group members in their daily activities. When they fail, they can trace the path back and see where they could have missed the link. They can, therefore, learn from their mistakes and correct them.

Critical Analysis

Critical analysis is part of the WFC Participatory Education Methodologies (PEM) model used to challenge conventional attitudes, traditions and beliefs which inhibit the full and equal participation of women and men in their own development and in the development of society as a whole.

With this model, women and men are encouraged to reflect on their lives and critically analyse the issues that affect them most deeply. WFC assists women and men to develop strategies that can help them solve some of the problem situations they encounter. This is because WFC recognises that rural people are the best experts in analysing their situations, identifying the real problems and finding viable solutions.

WFC employs and trains animators to facilitate gender analysis and human rights education with people in rural communities. The issues identified include basic survival needs as well as more long term strategic needs. Some examples include:

❏   access to food, shelter, clean water, health and education;
❏   women's inclusion in decision making at all levels;
❏   prevention of domestic violence;
❏   recognition of women's and children's rights;
❏   literacy;
❏   reproductive rights;
❏   improved economic status;
❏   safe environments; and
❏   sustainable development.

An analysis of people's lives using gender and human rights education as key factors begins to open doors as to how the prevailing state of affairs can be improved for the betterment of everyone in the community.

Under critical analysis, men and women are encouraged to find answers to questions such as where they are, how they got there, where are they going and how they will get to that point.

> We did not laugh off what we had seen. The lessons went deep and we were seized with a desire to change. We formed groups that finally came together to form an area association. We began cleaning our surroundings. We have been teaching people in our area how important it is for them to register as voters. The next elections are going to see an increase in the number of voters in our area. (*Man from Chalimongela Area Association.*)

As a result of critical analysis, people begin to question what is happening to them and why, what people think about it, the effects of what is happening, what can be done, what the plan is and why, what changes are taking place, who is involved and why. At this stage, a once docile community stirs to life. The critical analysis stage brings about an awakening in the minds of the people and in the community, allowing people to recognise their potential to deal with the problems that affect their daily lives. This is especially the case for women, who for the first time realise that they can speak out in front of men, contribute effectively to various debates, chair meetings, stand up as MPs or as Councillors and so on. Using the critical analysis model, women and men are empowered to challenge the status quo on issues that affect their constitutional rights, such as the rights to life, food, shelter, clean water, health, education and participation in the governance and development process of Zambia.

The 1999 evaluation report also commended the use of PEM as a 'viable way of engaging with the communities in the WFC target areas'. Findings indicate that the use of PEMs in remote rural communities by WFC has facilitated and increased awareness, understanding and appreciation of gender issues, civic duties and responsibilities.

The 'Aha!' is an exclamation made by individuals or groups after going through the critical analysis stage when they discover the benefits that they would derive from carrying out a particular project. These benefits could be better roads, schools, clinics, houses, food or many others. Upon realisation that, if they work hard, they can obtain these benefits, they exclaim 'Aha!'

The Blind Game

WFC uses the blind game to help the communities explore what it feels like to be in positions of advantage or disadvantage in our society. The game is played by two people, one of whom can see while the other is 'blind'. The two are asked to play the 'follow the leader' game in which the sighted person walks about making a sound as a way of leading the blind partner around. After a while, the partners switch roles. At the end of the game, the participants are asked to share in plenary how they felt in each case.

The blind game has been used very effectively in gender training and poverty analysis where those being led assume the role of those leading in order to help the leaders see clearly the injustices they inflict on others, be it men towards women or politicians towards the electorate. This game is very popular.

> Another bad thing in our area was the way government officials treated people. They treated us worse than we treat our goats. Then, in 1992, WFC came to our area for field assessment. They held workshops on human and children's rights, and on gender awareness. Between 1993 and 1995 we worked closely with WFC. We formed six groups and registered an area association in 1997. (*Woman from Moona Area Association.*)

The Five Friends of Planning

WFC uses the five friends of planning to get women and men to find solutions to the challenges they identify. The five friends of planning are who, what, why, when and how. This process enables the group to work out how they can move forward on the actions they have chosen to empower themselves economically. The exercise also helps to:

- motivate the group to work towards their solution;
- plan how the group will achieve its goal;
- provide a mirror for the group to evaluate progress towards the chosen solution; and
- assess the level of independence of the group and/or how much dependence there is on outside resources for their solution.

This game demystifies the widely held view that planning can only be done by educated people. Here we try to show that anybody – women or men, rural or urban, educated or uneducated – can plan their activities with utmost precision and can also trace back the performance of each of the individuals or groups involved in order for the community to move forward with their plan.

Human rights education

WFC believes that human rights awareness is central to getting people to participate more effectively in bringing about change in society. One of the complaints raised by people in our operational areas is that, once elected to Parliament, their MPs do not visit the constituents to plan development projects with them or to explain government policy. This is because the Constitution, which is the supreme law of the land and guarantor of human rights, does not provide for the continuing mandate of the electorate to regulate the conduct of an MP once elected. Consequently, the electorate is deprived of many rights the implementation of which is supposed to be facilitated by the MP. These include the rights to:

- information on government programmes;
- basic resources, such as land;
- services, such as water;
- clinics with adequate medicines;
- food security;
- agricultural inputs; and
- accessible markets for produce.

As a result of the non-fulfillment of these human rights, WFC decided to embark on human rights education as a tool for empowering the rural communities to speak up against such violations of their human rights and make their demands known. At first, the organisation ran human rights workshops for group members but these have now been extended to traditional leaders such as chiefs and village headpersons. This is because WFC considers traditional leaders as central to opinion formation and attitude change.

As a result of the human rights education workshops, many people in WFC operational areas have come to know, appreciate and demand their rights as citizens. This is clearly reflected in the interviews held with some of the members.

Literacy education

Statistics indicate that Zambia has a very high illiteracy rate and that it is mostly women who are illiterate. It is evident that this category of people cannot effectively participate in development work because they do not have access to information, which is one of the most critical ingredients to effective participation in development initiatives.

To address this shortcoming, WFC runs functional literacy classes to motivate development amongst women and men in our operational areas. We believe that education should be used as a tool to liberate people from enslavement to others as well as from the shackles of poverty, ignorance and disease. WFC is of the view that all education should prepare the learner for life in the community where she or he lives. Secondly, it should enable the learner to contribute more meaningfully and more effectively to the higher vision of their own personal development, the development of their families and, eventually, the development of the nation.

More and more people in WFC operational areas are able to read materials which have been produced in their own languages or which have been translated from English. They are increasingly becoming empowered with knowledge on issues that affect their day to day living, such as health, agriculture, food and nutrition.

WFC programmes and coverage

Field operations are currently running in three provinces: Central, Southern and Western. A total of eight districts are involved in the programmes. The districts are Mumbwa and Kapiri-Mposhi in Central Province, Mazabuka, Sinazongwe, Choma and Kalomo in Southern Province and Senanga and Kaoma in Western Province. In these districts, WFC is working with 171 groups of 30 to 40 people each. Hence a total of about 6,000 people are directly involved in WFC programmes. WFC has recently formed alliances with the National Peasant Farmers' Association and with support groups within the University of Zambia and other universities and colleges.

At grassroots level, WFC works with the groups of 30 to 40 people. Groups in the same area constitute an area association. The mission of the area association is to work and foster the development of the community using the available human, natural and financial resources. The area association is a community-based organisation (CBO) the main roles of which are to:

- monitor, supervise and coordinate the activities of groups in the area to ensure continuity and sustainability of their programmes;
- assist the groups in conflict resolution for the smooth running of group activities;
- form new groups in other areas so that more people are empowered to take greater control of their own lives;
- train other communities in gender analysis and awareness raising, civic education, advocacy and income generation activities to achieve social change;
- source funding for the groups from financial institutions and other organisations that provide financial assistance;
- collaborate with government extension services, NGOs and other CBOs to promote development in their area; and
- foster exchange visits with other communities and organisations with similar goals.

The impact of WFC programmes

To gauge the impact of WFC programmes for the purpose of this paper, a number of interviews were carried out with group representatives, individual members, local leaders, board members, donors and members of the general public. A summary of their responses is presented below. In general, the interviews revealed that people in the WFC operational areas are now able to:

❑ claim their rights as citizens;
❑ critically analyse their situations, identify their problems and work out solutions; and
❑ work together as partners in development.

Additional information gathered through the interviews is presented in the table below.

Past (before WFC)	Present (after WFC)
Did not know our rights and obligations	Know our rights and obligations as citizens
Feared our husbands	Work with our husbands as equal partners in the home as well as in development
Women's workload was heavy	Women and men share responsibilities and roles
Too many children and no spacing	Husbands and wives practise family planning
High levels of poverty	Economic empowerment through goat and pig keeping and other income generating activities
Wife battering and domestic violence in general was very high	Domestic violence has reduced
Negative traditional practices such as sexual cleansing, property grabbing and elopement were very common in WFC operational areas	Negative traditional practices have reduced in all WFC operational areas and have even been banned in some
Low number of girls, and children in general, at school	An increase in the number of children starting and staying in school
High levels of early pregnancies and early marriages	Cases of early marriages and early pregnancies reduced in all WFC operational areas
Men looked down upon women as subordinates	Men now treat women as equal partners in development
Used to fear politicians, especially ministers and MPs	Question and challenge politicians openly because we know our rights and obligations as citizens

Our area Councillor comes from an opposition party. This has led to our being labelled a political party. Not too long ago, the Deputy Minister for the province closed our meeting and was very abusive. He told us we'd see no development in our area because we sided with opposition parties. He said we had hitched a hike in a vehicle that has only one dim headlamp and we're headed for the ditch. This has confirmed what WFC always preaches – we cannot depend on the government to bring change in our lives. We have to do it ourselves and we will. (*Woman from Mangango Area Association.*)

Comments from individual group members

Emily Syakalenge got married to Ellison at the age of sixteen, having dropped out of school in Grade Three due to illness.

Emily and Ellison have ten children. For many years, their marriage was characterised by the desire to have more and more children because they believed that children were a gift from God. In addition, until 1993, Ellison was a habitual drunkard who often battered his wife and never cared for her or for the children. The little money the family earned from the sale of farm produce was all spent on locally brewed beer. Emily had no decent clothing and was always in tatters; the children were malnourished with protruding stomachs and had no clothing. There was never enough to eat.

Both wife and husband joined WFC in 1991. In the beginning, Ellison used to accuse Emily of having affairs whenever she attended WFC workshops. He would roar at her, 'Where have you been? I know you have a boyfriend and that's why you go for those WFC meetings.' Then he would beat her.

Emily says that WFC has helped a lot to make men appreciate women as equal partners at all levels, especially in the home. For example, in 1993, Ellison realised that what he was doing was of no help to anyone but had destroyed the lives and futures of his children. Through WFC gender-analysis workshops he realised that being a man did not mean being hostile, a drunkard and a wife batterer but it meant working with his wife and children as equal partners in development and in everything else. He reduced his drinking and started spending more time with his family to discuss issues and find solutions to their problems.

He also realised that his wife was being overworked and had no time to rest so he started to help with household chores and make sure that the family had enough food and clothing. His parents were so happy with this positive change that they gave him 42 head of cattle.

Now things have changed for the better for Emily and Ellison because the family has acquired some goats from the 'Pass on the Gift' project and keeps these goats and some pigs. They grow more maize, cotton and sorghum and, with the money earned, everybody benefits. The family used to live in a thatched house but now has a decent house and they are able to buy clothing and bedding for the children.

Emily says that their immediate preoccupation is to see that the children who are still in school do not drop out. 'Right now, our priority is to make sure that the girls in school complete their education. Even though they are too old for their grades we will make sure they reach secondary education.'

Emily and Ellison practise family planning to ensure that there are no more babies; with the last child, Emily almost died in labour and was in hospital for three months. She always tells her story to others so they can learn from their mistakes. 'So when people are talking of the effects of having many children too close to each other, I know what it means to have many children because I almost lost my life.'

From the traditional leaders

In many communities in Zambia there is domestic violence against women and children. There is also widespread property grabbing when a spouse dies and a tendency by communities to commercialise bride price and dowry payments. WFC works with communities to analyse the causes and effects of these problems. On one occasion, the communities reminded us that we had forgotten a very important ally in this process, the traditional leaders, the custodians of traditional law. We went back to the drawing board and discussed the issue with the programming team. We worked out programmes where traditional leaders were specifically targeted to become honorary members of our groups and we also organised workshops specifically for them. The response was overwhelming. Having gone through gender awareness and human rights workshops as well as economic empowerment and wealth creation, they embarked on a programme of visiting their chiefdoms to educate their subjects on what they had learnt and the implications of some of the traditions and cultures they had held on to for so long. The result has been that the traditional chiefs have:

❑ stopped their subjects from grabbing property from widowers and widows;
❑ stopped child marriages;
❑ created peace within communities to stop domestic violence; and
❑ fixed a uniform bride price as a token to parents rather than a 'get rich quick' scheme for the parents of girl children.

The chiefs are also demanding the fulfillment of the right to development for their people. The following points have been stressed at nearly every workshop that has been organised for the chiefs:

- Everyone has the right to development. The right to development, including political, economic, social and cultural development, is an inalienable human right guaranteed in Article 22 of the African Charter on Human and Peoples' Rights and the 1986 United Nations Declaration on the Right to Development.
- Everyone has a right to an equal share of the community and nation's resources without discrimination.
- Everyone has an equal right to participate in the development process of the country, such as the formulation of the budget process, as well as the right to information on government activities and administration.
- Everyone has the right to participate in the formulation of policies, plans etc., on development.
- All traditional rulers have a right to a fair share of the resources derived from their areas for and on behalf of their communities.
- Everyone, including traditional leaders and women, has a right to participate in the privatisation of the economy with full equality.
- Development shall be carried out on the principle of non-discrimination in the utilisation of national resources. The development of rural areas shall be accorded affirmative action measures in accordance with international conventions, especially the Convention Against Racial Discrimination, 1965.
- Everyone has the right to take part in economic activities. Therefore, government must ensure the availability of resources to boost agricultural and other forms of development.
- International financial institutions, such as the World Bank and the IMF, as well as donor states should ensure that conditions in the borrowing countries are not hostile to human rights and freedoms as a result of their policies.
- Government should ensure that the transport network in the rural areas is radically improved.

The traditional leaders have also made demands relating to their civil and political rights. These are that:

- Traditional leaders have an inalienable right to free political participation and government should immediately terminate any hindrance of the exercise of this right.
- Traditional leaders have the right to seek any political office as this is a birthright of all citizens.
- To ensure the effective exercise by traditional leaders of their roles, powers and functions, government should ensure that the provisions of the Constitution are amended to clearly spell out the institution of Chief, its roles, means, powers and functions.

All this is as a result of the human rights workshops WFC has been conducting for the traditional leaders. Before these, the leaders could not make such demands.

It is encouraging to note that the human rights education programme is yielding positive results.

Comments from the evaluators

In 1999, WFC underwent a detailed evaluation exercise with the objectives of:

- reviewing the extent to which WFC has been effective as an organisation in implementing its development programmes;
- determining the lessons that could be learnt from experiences since the last evaluation in 1996 and how such lessons could be fed into decisions on the future of programmes of WFC;
- assessing the effectiveness of the WFC organisation and management as a facilitator of empowerment of rural communities in remote rural areas in Zambia; and
- identifying any capacity gaps which needed to be closed for increased effectiveness in future.

The evaluation exercise covered the activities undertaken by WFC, how the activities were undertaken, who WFC networked with and what WFC had achieved. The exercises covered all three operational regions. The evaluation observed that there was

> ...a high degree of relevance of WFC programmes to the social, economic, and political needs of the target group. The entry of WFC into a community engenders community mobilisation around issues of concern to the villagers themselves through participatory methodologies. This approach enables the community to identify the cause of their problem (if not already known), and to initiate action at household and community level, to address the situation. WFC involvement also results in mobilisation of external resources, where possible, to support community effort.

The evaluators concluded that, 'WFC programmes are highly relevant to the needs of the target group. The point of engaging with the community is an identified need which makes the programmes immediately relevant to the reality of the community.'

The evaluators also noted that WFC's work had impacted positively on the communities the organisation was working with. They observed that:

> ...widows and other female breadwinners who had not much to hope for have become members of groups which now own hundreds of goats, and have access to some income; the groups have oxen which they use as draught power for improved cropping and higher yields. Group reports

also emphasised changes in the social relationships between husband and wife in the home as a result of the gender analysis and awareness raising programme as well as human rights education by WFC.

The evaluators also concluded that there was evidence that area associations initiated by WFC could stand on their own once weaned. In their own words, the evaluators stated that, 'there is evidence that these CBOs can outlive the presence of WFC in the area'.

Recently, WFC underwent an organisational assessment commissioned by the Institute for Democracy in South Africa (IDASA). The purpose of the exercise was to assess WFC's organisational programme effectiveness as stated in its vision, mission and other documents.

The evaluation described WFC as:

…a professionally run organisation and a force to reckon with in the NGO environment. It is deeply rooted in what it sets out to do. It is a voice for the poor and the voiceless. Government consults with them regularly to comment and provide advice on poverty issues and critique any policy that stands to disadvantage women.

The evaluator also attended one of the WFC workshops in the field and reported:

At the site visit, I encountered a truly empowered community and this is a result of one of the programmes of WFC. They had come to discuss and be educated about the cooperatives that they have formed. Here they are workshopped on sustainable livelihoods on projects that they are embarking on, for example, goat or pig keeping. This workshop was well attended with villagers travelling more than 30 km to attend. WFC takes the role of facilitator and the villagers take ownership. The field animator here is doing a sterling job and demonstrated commitment to his job. This demonstrates the organisation's effectiveness at goal achieving.

As a result of the impact of our work in the current operational areas, many communities have come to appreciate our efforts and are constantly requesting us to extend our activities to their areas. This was also confirmed by the evaluator, who observed that:

Women for Change is an organisation committed to social change and indicates no sign of shifting from its vision and mission. They are under tremendous pressure to expand to cover the entire country but resist due to calculated moves, priorities, realities and on following recommendations from the external evaluators.

The organisational capacity report made, among others, two important recommendations:

- that WFC share its experiences and successful leadership role with other NGOs; and
- that WFC conduct a 'train a trainer' system with other NGOs in remote rural areas to 'fast track' women's empowerment.

From international organisations and the press

Our work has also been noticed by a number of international organisations. Recently, as executive director for WFC, my contribution to the betterment of society was recognised by the American Biographical Institute, which bestowed on me the Woman of the Year 2000 Award.

In congratulating me on winning the award, the Zambian newspaper, *The Post*, on 13 June 2000, made the following remarks:

Emily's activism over the last eight or nine years will serve as an outstanding example for hundreds and thousands of activists joining non-governmental organisations (NGOs) and politics and, indeed, for millions of other Zambians. Emily symbolises and personifies the networking that is taking various forms in Zambia today. Women for Change's programmes are underlining what this networking is all about. It is about a common commitment to overcoming, as the absolute priority, the terrible legacy of poverty, repression and injustices of all sorts – it is a networking based on serving the social needs of our people. The NGO movement in Zambia is extremely fortunate to have within its ranks such an outstanding activist and leader, who has combined a rigorous mind with practical organisational work.

From the author's perspective

Three weeks before I completed writing this paper, WFC had an annual general meeting. Here the plans and budgets of the previous year, analyses of successes and failures, and future plans were presented. Observers from the donor community, government representatives and other NGOs all commented on how impressed they were by the quality of discussion.

But what impressed me was when the area associations' chairpersons asked for transport to visit the area MPs and Ministers for their provinces. As if that were not enough, they asked for transport to go and see the head of state. At this point I intervened and said, 'Heads of states are not seen like that. You need to make an appointment at least a month before.'

The entire women's delegation refused to heed my advice and said,

That is for you as a person living in town. First of all, we do not know about those procedures. The Office of the President never told us. We also remember that when the President was campaigning, he said we can visit him anytime, so we are just fulfilling our campaign agreement.

I gave up, as it was evident from their determined faces that they would not be stopped and I know them too well when it comes to such matters. So off they went and, as predicted, the security officers stopped them and asked them to make an appointment. They were also told they should be patient as the President would visit them in their localities. They retorted by stating that they had not seen the President except during elections every five years or whenever an MP died and there was a by-election. They asked the security officers if they should go and kill their MPs in order to get a visit from the President. The security officers were horrified and allowed the women to write a letter. The women sat down by the State House gate, asked for paper and pen, proceeded to write the letter and left it there. They were in a defiant mood and said if he did not give them an appointment they would be back.

That is what I call self-empowerment – the ability to decide, without fear, on an individual or collective action fully convinced that that is the best way to go. This story was widely reported in the press. The reaction from the public was that individuals were calling the office asking how they could become members of WFC where ordinary people are able to take such a brave action.

The other experience took place during our poverty and human rights education workshops in 1994 and 1995. This was after we had conducted several workshops and village meetings under trees in the communities looking at what poverty was, the causes and effects of poverty, and what could be done with regard to the Constitution and the right to the provision of basic necessities. Following the training of trainers workshop, we decided that the community trainers (area association members) should continue to hold these workshops on their own. At one of the meetings they decided to invite an area MP who came and graced the occasion.

During the meeting, one old woman scooped a cup of water from a tin container and offered it to the MP to drink. The old woman also made a big show of drinking the same water, but the coffee-like substance was water scooped from a shallow well. The MP knew from experience that the water was not clean and he refused to drink it. The old woman said to him, 'Please drink the water, you must be thirsty.' He still refused the water. Then the people turned on him and asked him why he had refused. They said,

We know why you have refused. It is because the water is not clean. You know that we got it from a shallow well and we share it with frogs and snakes. Just like you, we have a right to life as provided for in the Constitution and yet we are left to drink contaminated water which threatens our life. Where is the right to life?

The situation was nasty with people emotionally charged. I realised the power of knowledge and knew then that the community would not slide back to where it was before.

The next lesson I learnt in self-empowerment was on 17 January 2000. A group of us, 37 women and three men, had been arrested for unlawful assembly while protesting against the police for failure to curb numerous brutal rapes and killings of girl children aged between five and thirteen years. This was news all over Zambia and the WFC rural groups heard the reports too. We were to appear in court the following afternoon at two o'clock. I was pleasantly surprised when, at nine o'clock in the morning the next day, a group of people walked through the gates of the WFC offices singing and chanting. It was a delegation of rural women and men coming to give us support because they had heard of our arrest. They went to the High Court with us, singing and drumming and offering to be arrested as well, because they agreed with the cause – safety for our girl children as a constitutional right. At the time I was overwhelmed with emotion. We had started with very few groups discussing gender and human rights; now a whole critical mass was reacting to an issue of violence against women and children in a sustainable way. If this is not self-empowerment, what is?

Future challenges

WFC groups are convinced that there is a bright future in store for them. To them, just as to WFC, empowerment means growth even when the groups or area associations are completely unlinked from WFC. As one woman put it, 'We are now working for ourselves and we have to survive even after we are completely weaned to become a community-based organisation. The training we have been receiving over the years has empowered us enough to stand on our own.' For WFC, the struggle will continue elsewhere in another form.

There are several challenges to WFC programmes, such as:

❑ dependency on external resources which is one of the main challenges because, once these are withdrawn, WFC programmes will be affected;
❑ differences in values between the developed North, which provides support for running our programmes and the undeveloped South, e.g. Northerners

finding it difficult to appreciate early marriage as a hindrance to girl child education because the phenomenon is unheard of in their countries; and

❑ changes in attitude in our communities are far slower than in the North and therefore difficult to implement within timeframes set by the donors.

To address the problem of over-dependence on external financial support, WFC set up the revenue generation department to raise finance to ensure that WFC programmes will continue to run in the event that the cooperating partners withdraw their support.

Conclusion

As stated earlier, there were two major tasks ahead of me when I took up my appointment as executive director of WFC. The first was to stabilise the financial base of the organisation and win donor confidence. The second was to ensure that all the organisation's programming responded to the needs of the people that we were serving. These two tasks have been my preoccupation for the last eight years, during which time the organisation has won the hearts of a number of donors who are genuinely interested in improving the lot of the vulnerable and underprivileged. The financial base of the organisation has stabilised to the extent that WFC now owns real estate. In addition, the organisation has continued to respond to the needs of the groups as dictated by social, economic, political and other factors. This is done through area assessment surveys for new operational areas and through area reflections for the old operational areas.

As new and more challenging needs emerge, the organisation has also continued to expand from dealing with 2,500 members in 1992 to about 10,000 members in 2000. The organisation is currently undergoing an organisational development exercise to come up with a structure that will effectively respond to the realities on the ground, thereby contributing to the realisation of our vision and mission.

WFC has come a long way, through bumpy and rocky terrain, but our experiences in all our core programmes have been useful and rewarding. Looking at where we have come from, there are a number of developments that call for celebration. These can be summed up as the self-actualisation and the awakening of our people to be able, on their own, to deal with issues that affect their daily lives so deeply.

For us, the ability of women and men to stand up for their rights, both as individuals and as groups, is a dream come true. Women and men are able to stand up against bad traditions, cultures, or political discrimination or exclusion. They are able to advocate for better gender relations, greater political participation, equitable provision of basic needs and social services, and changes to traditions that inhibit women and men from developing to the full their human potential. The quest to economically empower themselves as individuals, groups and communities to levels never known before in remote rural communities is touching.

WFC also realises that there is a strong link between poverty eradication strategies, which are the core of our programming work, and government policies; between the sharing of the national cake and the governance of our country. WFC has deliberately chosen to work with rural communities to help them analyse their problems and what they can do about them. These informed choices by the people themselves give WFC the drive, at all levels, to do advocacy work to change the status quo.

The greatest enemy of our people is the central government. We believe that a system should be developed for people to govern themselves as they used to in the past. Decentralised people's governance will enable them to deal with the poverty question more effectively. On our part, we shall continue to question and to challenge the development paradigms adopted by our government that perpetuate our people's powerlessness. The power to access and control the country's resources by people living in remote rural areas without electricity, solar or otherwise, roads, clean water, and with extremely limited access to health and education, continues to inform our programming and approach.

WFC refuses to be a charity, giving people handouts. Our mission is to help people question why they do not have food or clothing, why their children cannot go to or finish school, and why their children die of preventable diseases. We will continue on this path as our people inform us that this is the best way to help them. We have refused the culture of silence in the face of absolute poverty. This is our contribution to the people who have contributed so much to making us what we are today.

Bibliography

Chigunta, Francis, 1999, *Zambia: Intentions Are Not Enough*, Social Watch Annual Country Report, www.socwatch.org.

CONCLUSION

Hope Chigudu

The stories in this book raise questions of what lessons in empowerment have been learnt and how successful each organisation has been as a tool in the empowerment of its stakeholders and the wider community. The stories also raise questions about the funding of the empowerment process within the constraints of stakeholder resource poverty.

Can a poor community or group be empowered significantly, without fundamentally improving their economic situation? Is it possible to empower people for social development solely from external funding? The five stories grapple with these questions, albeit from different perspectives – through community activism, adult basic education and literacy, human rights and gender-based development, and rural poverty and economic emancipation. This conclusion focuses first on the key lessons arising from the experiences of the NGOs, and highlights some common threads that run through all five stories; it then reviews the points which distinguish them from one another.

A people's perspective of development

The history of African NGOs often reflects the struggle to overcome poverty and ignorance with the ultimate vision of a more literate, aware and economically empowered people. This is the vision of those people whose belief in human beings as the centre of development efforts holds true in all respects. In pursuing the vision of improving and developing people, not just 'things', each organisation set out with specific goals targeting discrete compartments of the communities with which they were working. But, in every case, the NGOs found that the people viewed development in a holistic way and were not receptive to imposed 'development by compartment' strategies. They preferred development activities that addressed, simultaneously, the key elements of their lives. For the organisations whose stories are told here, this holistic development perspective of the people was a key lesson in empowerment and charted the way of conducting the business of social development.

However, all support agencies require project documents that classify and rationalise development activities according to sectors and this makes good administrative sense. The people's integrated and all-inclusive perspective of development does not fit neatly into strategic planning matrices and frameworks. For example, the neat organisational objectives of literacy or adult basic education of LABE in Uganda had to be expanded to include projects for poverty alleviation. The visibility sought for Tanzania's media women by TAMWA later incorporated assistance towards victims of violence through a crisis centre, and issues of economic empowerment. In Nigeria, COPODIN's targeted provision of free medical services quickly gave way to wider economic strengthening of the real targets of development for the people – when the pioneer team of medics found they could not ignore the people's economic disempowerment by corrupt regimes. In the same vein, it was not possible for Zambia's WFC to proceed with gender training and women's development until the issues of economic empowerment, human rights and literacy had begun to be addressed.

For ORAP, the people's perspective was very close to the NGO's original goals – reconstruction and reconciliation at village level in post-independence Zimbabwe. Such broad aims made it easier for ORAP's initial team to undertake development holistically, incorporating cultural precepts and the positive experiences of the rural underprivileged. The concept of *zenzele* permeated all their activities and provided an opportunity to target rural development in line with the people's own perception of their needs.

For COPODIN, ORAP and WFC, the holistic approach to development has created logistical and operational problems for the administrative units in partnership with communities but the organisations have managed to overcome these without losing sight of their development objectives.

Economic empowerment: a crucial leg of the empowerment route

It is not possible to achieve social development without economic empowerment. All five organisations realised that the lack of development in their target communities was a result of poverty. Each project had to integrate income generating projects, develop sustainable rural livelihoods and increase people's means of production in order to attain 'real empowerment' of the community. In some cases, they actually had to prioritise the eradication of poverty. This was the case with ORAP and COPODIN where rural populations were energised and supported to establish significant economic enterprises. WFC assisted partner groups to obtain loans and access markets for their produce, both locally and outside their villages.

ORAP's 'Zs and Q' philosophy explores the economic empowerment agenda to its fullest by encouraging collective savings, and the mobilisation and commitment of the individual to the community. The philosophy emphasises self-reliance and harnessing the family potential to 'fight poverty'. In this arrangement, the organisation gives family groups educational, technical and financial support while individuals direct and carry out the necessary economic activities to achieve their aims. It enables the poorest communities to work for themselves, in their culture and with what they know, to improve food production, and utilise and conserve local resources.

The level of poverty in some African societies may be so crippling that the poorest groups cannot access development aid. The NGOs realised this; their stories illustrate how failure to access educational opportunities leads to rural unemployment and an inability to access productive resources and technology. This leads to low productivity, hunger and poor health which all contribute to even greater poverty. In such circumstances, NGOs have to face the difficult task of reaching vulnerable groups and reversing the entrenched economic disempowerment of the people. For African NGOs, this remains a key component of the empowerment agenda and one upon which other aspects of rural development are dependent.

Funding the empowerment process

Funding can lead to problems, in terms of both its volume and its nature.

Despite the sometimes generous support from external agencies and partners, the problems of inadequate funding persisted in each project. One common cause of such problems was the expansion of projects or activities to cater for the increasing number of groups requesting support. For example, after the community activism of WFC protesting against the rape of young girls and forced marriages, more groups wanted to join the organisation. Similarly, in an attempt to be more relevant to the community groups in Matabeleland, ORAP had to expand its activities to include the Zenzele College, micro lending facilities, skills training and water provision projects. Such an expansion in activities requires greater funding and causes hopes of self-sustainability to fade. Unlike profit making organisations, NGOs are often unable to act decisively to increase their revenue. Even in the case of COPODIN, where communities began to raise funds locally to implement their own plans, the level of funding required to sustain the organisation was often beyond the reach of the people.

In terms of the quality of funding, the stories highlight the difficulties of partnerships. Most NGOs in Africa receive external funding to start up activities and later to buy capital equipment, including real estate. Many still require donor funds for operational and administrative costs, even where membership fees are charged. This almost total dependence on donor funding has been problematic for four of the organisations featured in this publication. While ORAP enjoyed the influx of development aid in the early 1980s in Zimbabwe, LABE, TAMWA and WFC struggled to gain credibility or form partnerships that might have attracted donor funding for their activities.

LABE, however, took on the government of the time and insisted that it play its role rather than abdicate its responsibility for adult basic education. On the other hand, COPODIN struggled on with its 'own resources', shunning external aid for almost a decade. The organisation's pioneers argued that the conditions attached to the funding destabilised the very communities that it sought to empower.

Complete donor dependency means that NGOs have to meet the conditions for funding and make plans according to the available funds. Even with ready evidence of the continuum of holistic development demands from the people, the donor community has been unable to provide block grants for organisations to make realistic plans with communities. Organisations are therefore not able to exercise adequate flexibility to handle the development problems and solutions emanating from the communities.

In an attempt to answer the question of whether 'real empowerment' can be achieved using external funds, each organisation has formulated cost-sharing measures between the communities and NGOs, and other revenue raising strategies. All the organisations have seriously contemplated their financial sustainability without donor funding. This is a key lesson in the empowerment process and is gratifying to note because donor fatigue, globalisation and the new sociopolitical realities of African and European countries are creating new imperatives for the future of donor funding for empowerment. The stories in these pages show the NGOs to be very confident of the ability of the people, in partnership with their governments, to gradually raise adequate funds and to target their own development projects with declining support from the North. Given the extreme levels of poverty in the rural areas, where most of the projects are located, the extent to which the NGOs will be successful in raising funds locally cannot be accurately established. Yet, it is clear that this might be the only way to achieve the empowerment of the peoples of Africa.

Working in African NGOs: a dilemma of lifestyles

Another lesson of empowerment is the dilemma of lifestyles for African NGO staffers. The stories told here, with the exception of COPODIN, avoid frank discussion of the issue. Debate rages among African NGOs concerning the lifestyles of their leaders and administrators, some of whom in recent years have acquired organisational assets and vehicles to match their professional peers in other sectors – the 'Pajero syndrome'. One group argues that this enables NGOs to attract and maintain qualified employees since these are known, professionally, to be highly mobile. This may be justifiable considering that NGOs and the public and private sectors compete for the same staff in an open job market. However, other groups, notably funding agencies and NGO members, argue that the level of comfort demanded, and sometimes 'taken', by these staff in terms of salaries and fringe benefits, outstrips the value added on development projects. In fact, some organisations have been severely criticised for 'fattening themselves' at the expense of the poor whose cause they purport to be championing. Three questions arise from the stories of empowerment told here: Should members of staff of an NGO live in the communities in which they work? What lifestyles should NGOs leaders lead? Where is the line between labour market pragmatism and personal aggrandisement of NGO leadership and staff?

The story of COPODIN shows an organisation which managed to overcome its financial obstacles primarily through the commitment of the peasants and then, secondly, through the self-sacrifice of the team of professionals who 'dared to be different'. It indicates that the organisation did not pursue a financial programme for the benefit of the project administration. COPODIN reduced its management costs by retaining only very necessary staff who had to live among the peasant communities. However, it is noted that, in Africa, when a person receives formal education, it is at great cost to the family. This sacrifice is made in the hope that the child will become a form of social security for the family, working to repay the other members. When the child is employed by an NGO such as COPODIN and goes to live 'in poverty' with the poor communities where the project is located, is this fair on the family?

Literacy: a means to empowerment

The term literacy is commonly used in all of the projects in this book, underlining its importance in the wider empowerment agenda. The reactions recorded by LABE and WFC indicate the full impact of literacy programmes as a catalyst to empowerment. The actions of the women who demanded to see their president and sat at the gate to write him a letter, or the woman who insisted on getting clarification of the group's constitutional provisions, or the groups questioning the management of their budget as illustrated on banana fibres, all resulted from increased literacy and adult basic education. The stories of LABE, ORAP, COPODIN and WFC all buttress the fact that people understand their situations and improve their self-esteem and confidence through literacy programmes. In all cases, the people, though rural and poor, became confident enough to demand their rights from the custodians of the law and public services. Even for TAMWA, where the targets were mostly educated women, with a large proportion being professional women from the media and universities, the need for a different kind of literacy – legal literacy – was clear. There is consensus that adult basic education and literacy in all their forms are necessary means to the total empowerment of people in any circumstance.

Gender: a basis for social change

In WFC, TAMWA, LABE and ORAP, there is a clear goal of emancipating women. The approaches chosen in each case relate to the processes through which the organisations' programmes developed. There is a healthy mix between gender education and women-in-development issues in each organisation. TAMWA chose gender education on legal issues, targeting women in the media and society as well as men in decision making positions. Law enforcement agents had to be re-educated along with students at the local police academy and university. WFC prioritised human rights advocacy and taught women their rights and responsibilities. LABE and ORAP also introduced human rights issues and reached many women. ORAP targeted the family unit where women predominate in actions to guarantee the welfare of their families.

Their stories prove that gender-based social change has been mainstreamed in rural development. They confirm that gender education and the training of women in development was not donor driven but emanated from the communities in which the projects were implemented. Agitation for women's rights and social change has become fundamentally entrenched in the agenda for rural development as African traditions evolve to meet the challenges of a new world order and altered lifestyles. For example, the problems associated with HIV/AIDS have awakened African women to the dangers of the marriage and family ethos within which we have lived for centuries. The disease is destroying the social fabric of African communities to the extent that it has left even the hardest of patriarchs with no doubt as to the advent of the female-headed household and the need to provide production space for such families.

The story of WFC raises the issue of gender dynamics at community level. Gender profiles of communities in most African countries depict a clear division of responsibilities between women and men. While the project teams were targeting women for development assistance, WFC identified a need to include men in their meetings to ensure entry into the project areas. But the men invariably changed the core business of gender awareness to income generating issues. Experience in other projects in poor rural communities has shown that such involvement of men in women's projects often leads to the marginalisation of the women's plans or aspirations. However, the story of WFC reflects a commendable success in dealing with these competing interests. One wonders then why it was not possible to make women self-reliant in their own projects, with the men receiving gender awareness training for their support roles. In cases where, for example, women are working with families, there is a need to empower them specifically and to adopt a targeted approach to women in development issues.

Legislating against violence: how far can we go?

TAMWA's successful lobbying for legislative reform and WFC's campaign against rape and abuse of the girl child both deal with the issue of gender-based violence. For TAMWA, their research and documentation services to the police and legal system had the effect of influencing changes in the existing laws and enactment of new ones. However, although laws may be on the statute books, successful enforcement remains elusive. Recourse to the law, particularly by marginalised and poor women, is critical to the claims of success, and TAMWA and WFC have had difficulty gaining it to protect the victims of violence, rape or sexual harassment.

Among the groups of women who need guarantees of recourse to the law are poor women who cannot afford legal fees, rural women surrounded by deeply patriarchal traditional structures and professional women who are isolated in male dominated environments. There is a dire need for more intensive gender education and lobbying to ensure that women who are violated have adequate access to the law. In fact, the story of TAMWA poses the challenge to all NGOs of how to strategise on other fronts to improve recourse to the law on gender-based violence.

Networking

The stories reveal that networking is very important for targeting NGO interventions. Since NGOs can rarely provide nationwide coverage, it is essential for them to operate within networks and avoid stepping on each other's toes during project implementation. Networking greatly enhances NGO advocacy roles. Many NGOs are engaged in advocacy where their success is often measured by the ability to give appropriate advisory or referral services. Therefore, linkages with other organisations are very important.

TAMWA offers a good example of effective networking and advocacy that has achieved tangible results. The core team of media women, lawyers and other professionals provided a solid foundation for networking and advocacy. Using their skills and positions, the women were able to train, support and advise other women's groups and establish the credibility that was crucial for media campaigns. LABE's sustainable organisational development strategy was directed at establishing a tertiary service level from which local literacy units could be supported. In fact, the OD consultant made specific recommendations to LABE in this regard with emphasis on financial sustainability. As a result, LABE became the voice of Ugandan literacy organisations and a source of support for local NGOs.

WFC, ORAP and COPODIN have associations, unions and village level groups through which projects are implemented. Apart from the number of followers and groups reached, it is not clear to what extent 'real networking' is taking place within these three associations. COPODIN and WFC argue that, in some cases, the expectation of financial rewards attracts groups into the associations. Such an influx of smaller groups joining a network may necessitate the formation of hierarchies of bureaucracy and create power positions that make it difficult for the networking objectives to be met. However, it is also important to understand the networking benefits that can accrue within such associations, as shown by COPODIN's relationship with NAVISOC and PERFORM. Such synergy of networking has not been possible in cases where NGOs do not have adequate access to appropriate technology and raises questions about the feasibility of networks among partners who have unequal access to technology and resources. The African NGOs presented here have managed to identify the crucial elements for networking. These include adequate access to information technology, improved organisational skills, and appropriate human and financial resources. Unfortunately, it is not always possible to attain this for all members of the networks; some will remain passive recipients because of their poverty.

Governance issues in NGOs

Governance among NGOs in Africa has come under scrutiny alongside the continued demands for good governance from African leaders. From the stories told here, it is clear that accountability, transparency and responsiveness have been the watchwords of the NGOs. They highlight changes in strategy, reviews of plans and capacity building proposals that guide the organisational development of each NGO. Founder members of each organisation grappled with the issues of custodianship and their organisation's mission and vision. In some cases, events which could have degenerated into scandals were deftly handled to ensure the survival of the organisation. The quality of leadership and accountability and responsiveness to the communities are crucial aspects of empowerment which must be reflected upon in the process of setting up NGOs. Although the constitutions of most NGOs guarantee this process legally, it is generally the skill of the individuals at the helm that ensures the pursuance of good governance.

The legal requirement to establish boards and management committees is shown to have an effect on the actual empowerment of the organisation and the community. Often there is infighting and the development of personality cults as workers and management become embroiled in haggling with the board over financial benefits, at the expense of development objectives and the communities that are supposed to be served. Many boards now demand sitting allowances for the members' 'sweat' and so end up competing for resources with the staff and management. LABE's experience of 'ending up with a weak board by default' frankly describes the issues of governance in the light of staff welfare and the personal agenda of some NGO managers. In TAMWA, the problems in leadership were openly and honestly dealt with and resolved. Theirs was a good example of the teething problems of many organisations in the formative stages. Similarly, LABE, COPODIN and WFC describe how their initial problems were solved only by the tenacity of the leadership and vision of the founder members. These stories reveal that it is important to balance organisational vision, mission and institutional memory against good governance, popular participation, transparency and accountability in the empowerment process.

At another level of governance, the stories raise the issue of the relationship between government and NGOs. As non-state actors, should NGOs be working very closely with government and what might be the advantages of such an arrangement? Should a government representative be invited to sit on the board of an NGO and what would be the implications of this? The stories of WFC and LABE illustrate the advantages of government-NGO cooperation in Zambia and Uganda. Owing to the failure of the Ugandan government to stem the collapse of social services in the post-war era, NGOs started providing services which would normally have been the responsibility of government. Where the organisational agenda was to provide adult literacy, the critical question was who should pay for the services. LABE leaders pushed the government for action on this front and became a watchdog for the populace to ensure that the government did not abdicate its social responsibility for mass education. In Zambia, WFC sought external financial support in order to work with remote rural communities.

However, the stories of ORAP, COPODIN and TAMWA reflect the need to guard the power base of NGOs to ensure that governments do not control them for selfish political ends. The story of ORAP confirms that, in cases where NGO administrators or board members become too close to the government or political parties, the organisation's credibility may be compromised in the eyes of civil society. The boards and executive arms of NGOs should not involve themselves in prevailing political movements. This is part of the code of conduct of NGOs in most countries and is often stated in the registration documents of these organisations. In terms of external partnerships, LABE exemplifies the ideal relationship with funding agencies whereby the NGO may implement activities 'together' with their funder in the project areas. LABE insists that external support relationships should not end at funding but must extend to 'real partnerships' in literacy and adult basic education actions. This, in turn, improves LABE's credibility with the support agencies and groups.

Founder-member syndrome in NGOs

It is striking to note that there has been no change in the administration in the organisations (except in the case of ORAP) for the past twelve years. The incumbents of each organisation whose story is told here date back to the origins of the NGOs. Why have they remained in office, in some cases for nearly two decades? Is it for love of the organisation or have these institutions of empowerment been personalised? The writer of each story states the manner in which the founders persevered 'against all odds' to carry the organisation over many years of activism and empowerment. This is very commendable. But are the leaders of these organisations not running the risk of injuring their credibility in much the same way as African heads of state who have declared themselves 'life presidents'? The arguments presented in the stories reflect that the organisations neither worked towards institutionalising change processes nor developed 'new generation' capacity for managing the empowerment process. They often argue that changes in administration do not create opportunities for a smooth transition within the organisations, but if this is the case, then these are the real issues that the organisations should work to overcome. The NGO experiences described here have exposed the much talked about 'founder member syndrome' which is yet to be explored fully on this continent.

A continuum for organisational development

A key lesson in empowerment emanating from the five stories is that OD should be a process, not an event. With little experience of NGO management, most of the projects ran into problems quickly. In some cases, the organisation's problems grew until an OD specialist was called in to assist. Initial OD sessions typically dealt with the organisational mission and vision statements. However, these statements were soon turned into mere written texts for display to outsiders, underlining the fact that continued OD support and guidance is crucial for developing organisational culture and knowledge, and the attitude and skills of staff. This was the case in TAMWA where OD support assisted the media women to extract themselves from the quagmire of conflicting interests, personality conflicts and a lack of coordination to finally ensure organisational consistency and the commitment of members.

Among other benefits, OD support provides the opportunity to empower stakeholders and maintain basic performance standards. It rationalises organisational vision and mission into objectives and verifiable indicators that can be pursued by all members of the organisation and helps avoid the cult of mediocrity. It also allows for transparent and diligent programme reviews, which are necessary for improving administrative practices. The case of TAMWA clearly offers alternatives to the unnecessary cover-ups which organisations tend to engage in whenever there is an external evaluation of activities.

Comparing and contrasting the experiences of the five NGOs

The distinguishing features of each story are summarised below, combining the context of each NGO's actions with its specific agenda for empowerment, the different organisational structures employed to achieve their goals and the extent to which they succeeded in empowering their communities.

Rationale: context of NGO actions

For WFC, the impetus to empower women in the remote rural areas came from Zambia's general economic decline, which led to the suffering of many people. As often happens in times of poverty, the poorest rural communities became more marginalised owing to their remoteness from the seat of government. Rural development programmes could not reach them and the government could not cope with the burden of the welfare state, hence only people in accessible areas or urban centres received state attention. TAMWA, on the other hand, was spurred to action by the inferior status of media women in the newsrooms of Dar es Salaam. A few women decided to speak up against the bad light in which women were generally depicted by the media. Solidarity with the oppressed professional women of Tanzania energised a group of twelve media women from different backgrounds to meet and form TAMWA. In each case, the empowerment process finally spread to the men of the community, who were privileged to receive the appropriate gender education.

ORAP started as part of the reconstruction and reconciliation programmes for the southern provinces of post-independence Zimbabwe when political discontent and development imbalances in the rural areas of Matabeleland and Midlands provinces required just such an action. The early years of independence left the rural areas in these provinces still marginalised, despite the wider claims of black empowerment and rural development within government ranks. ORAP, therefore, stood in the gap and organised communities and groups to implement self-help rural development programmes using donor funds. This process resulted in empowerment for the people who participated. Similarly, in oil-rich Nigeria, there was an entrenched system of political and economic patronage in the rural farming communities of the western region. Successive military regimes and large scale government corruption betrayed the hopes and aspirations of poor rural citizens. A group of university medics decided to act to alleviate the suffering of a selected village community of Yoruba origin. Initially they planned to provide free health services to the people. This simple plan led to the empowerment of the people as greater needs were unearthed and attended to by the project team. It was this initiative that later developed into the Coalition for Popular Development Initiatives in Nigeria (COPODIN).

The same pattern can be seen in LABE's formation and development. Uganda's proverbial 'ten wasted years' characterised by state-inspired violence and the collapse of government services in several fields, including education, gave rise to more NGOs coming to the rescue.

For each of the NGOs, the need to empower people stemmed from the failure of local social systems and the lackadaisical attitude of the state. The communities found themselves mired in a vicious cycle of disempowering poverty – until an NGO stepped in.

Agenda for empowerment

LABE's organisational agenda was the clearest and the most closely followed of those presented here: 'to elevate adult literacy and adult basic education using local resources'.

WFC chose gender-based activism as the major path to empower the poorest and most neglected rural women and their families. Their programme of action had to encompass human rights education and advocacy for women's rights. It called for the improvement of rural livelihoods, and economic empowerment of women, the youth and, later, men. TAMWA chose to create awareness about the indecent portrayal of women in the media. By publishing feminist magazines, they provided alternative images for women. TAMWA prioritised research and documentation of cases of gender-based violence and the killing of women by families. With well-researched information, the organisation was able to carry out successful media advocacy and campaigns. They raised public awareness on issues of domestic violence and the law, and also carried out community action and legal literacy outreach programmes. While dealing with domestic violence matters, the idea of a crisis centre emerged. Counselling services and support groups developed alongside the crisis centre. TAMWA's agenda further included legal education of NGOs, teachers, law enforcement officers and students, and lobbying for legal reforms.

ORAP's key agenda for empowerment was to facilitate self-reliance in rural development in southern Zimbabwe. This they did by building on the positive experiences of rural people to develop their capacity. Although it is not clear how ORAP's agenda developed, cultural precepts were used to determine development directions for rural poor. The NGO actions were aimed at eradicating poverty in order to improve living standards. This in turn empowered the families that joined the project.

COPODIN went into the remote farming community of peasants to provide free medical services. However, this exclusive agenda slowly evolved to encompass functional literacy, health education and the development of fairly large income generating enterprises, all aimed at eradicating poverty. The organisation facilitated the establishment of sustainable rural livelihoods, wholly dependent on local resources.

Stakeholder focus

NGOs must maintain a stakeholder focus or die; by their nature, they are 'instruments of response' to human development. WFC, therefore, viewed women as its entry point into rural communities. Women and children are the most vulnerable in poor rural areas. In WFC's analysis, improving the lot of women would have a positive effect on the whole community. The organisation, therefore, regards women as the main stakeholders of rural development. LABE uses a people-centred development philosophy that seeks to give people tools to function within a defined system. Stakeholders are enabled to work with what they know. Examples of new models of education have been developed; for example, carving budgets on banana trunks and fibres helped to localise the processes even in the face of donor funding which provided books and manuals. The people determined their syllabus as well. LABE also paid attention to another group of stakeholders – the donors, insisting that relationships must extend to 'real partnerships'.

Some of the NGOs draw their agenda and activities directly from the communities they work with. ORAP focuses on the family as the unit of development. The NGO organisational structure reflects this emphasis, since the family and village are the highest decision making levels of the organisation. All activities of the organisation are planned for the development of the family unit, both economically and socially, and the philosophy and strategies of the organisation also emanate from the family and village levels. COPODIN's organisational goals focus on the rural farming communities within which they work. The philosophy and strategies for operations largely emanate from the peasants with guiding concepts being taken from the local language.

Organisational structures

Deriving its authority from the family, village and umbrella associations, ORAP is governed by an advisory board with a policy making board of trustees. Project units then undertake activities such as the Zenzele College, community education and income generation for the organisation.

WFC is a trust registered under Zambian law. The AGM is the highest decision making body for WFC. There is a board of trustees and a director, with staff for the day-to-day management of activities. The grassroots groupings are mainly women's associations responsible for coordinating a number of village groups.

TAMWA's organisational structure is still evolving and is not very clear from the paper published here. The organisation was initially set up as an ad hoc unit of media women working on selected issues or projects. This founder group experienced many organisational development problems. They later incorporated other professional women and some regular project staff to form the current configuration of implementing committees. All activities are coordinated by a unit referred to as a 'secretariat', comprising the director, programme officers and administration support staff. The organisation continues to have OD input in a bid to develop a stable structure.

The COPODIN family of organisations operates with two structures. There is an internal one, with a coordinator of projects and project officers drawn from the local community, taking charge of specific projects where the organisation interacts with the farming communities directly. The other structure consists of a community-based peasant association, union executive committees and a national board that coordinates the activities of member peasant organisations.

LABE's structure includes a board, a committee of partner NGOs, a management committee and project staff. The mechanical approach of running organisations on a 'project' basis with quarterly planning affected the organisational structure owing to the uncertainty of obtaining funds. Staff welfare was also affected by the dependence on irregular funding and these factors ultimately impacted on the attainment of stakeholder aspirations and empowerment.

Challenges faced

TAMWA experienced initial fragmentation owing to the lack of OD support and minimal experience in managing NGOs. The organisation still faces the challenge that is the core of its intervention, i.e. an entrenched patriarchal system that overrides awareness campaigns and condones the inaction of law enforcement officers. Having identified inappropriate laws regarding gender-based violence, TAMWA also needs to establish ongoing credibility for the crisis centre for abused women, as well as security of the women activists from their own families and marauding men.

In Uganda, a key challenge for both the government and its citizens was to make up for lost time in adult literacy and basic education. For LABE, the challenge translated into keeping the vision of adult basic education alive. This was affected by high staff turnover, and the appointment of a new management and board as the organisation struggled to maintain its institutional memory, vision and mission. Workers are expected to share a common vision and mission for LABE but this has not always been possible. The dynamism required of leadership in such an organisation also poses a challenge to LABE.

Empowerment of people in the context of entrenched cultures is not an easy task because some of the traditions may not coincide with the evolving socioeconomic order. ORAP's holistic approach to rural development following a people's perspective was not easy to implement. It required many resources with the concomitant problems of management and accountability. Networking and cooperating with external support agencies, regional organisations and government made it difficult to guarantee respect for the ORAP philosophy and the communities' agenda. Financial sustainability was important in order to ensure that ORAP's donors did not set the pace of the operations.

WFC faced the challenge of a conflict of interest where other organisations were providing handouts to the rural women while WFC preached self-reliance to the same people. WFC would like to empower the people to identify their own problems, find possible solutions and seek their own resources to solve the problems. Any additional funding from the organisation or donors should be viewed as a bonus.

COPODIN's refusal to work on the basis of donor grants has posed the greatest challenge to its work. The peasants have had to be self-reliant and the organisation has survived, against all odds, on locally sourced funds and the peasants' contributions. This has strengthened ownership of the organisation among the peasant communities. COPODIN balances the various needs that emerge as part of the holistic empowerment process to achieve some degree of success in empowerment without overwhelming the organisation. The organisation reaches out to wider groups as more peasants decide to take up the challenge to empower themselves in collaboration with COPODIN.

Overcoming the obstacles

WFC overcame its obstacles by organising and empowering a critical mass of women from remote rural areas. The women can now demand their own rights in development from the relevant bodies with minimal support. Examples of real empowerment can be noted in the visits to MPs to demand better services and the giving of 'brown water' to an MP at a gathering. WFC has assisted the women to confidently address their own problems as a community. For any African who understands the 'deity status' which local politicians ascribe to themselves, how intimidating they can be and how they are feared for the violence they perpetrate on anyone who dares challenge them, WFC's achievement is no mean feat. Their achievement indicates that African NGOs can indeed empower communities to speak up and speak out for social development.

This truth about empowerment is confirmed by TAMWA's story. Through media campaigns, the founding members managed to overcome the stereotypes and reactions of both the public and their workmates to establish a credible organisation and a crisis centre for victimised or abused women and children. Their media campaigns have been extremely successful and are the main tools for overcoming the obstacles to improving the images of women – in the media, in homes, on the university campus, and within the law and the law making organs. Most importantly, in both WFC and TAMWA, the women did it for themselves.

To overcome the obstacle of economic disempowerment, ORAP developed a business plan that spanned significant income generating activities such as credit schemes, the establishment of venture capital companies and partnerships with financial institutions in Zimbabwe. This gave the organisation the required level of financial independence to maintain its organisational goals and plans in a coherent way. By doing this, the organisation demonstrated true empowerment where people can be assisted with initial capital to achieve sustainable economic development. Following the 'teach a person to fish, rather than give a fish' paradigm of economic empowerment, the people in ORAP's story were given the best form of empowerment – the means of production to create wealth and eradicate their own poverty. In a similar manner, COPODIN managed to overcome its financial obstacles through the commitment of the peasants and the team of professionals. The organisation did not pursue a financial programme for the benefit of project administration but preferred to reduce its management costs and to retain only very necessary staff, living among the peasant communities according to the lifestyles of the people. Through a 'learning by doing' partnership with the community, COPODIN achieved greater empowerment of the people and also empowered its professional staff for 'real' social development in their communities.

However, for LABE, despite gaining a more adaptable funding framework to allow proper planning and staying afloat through the difficult phases of organisational development, it is not clear to what extent the local partner CBOs and NGOs were empowered. Most of LABE's empowerment processes were internal and, by the writer's own admission, were organisational, project and financial improvements. The story of LABE raises fundamental questions around NGO governance issues. For example, the legal requirements to establish governance structures meant the making up of boards of governors, management committees or executive bodies to counterbalance the policy making bodies. While this is necessary and desirable, it has an effect on the actual empowerment of an organisation and a community because these structures easily become enmeshed in power struggles and 'resource rows'.

Lessons in empowerment

What shall we say then are the learning points from these stories? The writers have described in some detail what they consider to be the lessons in empowerment. In addition to these, some others are singled out here as a conclusion to the story of African NGOs on the paths to empowerment.

- The **staffing structures** of NGOs need to reflect the emphasis of the organisation's core business. WFC's development and use of local models for training is effective and builds the capacity of trainers to adapt academic models to the situation on the ground. For example, WFC personnel are mainly outreach staff; in order to animate or mobilise the people to act for development, they stay for periods of three to four weeks in the villages, living amongst the people. This is a powerful lesson for some African NGOs that may tend to become top-heavy despite their organisational vision and mission. There is a need to maintain a pragmatic stakeholder focus and establish structures that get the job done.
- Experience in **NGO management** is crucial for the setting up of an organisation and should be supported with continuing organisational development. For organisations such as TAMWA and LABE, this would ensure consistency and commitment of staff and partners.

- **Advocacy** is a skill which should be taught and learned, in addition to skills and experience in NGO management.
- Where the empowerment path is advocacy and lobbying for state commitment or legal reforms, **networks** are of paramount importance. Research and publications contribute immensely to the building of NGO credibility and empowerment of the beneficiary community. Such networking calls for capacity development of the partners, transparency and diligent reviews of programmes to improve administrative practices. The case of LABE shows that while initial meetings were poorly attended, when the state started to arrange a national literacy investment plan that would affect NGOs, every NGO woke up to the need to join LABE's efforts.
- ORAP teaches that **empowerment cannot be carried out by external agencies.** Given the opportunity, people will empower themselves with the support or facilitation of their local organisations. Community enterprises can only be sustainable if they derive from a people's cultural precepts and knowledge. Western models of development present real challenges to our rural development processes because they are not inclusive. Empowerment processes need to recognise that social, political and economic arrangements in each community will always dictate the level of human development.
- The **empowerment** and social development of African communities **cannot be sustained by the financial magnanimity of the North.** Empowerment must be rooted in Africa's vision and economic base, eschewing all symptoms of dependency. A good mix of resources from both sources is ideal for carrying out the task of empowering the people towards social and economic self-determination.
- COPODIN's story illustrates **the incremental nature of empowerment.** Like all behavioural and environmental changes, achievements in socioeconomic empowerment can only be understood from a cumulative perspective. Very small gains are made periodically over a long time and it takes a persevering community and organisation to keep working at empowerment. Do the donors have the patience for this and, if not, what is the recourse for African NGOs?
- NGOs can only energise social and economic changes with the **cooperation of governments.** To achieve real empowerment of communities, NGOs have to be recognised by the state as complementary entities, reaching where the state may not dare or be able to. NGOs also have to respect the state and its authority, even as they take 'uncompromising positions' on issues affecting the welfare of the communities served. Sometimes, NGOs' excessive claims of success with communities, or their overriding of the state, could lead to resentment. It is not necessary for NGOs to 'dig their own graves with their mouths'.